W9-AWW-219

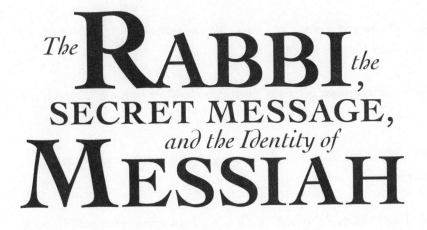

The RABBI, *the* SECRET MESSAGE, *and the Identity of* MESSIAH

Also by Carl Gallups

***Gods of Ground Zero:** The Truth of Eden's Iniquity, Why It Still Matters, and What's Coming Next*

***Gods and Thrones:** Nachash, Forgotten Prophecy, and the Return of the Elohim*

***When the Lion Roars:** Understanding the Implications of Ancient Prophecies for Our Time*

***Be Thou Prepared:** Equipping the Church for Persecution and Times of Trouble*

***The Rabbi Who Found Messiah:** The Story of Yitzhak Kaduri*

***Final Warning:** Understanding the Trumpet Days of Revelation*

***The Magic Man in the Sky:** Effectively Defending the Christian Faith*

★★★★★ *"And you shall know the truth and the truth shall set you free! Riveting, Exciting, Revolutionary & eye opening. Truth in every chapter. A must read for Jew and Gentile alike!"*
— Messianic Rabbi Eric Walker, Executive Director of Igniting a Nation Ministries

The RABBI, *the* SECRET MESSAGE, *and the Identity of* MESSIAH

The Expanded True Story of Israeli Rabbi Yitzhak Kaduri & How His Stunning Revelation of the Genuine Messiah is Still Shaking the Nations

CARL GALLUPS

Internationally acclaimed investigative author who broke the original story on *The Rabbi Who Found Messiah*

With Messianic Rabbi Zev Porat • Tel Aviv, Israel

DEFENDER

CRANE, MO

The Rabbi, the Secret Message, and the Identity of Messiah: The expanded true story of Israeli Rabbi Yitzhak Kaduri and how his stunning revelation of the genuine Messiah is still shaking the nations
By Carl Gallups

© Copyright 2018 Thomas Horn, Carl Gallups. All rights reserved.

Printed in the United States of America.

Unless otherwise noted, all Scripture quotations are from The Holy Bible, New International Version®, NIV®, Copyright © 1973, 1978, 1984, 2011 by Biblica, Inc.™ Used by permission. All rights reserved.

Cover design by Jeffrey Mardis.

ISBN: 9781948014120

In Memory of My Father-in-Law, James Nelson Blount (1933–2017)

James Nelson Blount served as a deputy sheriff, chief criminal investigator, and finally as the chief deputy for the sheriff's office of Jefferson County, Florida.

For many years after leaving the sheriff's office, Nelson was elected and reelected as the chief of police for Monticello, Florida.

He is dearly loved by the family he temporarily left behind and is sorely missed by the multitude of grateful people he sacrificially served for so many years.

From him, a man of faith and loyalty, I learned many amazing things about life and service to others, not the least of which was how to investigate a matter fairly and thoroughly. In that regard, I pray this book would have made him proud.

CONTENTS

Part Three

The Divine Perspective

Part Four

The Divine Changes

Part Five

The Divine Awakening

Part Six

The Divinely Prophetic

Part Seven

The Divine Name

A Word from Messianic Rabbi Zev Porat

The story of Rabbi Kaduri has impacted my life and ministry in several hard-to-imagine and unmistakably Heaven-ordained ways. Doors of impossible witnessing opportunity have been opened through the Kaduri Yeshua revelation. Through those portals we have been able to lead Jews—around the world and especially in Israel—straight to the Word of God and then to salvation.

Not only has this amazing Kaduri story been an effective evangelism tool among unbelieving Jews, but it has also proven to be a rich blessing of encouragement and a prophetic thrill to many who are already believers in *Yeshua Ha' Mashiach*.

I believe this book will also touch your life in several unexpected ways. Prepare yourself for an anointed and supernatural journey of discovery!

Prologue

What You Don't Know

Even if you're familiar with the account of the late Israeli Rabbi Yitzhak Kaduri and believe you already know what it's all about, I can assure you: *you don't*. The reason I can state this so emphatically is because I had the distinct privilege, in 2013, of writing the very first exhaustive investigative work on the original story.[1]

Since the days of the Messiah note's initial revelation in 2007, the saga has exploded to an entirely new depth, exposing a treasure trove of additional information never before released to the public. Additionally, several new witnesses have come forth confirming the account with an even clearer perspective—and the note's startling proclamation continues to make its way into some of the darkest spiritual corners of the earth. Rabbi Kaduri's story is still as fresh as the morning dew and is ceaselessly unfolding with every day that passes.

On the other hand, if you've never before heard of the Kaduri account, strap yourself in. You'll soon learn to *expect the unexpected* as you turn each successive page on the journey ahead. Not only will this true story thrill your soul, but it is also guaranteed to open up a brand-new world of insight regarding the contextual understanding of God's Word as well as the amazingly prophetic times in which we now live.

This is a ride you'll not soon forget. You'll be pondering it and sharing it for a long time to come.

Thank you for taking this journey with us.

Carl Gallups

PART ONE

THE DIVINE LINKS

Divine: "Of, relating to, or proceeding directly from God."[2]

1

The Rabbi, the Note, and the Messiah

The worldwide reaction to news of Kaduri's note has been "crazy." I have never received so many emails and calls from around the globe.[3]
—Aviel Schneider, *Israel Today*

The entire affair started with a mysterious, encrypted note.

Shortly thereafter, a beloved Israeli prime minister directly connected to the note's message suffered a devastating medical malady.

Within days, that tragedy was followed by the unexpected death of the man who had written the note: modern Israel's most famous Orthodox rabbi. Then came a long, *one-year period* of waiting for the departed rabbi's mystery note to be revealed according to his own instructions.

After those twelve months finally elapsed, the missive was proudly posted by his ministry officials—right in the middle of the front page on the rabbi's own website. A few weeks later, the underlying secret message it contained was "decoded," and, thanks to the ever-present global reach of the Internet, the mystery was laid bare before the world. The Jewish and Christian faith realms were stunned by the note's revelation.

That's when the firestorm erupted.

The heart of the story actually began in 2005 on a pleasant October afternoon at a very special Yom Kippur[4] service in the Bukharian Quarter of Jerusalem. That ultra-Orthodox Quarter is situated in the center of Jerusalem and is less than four miles northwest of the ancient Old City—the site of the Temple Mount.

The Day of Atonement

The aging rabbi knew the time had come to reveal his secret—a secret the size of an earthquake.

Rabbi Yitzhak Kaduri had just emerged from a lengthy, trance-like state of meditation as his Jerusalem synagogue attenders looked on. He had been sitting in the "Teacher's Seat"[5] with his hands gently shielding his eyes as he prayed.[6]

Still seated in the place of authority, he lowered his hands and smiled slightly as he glanced around the room. He was certain that his congregation trusted him, but would they accept what he was about to tell them in these next few moments? He opened his mouth to speak. A reverent hush fell over the room. The listeners could tell that their beloved teacher had something monumental to convey.

On that particular day, Rabbi Kaduri would not deliver the traditional Orthodox liturgy approved for this special Feast of the Lord (Leviticus 23:26–32). Rather, at this service, he would break from the deeply entrenched protocol of the occasion and do something absolutely scandalous: *He would preach.*[7]

In due course, what the rabbi claimed to have been given through that heavenly vision would cause a significant religious upheaval in Israel. It would also correspond to the fulfillment of certain biblical end-time prophecies.

But the *Kaduri ordeal* wouldn't unfurl itself overnight. Even though it had begun on that dramatic evening of Yom Kippur commemoration, the divine chess pieces were still being supernaturally moved into their places. The people in attendance that day could not have known they would become the first witnesses to a stunning, prophecy-connected event. In only a few short weeks, Rabbi Kaduri's unexpected death would set into motion the spiritual mechanics that would ultimately shake the foundation of the Judeo/Christian world…

…as well as of the gates of Hell itself.

2

The Unveiling

For our struggle is not against flesh and blood, but against the rulers, against the authorities, against the powers of this dark world and against the spiritual forces of evil in the heavenly realms.

—Ephesians 6:12

By January 28, 2006, Israel's most beloved and celebrated Orthodox rabbi had passed away at the age of 108.[8]

To this day, there is hardly a Jew in Israel who doesn't recognize Rabbi Yitzhak Kaduri's name and image and revere his memory. At the time of his passing, practically every taxi driver who shuffled the tens of thousands of people back and forth from Jerusalem to Tel Aviv displayed a picture of his benevolent face dangling from the rearview mirror.[9]

At Kaduri's funeral service, hundreds of buses, escorted by over a thousand police officers, transported the attendees.[10] More than three hundred thousand people from around the world lined the barricaded streets of Jerusalem to get a glimpse of the historical event and pay their final respects.[11] This was the largest funeral gathering modern Israel had ever experienced.[12]

The Secret

The vast majority of people in that massive funeral throng didn't have a clue that, only a few months before, Kaduri had scribbled a small, mysterious note on a nondescript scrap of paper. The content of the note was supposed to reveal what the beloved rabbi had declared as a long-awaited divine revelation: the *actual name* of the soon-coming, *genuine* Messiah.

However, when the note was first unfurled before the world, the words revealed no name of the Messiah, at least not in its obvious, surface rendering. In fact, the message appeared to be rather benign. Many of Kaduri's followers expressed their disappointment. At the very least, they were simply confused by the fact that Messiah's name was not there.

Simply put, this "message" they were looking at on Kaduri's website was not what they had waited an entire year to see. They wanted to know the *actual name* of the Messiah, the name Kaduri claimed had been divinely revealed to him. But this note did not even come close to fulfilling that simple promise…*or so they thought.*

The disappointed ones would soon be in for a huge surprise. Within weeks of the original posting, a group of Kaduri's closest followers discovered the note's true message. They were ecstatic when they saw it. Not only had their beloved Rabbi Kaduri done exactly what he had promised, but the name of the Messiah had been right before them all along. The encryption key used to unravel the coded revelation was boldly dangling in the very first sentence, hidden in plain sight. To their amazement, Rabbi Kaduri had ingeniously encoded his note. But why would he put the promised name of Messiah in the form of a coded secret? As you will soon discover, there was a very good reason.

When the name was finally revealed, the revelation stunned practically all who saw it. I say "practically" all because, as you will learn a little later in this story, a small group of Kaduri's students knew full well what the note was supposed to reveal. The renowned rabbi had spoken with them behind the closed doors of classes about the revelation. But now, he had pulled it off—from beyond the grave. He finally told the world what those students already knew.

The Messiah

The news of the decrypted riddle blazed around the world like wildfire. Kaduri's note dramatically disclosed what billions had been proclaiming for more than two thousand years: *Yehoshua/Yeshua* (Hebrew for "Jesus") is the name of the real Messiah.

Kaduri's Orthodox followers were livid. *How could this be? This isn't possible! This must be a trick!* No Jewish rabbi of Kaduri's prominence would dare suggest such a thing, they said. Would the world now suggest that Kaduri had somehow become a "Christian?" *Preposterous! Blasphemous!*

That's when it started. Powerful, malevolent forces—human and spiritual—began marking out their territories.

This was war.

Missing

Within a very short time after the decryption process had been exposed, the note was removed from Kaduri's website. It would later be claimed by a trustworthy authority in the matter that the note had secretly been destroyed in an occult-styled, ritualistic ceremony.[13] But it was too late. A huge number of people who were following the amazing story had already preserved screenshots of the revelation.

The spiritually ignited power storm had begun. Rabbi Kaduri's ministry officials and other Orthodox elite, along with powerful anti-Christian missionary organizations and several prominent media voices, began to claim that the note was nothing more than a fraud. Anyone saying otherwise was summarily branded as a liar and a charlatan. However, those who were conversant in the facts began to detect what they suspected to be a massive cover-up in progress.

This intricate story involves several occultic rituals, one of which included death threats upon an important Israeli government official. The account is also marred by vicious ecclesiastical infighting and carefully orchestrated cultural obfuscation, as well as incessant outlashing against those who have tried to uncover the truth. As it turns out, even the land of Israel is plagued with its own "deep state" and "fake news." In short, the entire ordeal is wrapped up in spiritual warfare of the highest magnitude.

That supernatural Kaduri note narrative, all these years later, continues to unravel like a spool of twine bouncing down the side of a mountain. And so far, its range of influence appears to have no boundaries.

It's Supernatural

> Do not be anxious about anything, but in every situation, by prayer and petition, with thanksgiving, present your requests to God.
>
> —Philippians 4:6

Soon after the late 2013 publication of my book about the Kaduri note, a growing litany of national and international television and radio programs began to offer interviews. Because nothing had yet been released to the world that had approached the Kaduri story from the standpoint of a truly credible investigative and biblical examination, interest in my exploration of the matter began to bloom.

By late 2014, after watching an earlier nationally broadcast television interview, TBN host and singer/songwriter/actor Pat Boone arranged to have me flown out to the TBN studio in Costa Mesa, California. He wanted me to unpack the Kaduri story on his globally broadcast headliner show. That interview with Pat and Shirley Boone opened additional doors for me to do many more interviews. A growing audience was beginning to want to know every detail about this intriguing and true story.[14]

I am now embarrassed to admit that the publication and worldwide distribution of that initial work unnerved me a bit, at first. I was concerned that a good number of Orthodox Jews,[15] regardless of the documented facts, would hate the book. I also surmised that they would probably dislike me intensely for writing about the event. I was proven correct in both of those assessments. Along with the burgeoning list of glowing accolades came an outpouring of abject loathing because I had dared to expose the story in the first place. It turns out much more was at stake than I had imagined.

I was also fairly positive that most of the Christian world simply would not "get it." My concern was based upon the sheer complexity of the matter. After all, the story is steeped in intricate Jewish thought and strange and unfamiliar Orthodox traditions, as well as certain mystical and cultic connections—so much so that I feared a number of Christians wouldn't even pick up the book in the first place. It turned out that I was right about that hunch as well.

I similarly suspected that for my work on the story to be taken seriously, there would have to be several credible media interviews attached to it, both Christian and secular—and there might even need to be a contact inside Israel who could get this account into the hands of the Jewish people living there.

Divine Intercession

Soon after the book's release, my wife, Pam, and I began to immerse the matter in prayer. I needed wisdom concerning how to appropriately address the complex story in upcoming interviews. We were also praying that somehow the Lord might use the book in opening up a pathway to salvation through Yeshua, particularly for Jews living in Israel. However, we couldn't begin to imagine how those doors might be unlocked. We certainly had no way of forcing that dream to come to fruition. We wondered who in Israel would have an interest in using such a story for ministry purposes.

But, of course, Heaven's Throne knew a thing or two that we didn't.

Prayers from Israel

I had no idea at the time that the bigger picture of what the Lord was doing also involved the prayers of a humble Hebrew[16] man, Messianic Rabbi[17] Zev Porat. Zev has lived most of his life in the heart of Israel, where for years he has been a minister of the gospel, along with a team of ministry assistants.

Rabbi Porat is the founder of Messiah of Israel Ministries, headquartered in Tel Aviv.[18] Zev, unbeknownst to anyone else in the world, had been longing for someone to thoroughly research the Kaduri story and put the account into writing. He, of all people, understood its vast importance.

Practically every Jewish person in Israel had at least heard of Yitzhak Kaduri, although few at that time knew of his amazing Messiah revelation. This was largely because the Orthodox Jewish elite had already determined to declare the story blatantly "false" and abjectly "dangerous." Accordingly, most of the facts had been explained away and hidden from the masses.

However, Rabbi Porat already had important connections with the Kaduri network. He even had direct familial ties to Kaduri himself. Zev was also well aware of the note's veracity. But there was a problem. As he tried to tell the story in Israel, he had a difficult time gaining a Jewish audience without being able to show credible documentation of the claim from an "outside" source.

Rabbi Porat wondered who in the world would write this amazing story. Who would dare attempt to uncover its incredible secrets and then expose them to the world, maybe even at their own peril?

Neither Jew Nor Gentile

Rabbi Porat believed that certainly no Jewish authors would venture to tell the Kaduri story. By now, the Kaduri Messiah note announcement had become toxic. If anyone even dared touch it, powerful forces would ensure that he or she would regret having done so.

Furthermore, Zev reasoned, there were probably precious few Gentiles who knew enough about the Kaduri phenomenon in context to do justice to the matter. How *could* there be? What Gentile would care about the Kaduri claims to the extent that he or she would write a book about it? Furthermore, what Gentile could begin to understand the deeply complex Jewish customs tied to the subject, as well as comprehend its eternal importance?

To Rabbi Zev Porat, it seemed that the dream of journalistically exposing the truth of Rabbi Kaduri's explosive revelation was an impossible act of wishful thinking. So, the Hebrew man of God did the only thing he knew to do: He continued to pray. He believed if Yahweh[19] wanted the story exposed, it would happen.

Prayer Partners

Unbeknownst to Zev Porat, a Florida pastor and his wife were also praying—on the other side of the globe, eight time zones away. They were praying about the same kinds of things that Zev was lifting before the Lord. We were probably the only two households on the planet engaged in those specific prayers.

But, as it turned out, I had just completed the very book for which Zev had been praying. Actually, as the Holy Spirit *must* have directed, I had even mentioned Zev Porat's Israeli-based ministry in that book, because I had viewed several online videos of him as he, in the aftermath of the note's decoding, had personally discipled a handful of Kaduri's "believing" yeshiva[20] students. However, it would be more than a year later before I discovered just how closely Zev was connected to the Kaduri ministry.

In truth, even though I had at least heard of Zev, he didn't have an inkling of who I was. At this point, we had never met, nor had we communicated in any manner. And he certainly did not know about the book I had written—the very book he had prayed would eventually burst forth into reality. But, how would our two very different worlds become connected?

Yes indeed: *How?*

That's when the wheels of Heaven's Throne began to turn. Slowly, but powerfully, the story propelled forward like a massive locomotive leaving the station, grinding toward an amazing journey of divine destiny.

The unseen realm snapped to attention.

4

Heaven Calling

Who has believed our message and to whom
has the arm of the LORD been revealed?
—Isaiah 53:1

From my standpoint, the numinous journey started with an unexpected phone call to my northwest Florida church office in early 2014. The call came from prominent Indiana commercial produce farmers Chuck and Tami Mohler.

You read that correctly. I said "a farmer and his wife." *From Indiana.* The call didn't come from a preacher, a reporter, a theologian, or a member of the rabbinic elite in Israel. It didn't come from the Israeli media or the nascent Sanhedrin Council.[21] It didn't come from Rabbi Zev Porat, either. Zev still didn't know anything about me or the book at this point.

Instead, the phone call came from a couple of regular, hard-working people who lived in America's heartland. What I heard next on the other end of the line floored me. The conversation began with Mr. Mohler asking me, "Are you really the one who wrote this book about Rabbi Kaduri?"

I answered in the affirmative, but I admit that I somewhat resented his initial incredulity.

Mr. Mohler continued, "How did *you* know about this story? Why in the world would you even write it? What connections do *you* have to it?"

Now *my* radar was in red-alert mode.

I had never met the Mohlers. I didn't have a clue as to who they were. When I first received the call, I thought it was perhaps a prank, maybe even the beginning of the persecution and harassment that I had expected would eventually be coming my way.

On the other hand, Chuck didn't have any idea who I was either, but he told me that he and his wife had read the book and were overwhelmed to see this story in print.

I thought: *How could farmers from Indiana have been so moved by a book about an elderly Jewish rabbi from Israel who was now dead? How could they possibly know anything meaningful about this story?*

The funny thing is that at the same time I was thinking those things, the Mohlers were discussing among themselves: *How could this Baptist preacher and former cop know anything about this deeply Jewish story? How could a Gentile from the Gulf Coast possibly have any idea concerning the full measure of what he had stumbled upon?*

The Divine Vacation

Here's what Chuck Mohler related to me about their discovery of the Kaduri book. The Mohler family had been on a much-needed vacation. The off-season for their farming industry was finally upon them, and they were headed out to Key West, Florida.

In the final leg of that 1,400-mile trip, they stopped briefly in Sarasota, Florida, to do some shopping. A local bookstore was in the shopping center. Tami Mohler, "on a whim," decided to walk over to the bookstore and do some browsing while Chuck picked up a few supplies at the grocery store.

When she walked into the shop, the first thing Tami noticed was a conspicuously displayed "new book" about Rabbi Yitzhak Kaduri. The book was written by an author she had never heard of. The book was titled *The Rabbi Who Found Messiah: The Story of Yitzhak Kaduri.*[22]

Only one copy of the book was left on the display stand. Tami purchased it and went straight to share the news with Chuck.

Why was she so eager to share that treasured possession with Chuck?

Connections

Chuck told me the reason. "You see," he said, "we are not merely Indiana natives and commercial produce farmers. There's more that I need to tell you."

Chuck related that he and his wife had lived and worked in Israel in the 1980s. Since returning to the United States, they had made frequent trips to Israel, where they had developed numerous connections among important people.

The Mohlers were familiar with the controversial Kaduri story and were keenly aware of the low flashpoint concerning telling that story in the presence of any Orthodox Jewish person in Israel.

Chuck then told me the following:

> In 2006, I was invited to speak before the nascent Israeli Sanhedrin Council. It was a twenty-six member Sanhedrin that day. Their purpose was to meet with a few select Gentiles to discuss how the Jewish community, mostly the Orthodox rabbis, could be a light to the Gentiles. The group of specially selected Gentiles were from the United States, Great Britain, and a couple of other countries. I was there at the invitation of Larry Borntrager.[23] Mr. Borntrager was given the responsibility of choosing the Gentile speakers. A total of twelve of us spoke before that Sanhedrin meeting.
>
> Mr. Borntrager was involved with the deeply revered Rabbi Schneerson and his B'nei Noach Movement.[24] Tami and I were considered B'nei Noach ("Sons of Noah") because of our longtime affiliation with the renowned Noahide[25] archeologist Vendyl Jones,[26] even though we did not ascribe to all of his teachings. This

is how Mr. Borntrager came to select me to be one of the speakers on that important day.

When it was my turn to speak before the Sanhedrin, I declared my belief in *Yeshua Ha' Mashiach.*[27] None of the other speakers that day had made this kind of forthright declaration of their true faith. But I felt led of the Lord to make this point clear—yet presented with a measure of deep respect for my audience.

I told them that I believe that *Messiah ben David*[28] is Yeshua—the true Messiah. I also told them that the Lord had sent me to them not to make Christians out of them, but for me to learn from them. I told them that the Lord would eventually be sending others like me, by the thousands, to learn of our biblical heritage through the Hebrew people. They tolerated all this without uttering a single word of protest.

I went on to say that the Christian community would ask very difficult questions of them—but for them to please be patient with those of us who had the right heart in asking our questions. I imagine it had probably been centuries since anyone had stood before the nascent Sanhedrin council and directly testified about Yeshua.

Rabbi Michael, the chief rabbi for that meeting, explained to me that the Sanhedrin corporately believed that Israel's only hope for survival was that the Messiah would come very soon, but that the true Messiah would only come if they start fulfilling their God-given role. One of those major roles, he explained, is that the Jews must be a light to the Gentiles. Rabbi Michael said they realized that they were not being a light. I pleaded with the Sanhedrin not to shut the Christians out just because they ask difficult questions and sometimes do not know how to conduct themselves appropriately in asking those questions. The message was well received.

At the end of it all, this entire experience was really quite puzzling to us. We didn't understand the spiritual significance of why Tami and our two boys were there for this meeting in 2006.

> We kept asking the question: *What was the bigger purpose of this day? What was this meeting really leading to?*
>
> We waited eight long years. And then it happened. We picked up the book *The Rabbi Who Found Messiah* as we were on our way from Indiana to a Key West vacation in 2014. That book opened the door to the answer.[29]

Chuck laughed, "Pastor Carl, I can't believe you would even know anything about this story, much less that you would be able to present it so accurately."

Then, in a more somber tone, he said, "I hope you're ready for what's coming next. This story is just beginning. It's going to heat up very quickly. And it won't be over until Yeshua returns."

Suspicions

That's when Chuck dropped another surprise on me. He said, "Pastor, we want to cut our vacation short and drive up to where you live. I want to meet with you in person."

I explained that I lived in the Pensacola, Florida, area in the extreme westernmost tip of the Florida Panhandle. I told him I was only about sixty miles from Mobile, Alabama. In other words, driving from Key West to Pensacola would take at least fourteen hours.

"I don't care," he said. "I have an idea. I believe it's a word from Yahweh. But, I need to know if all of this is on the up and up. It's very important that we know who you are. I need to meet you face-to-face. We'll be on our way in the morning."

So, they were off, headed to Florida's Panhandle. Just like that.

Chuck later divulged to me that they initially thought my involvement in the affair might turn out to be some kind of a literary ruse, a mere money-making venture that involved me attempting to piggyback upon a highly controversial and sensational claim. They were concerned that perhaps I didn't really understand the significance of this incredible story and the impact it might have on the lives of so many people, perhaps even upon the nation of Israel itself.

Equally, I initially questioned *their* sincerity. Chuck's story was impressive. But I had been approached before by people who had attempted to mislead to try to extract a tidbit of personal gain. Anyone could concoct an intricate story to use for nefarious purposes. I didn't even know these people, nor did I know anyone else who might be familiar with them.

I came very close to calling off the meeting altogether. But every time I picked up the phone to call the Mohlers, an uneasy feeling washed over me. I couldn't shake the feeling within the depths of my soul that perhaps, just perhaps, the Lord of Heaven was up to something bigger than anything I could imagine. I never made that call.

However, because of my initial suspicion, I still elected to meet the Mohlers at a local chain restaurant instead of inviting them to my own home or even to my church office. I was on edge about the recent public release of the story. Furthermore, I was still trying to wade through the phone calls, emails, and social media messages of hatred and threats that were beginning to manifest. I didn't want to put myself, my family, or my staff in a potential "set-up" situation.

So, we met for breakfast at a Waffle House restaurant just off Interstate 10. I was taking no chances.

Thankfully for me, as it turned out, the Mohlers' actions and intentions proved to be genuine. We are now good friends and have enjoyed fellowship on a number of occasions, despite the long distance between us. However, that day of checking each other out was the meeting that began to change everything.

I just didn't know it yet.

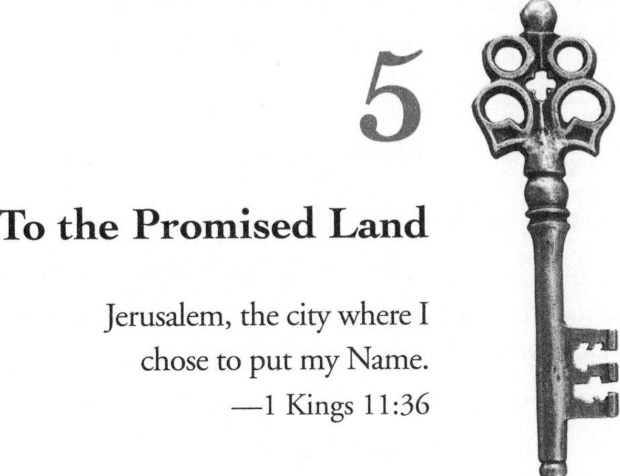

5

To the Promised Land

Jerusalem, the city where I
chose to put my Name.
—1 Kings 11:36

Within a few weeks after that portentous breakfast meeting in Florida, Chuck, Tami, and their teenaged son Dan were at their local airport in Indiana. They had boxed up a hundred copies of the *Rabbi* book, had checked them on their flight, and had taken off to make several connecting flights. They were headed for the Promised Land—the land of Israel.

The Mohlers were convinced that somehow the Lord was in the process of doing something amazing with this story. They sensed a divine urgency to get those books inside the Holy Land and into the hands of a few of their contacts, people they thought might help distribute the material throughout Israel.

I held my breath as I now had to face the fact that my investigative exposure of the story—*in print*—was finally making its way to the heart of Israel. I felt certain that genuine spiritual warfare would soon kick off.

Our prayers had been miraculously answered. But, was I prepared for what might happen next? If I had only known…

Unexpected Response

Upon arriving in Israel, the Mohlers quickly began contacting old friends. They were thrilled to share the thoroughly researched material on the Kaduri story because they were convinced the information might assist their friends in Israel as they ministered within the Orthodox community.

What they had expected was an enthusiastic reception to the finally documented information. However, what they got was a cold shoulder and exclamations of, "We can't use that *here*! The Jews will not allow it!"

The battle had begun.

Disappointed but not defeated, the Mohlers continued to contact everyone they knew in Israel. They wanted to speak with anyone who might be the slightest bit interested in using the authenticated Kaduri story that had finally been put into print. Over and over, however, the doors were closed.

Most of their Israeli acquaintances were familiar with the Kaduri account and understood its significance. But they were patently apprehensive about sharing the story among the Jews in Israel. The Orthodox rabbis had already put the word out: *This story is false! It's a lie! Stay away from it—or else!*

A Door Cracks Open

Refusing to give up, the Mohlers continued to seek other contacts. One was a Messianic Jewish man named Victor Kalisher, the general director of the Bible Society in Israel.[30] When Victor saw what the Mohlers had brought him, he was thrilled. He, too, was familiar with the story of Rabbi Yitzhak Kaduri and the aged rabbi's revelation of the Messiah. He immediately wanted copies for his store and ministry. A door had, *at last*, been cracked opened.

Seeking Zev

Believing the Lord had revealed an open pathway to planting the Kaduri story seed, the Mohlers sought another man who lived in Israel. This man spoke Hebrew as his first language and thoroughly understood the Orthodox and rabbinic culture of Israel. In fact, prior to believing in Yeshua as Messiah, he, too, had been studying to be an Orthodox rabbi. The man they sought was one whom, until now, the Mohlers had only read about in my book. That man was Messianic Rabbi Zev Porat.

Chuck and Tami were especially intrigued by Zev's ongoing discipleship ministry among a small group of Rabbi Kaduri's students. Those Kaduri students were also believers in Yeshua—and Rabbi Zev had come to know them personally.

The Mohlers had seen Rabbi Zev's videos, in which he conversed in the Hebrew language with Kaduri's rabbinic students as they unashamedly and in the face of potential persecution shared their testimony that Yeshua was Messiah. The students also affirmed that they had learned this truth from Rabbi Yitzhak Kaduri himself. These men were well aware of Rabbi Kaduri's note. They dared to allow their testimonies to be posted on the Internet. Zev relates that several of these students have since undergone intense persecution from Israel's rabbinical elite because of their published testimonies.

The Mohlers reasoned that surely Rabbi Zev would want this book. Of course, they had no way of knowing this was exactly the miracle for which Zev had been fervently praying. But the Throne of Heaven knew—and Yahweh heard the prayers. The cosmic chess pieces were falling into place.

Chuck and Tami began their search for Zev, asking the Lord for divine guidance not only in finding the rabbi, but also in convincing his heart to be open to meeting with them. Chuck had come all the way from Indiana for this very type of conference, and he and his wife were certain that meeting Zev was among the reasons the Lord had brought them to Israel. Now *three* households were explicitly praying toward the same goal.

Contact

Through a series of laborious email and phone-call attempts, the Mohlers finally made contact. Rabbi Porat graciously agreed to meet with them at a Tel Aviv restaurant.

During that meeting, Zev was overwhelmed by what the Mohlers related. They explained that they had been in fervent prayer, believing that someone would write a book documenting the Kaduri event. They admitted they had never heard of me or the book, but were thrilled to receive a copy.

Not long after that supernaturally orchestrated meeting, I received another unexpected phone call. As you might suspect, it was from Rabbi Zev. It appeared that his "impossible" prayer had finally been answered—and so had mine.

What was Yahweh up to? Where was this saga ultimately headed? Initially, I had believed it impossible for this story to gain any real traction.

I had no idea how mistaken I had been.

Part Two

THE DIVINE MESSAGE

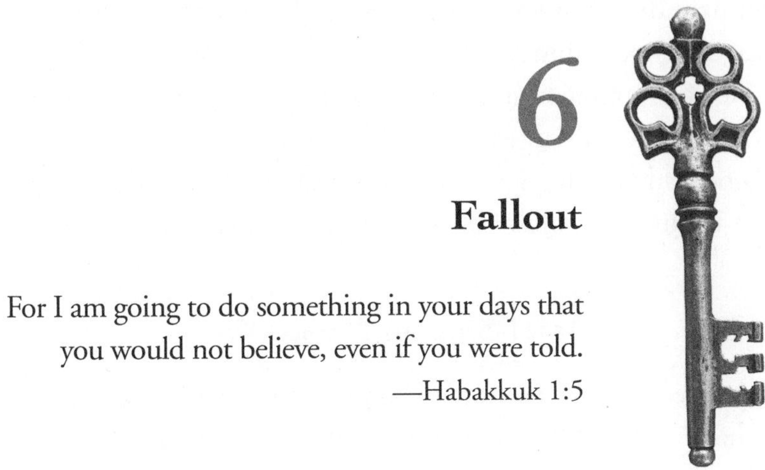

6

Fallout

For I am going to do something in your days that
you would not believe, even if you were told.
—Habakkuk 1:5

In the summer of 2016, I received an email from an internationally renowned figure I had recently met. He informed me that Israeli Prime Minister Benjamin Netanyahu had requested a copy of my first Kaduri book and now had one in his Jerusalem office. Three years after its release, the story was still making its way into unexpected and prominent places.

Suffice it to say, Rabbi Yitzhak Kaduri was not merely an obscure rabbi going about his business in some back-alley Jerusalem synagogue while remaining largely unnoticed. No, this rabbi was unlike any other Israel had known in modern times. Underscoring this truth is the fact that the president of Israel, Moshe Katsav, gave the eulogy at Kaduri's massively attended funeral.[31] Also in attendance was Rabbi Ovadia Yosef, the spiritual head of the Sephardic[32] ultra-Orthodox Shas party.[33]

Additionally, Rabbi Kaduri was personally acquainted with Israeli prime ministers, government officials, Israel Defense Forces (IDF) officers, Orthodox elite, and several notable dignitaries around the world. Kaduri had reached luminary status and political notoriety during the 1996 Knesset elections, when he was reported to have been instrumental in swinging the decisive balance of twenty-nine thousand voters. Those voters ensured that the Likud[34] party leader, Benjamin Netanyahu, was to be elected as prime minister of Israel.[35]

As previously noted, at the time of Kaduri's funeral, news of the famous rabbi's Messiah note was still largely unknown to the world. Most of his claims had been revealed only to a select number of his students and followers, behind the walls of his yeshiva, and in his modest synagogue.

Ariel Sharon Must Die

As if the foregoing facts were not unlikely enough, Kaduri had also claimed that on the October 2005 night of the Yom Kippur celebration, Messiah's eventual appearance would be directly linked to then Prime Minister Ariel Sharon. Gasps were heard in the congregation as the famous rabbi further disclosed that the Messiah would only appear sometime *after*—not before—the death of Sharon.

At the time of Kaduri's shocking claim about Sharon, the prime minister was reported to be in "perfect health." But by early January 2006, less than three months after the rabbi's announcement, Sharon had suffered a massive stroke and lay comatose in a Jerusalem hospital.

In addition to his Messiah note connection, Prime Minister Sharon had just been involved in the highly unpopular "land-for-peace" deal of relinquishing the Gaza Strip to the Arab Palestinians. Several leading Israeli Orthodox rabbis lambasted Sharon for the deal. So, the talk of his death within this unfortunate time frame of his debilitating stroke was particularly unnerving to a number of people who were following this story.[36]

Lashings of Fire

What makes the account even more intriguing is that in July 2005, just three months prior to Sharon's hospitalization, a rabbinical Kabbalah death curse called the *Pulsa Denura*[37] was conducted against the prime minister in an ancient Israeli cemetery. That occultic conclave was widely reported in various mainstream Israeli news sources.[38]

In that ritual, the Orthodox Israeli news source *Haaretz* claimed that a specific group of Kabbalistic rabbis had called for angels to kill the prime minister and thwart his Gaza withdrawal plan.

> A group of extreme-right activists said...that they had held a ceremony to place a pulsa denura, a halakhic[39] curse, on Prime Minister Ariel Sharon in order to bring about his death. They had called on the Angels of Destruction to kill Sharon.[40]

Rabbi Yitzhak Kaduri was not directly implicated in that particular ritual. However, in January 2006, the US edition of *The Guardian* reported that Kaduri was indeed implicated in a previous *Pulsa Denura* ceremony and suspected his involvement in a subsequent one. *The Guardian* obituary of Yitzhak Kaduri recounted those assertions:

> If dispensing blessings was one of Kaduri's stocks-in-trade, so was sending curses. In 1991 he sought out the name of Saddam Hussein's mother, so that he could send efficacious Pulsa Denura—Aramaic for "lashings of fire"—against this enemy of the Jews.
>
> Kaduri was also implicated in the death curse on Yitzhak Rabin, which was eerily pronounced just a month before the Labour premier's assassination in November 1995. Although he was never proved to be a signatory, in the eyes of secular detractors, guilt by association was good enough.[41]

The plot thickened.

7

Complicit?

Many testified falsely against him,
but their statements did not agree.
—Mark 14:56

Guilt by association is not *proof* of anything.

When it comes to the "Sharon curse" of July 2005, Messianic Rabbi Zev Porat offers some important light: "I know for a fact that Kaduri was *not involved* in the *Pulsa Denura* curse against Ariel Sharon in 2005. I was there when all that took place. I was closely following those news reports."

Zev continued:

> There are no legitimate claims that Kaduri was even remotely involved. There are no photographs of Kaduri with that group, no one close to Kaduri ever claimed it, before the Yeshua note was exposed, and Rabbi Kaduri himself never claimed it. Believe me, I know a lot of important people who would know the connections if they were true—but they're just not there.
>
> I can also assure you that if Kaduri had in fact participated in that highly publicized ritual against Ariel Sharon, there would be plenty of evidence to indicate that he was there. And there would have been many important people making that claim right

after the ceremony was conducted. After all, he was Israel's most important Kabbalistic rabbi at that point in our history. They would have trumpeted his presence from the rooftops! His presence would have been a major endorsement of the ritual's proceedings. But his name was never associated with it—in any way.

I can tell you a dirty little secret about this, though. It was only *after* the Kaduri message was translated to reveal that Messiah's name is Yeshua that several rabbis began claiming Kaduri was involved in the *Pulsa Denura* against Sharon. Some have even made this accusation to me personally. But, the reason they do this now is a hypocritical one.

Duplicity

Zev went on to say:

> They claim that if Kaduri was really a believer in Yeshua as Messiah, he would not have involved himself with that Kabbalah curse. Imagine that! They are actually admitting that the *Pulsa Denura* is evil and that following Yeshua would necessarily prohibit a true convert from practicing evil! I'm not sure they really thought about their charges in this matter. As often happens, they have become trapped in their own words.
>
> So now they find it an advantageous tactic to try and discredit the Kaduri message by saying that he really *was* involved. Think of it! Kaduri's name was not connected to the 2005 Sharon Kabballah curse—until all these years later, only after the note was opened. To me, this is even more proof that the rabbis know the power of Kaduri's Yeshua note and will do or say most anything to try and discredit it.
>
> What's more, since there is no hard evidence of any kind that he *was* involved, the rabbi's own words give more evidence that Kaduri had become a believer in Yeshua during that same time

period. The more they invent ways to try and discredit Rabbi Kaduri's note, the more they give it proof.

Corroborating Evidence

In fact, a well-known ultra-Orthodox Israeli news source reported in 2006 that Rabbi Kaduri had expressed his *support* of Sharon's Gaza handover. But, relinquishing the Gaza Strip was also the very reason for the *Pulsa Denura* in the first place. Therefore, it would make no sense that Rabbi Kaduri would *want* Sharon to die for orchestrating the Gaza arrangement, a negotiation Kaduri himself was publicly reported to wholeheartedly champion.

Kaduri's support for Sharon further bolsters Messianic Rabbi Zev Porat's claims concerning Kaduri's *non-involvement* in the Sharon *Pulsa Denura* curse. Additionally, the Orthodox news source *Ynet News* indirectly ties Kaduri's support of Sharon in the Gaza ordeal with his Messiah revelation:

> In recent months, **Kaduri's name was tied to a blessing** to opponents of the disengagement from Gaza, but his son later said his father believes "Gaza belongs to Palestine." Kaduri himself surprised many followers when **he offered his support for Prime Minister Ariel Sharon's** Gaza pullout in April.
>
> "…**We can trust Sharon**, he is okay," the rabbi told an ultra-Orthodox newspaper.
>
> He added: "I have no faith in the Arabs but we must have a little quiet. **Sharon's government isn't so bad.**"
>
> Recently, rumors have circulated in the ultra-Orthodox world that the **Messiah has revealed himself to Rabbi Kaduri** in dreams.[42] (Emphasis added)

"The reason Kaduri would not have participated in this Kabbalistic ritual was because it was at about this very same time that he was also reported to have met Yeshua in a vision—just as *Ynet News* confirms," Zev says. "I think it is because Rabbi Kaduri, at that new time in his life, would have sensed that to participate in an occultic ritual of this sort would have been wrong."

More Connections

It "just so happened" that Chuck and Tami Mohler, the farmers from Indiana, were seated on an airplane at Ben Gurion International Airport in Tel Aviv in that January of 2006 when the flight attendants announced over the intercom that Prime Minister Ariel Sharon had just suffered a stroke. The Mohlers were returning to the United States after having met with the Sanhedrin Council.

The couple said the passengers on that flight erupted into expressions of genuine sorrow when the doleful news about Sharon was announced. Of course, none of the upset passengers could have known it at the time, but Ariel Sharon would never recover from that coma.

Then, as if Heaven itself desired to punctuate Kaduri's "prophetic" claims, just a few weeks after Sharon was hospitalized, Rabbi Yitzhak Kaduri himself was also hospitalized. He was diagnosed with pneumonia and, within a few weeks, was dead. But Sharon was still alive—in a coma.

Kaduri's closest followers and students were collectively holding their breath, and they would do so for an entire year. In the interim, they speculated upon the enigmatic note and its promised revelation. They also wondered about Sharon's health and if he might soon recover from his coma. In the meantime, Sharon's comatose condition would linger on—for eight long years.

Hard to Believe

If you've never heard this information before, it probably sounds increasingly untenable the more I continue to lay out the particulars. I understand.

The story is intricate, and there are still other fascinating complexities that I will disclose in the chapters to come.

In addition to the foregoing complications, the Rabbi Kaduri account is, of course, fiercely disputed by those who continually attempt to cover it up. Without burying the truth, their entire way of life—especially their deeply held belief system, along with its financial perks—could be seriously compromised.

The global sphere of Kaduri's influence was immense. As far as the Orthodox elite were concerned, the story *had* to go away—and with as little fanfare as possible. However, to their deepest consternation, the thing just wouldn't stay hidden.

There was still so much more that might yet be revealed.

So the obfuscation continued.

8

The Case of the Missing Crosses

He reveals deep and hidden things;
he knows what lies in darkness,
and light dwells with him.
—Daniel 2:22

What follows next is certainly an intriguing twist to this story.

As stated, in January 2007, Kaduri's mysterious Messiah note was indeed posted on his ministry's website one year after his death. It was prominently displayed on that website for several weeks, along with a feature story about the note, until its Messiah message was decoded. Then the note and the story about it were removed and the note was vehemently denounced as a fake.

Upon its initial unveiling, there seemed to be nothing unusual or blasphemous about the note at all. It appeared to be a typical mystical, Kabbalah-type message, one that might be expected from the beloved rabbi. The so-called revelation seemed only to express some vague description of Messiah's *function and ministry*—mere administrative matters that would accompany His ultimate appearance. In other words, the note sounded very Jewish.

But a few weeks later, the dominoes began to fall.

The Firestorm

On April 30, 2007, the widely read print magazine *Israel Today* published a feature story about Kaduri's note. The article's writer claimed the note had been decoded and suggested that the message it contained might well prove to be spiritually earth-shattering. The publication also posted an article, in conjunction with the magazine story, on its Internet website at *israeltoday.co.il.* Both the magazine article and the Internet piece bore the title, "Rabbi Reveals Name of the Messiah."

The article's author, Aviel Schneider, was quoted as saying, "The worldwide reaction to news of Kaduri's note has been 'crazy.' I have never received so many emails and calls from around the globe."[43]

But soon, a peculiar fact was discovered. Only the original Internet article, not the magazine article, contained a section titled, "The Rabbi's Followers React." A striking and important piece of information was included in that Internet edition of the Kaduri story:

> *Israel Today* was given access to many of the rabbi's manuscripts, written in his own hand for the exclusive use of his students. Most striking were the cross-like symbols painted by Kaduri all over the pages.
>
> In the Jewish tradition, one does not use crosses. In fact, even the use of a plus sign is discouraged because it might be mistaken for a cross. But there they were, scribbled in the rabbi's own hand. When we asked what those symbols meant, Rabbi David Kaduri said they were "signs of the angel."
>
> Pressed further about the meaning of the "signs of the angel," he said he had no idea. Rabbi David Kaduri went on to explain that only his father had had a spiritual relationship with God and had met the Messiah in his dreams. Orthodox Jews around the Nahalat Yitzhak Yeshiva told *Israel Today* a few weeks later that the story about the secret note of Rabbi Kaduri should never have come out, and that it had damaged the name of the revered old sage.[44]

Why would Kaduri swathe his manuscripts with something that looked like the sign of the cross? Using such blatantly Christian symbols would be considered highly offensive to any Orthodox Jew. Consider the title of a 2014 opinion piece published in *The Guardian*: "Christians Must Understand That for Jews the Cross Is a Symbol of Persecution." That piece states, "While Christians regard the cross as an inevitable part of human salvation, for Jews it remains a symbol of centuries of oppression."[45]

Vanished?

Surprisingly, the original *Israel Today* article eventually disappeared from the Internet. The conspiracy theories began to churn like a mushrooming storm front. Not only had that article been hotly contested by the Orthodox elite, but some who were closely following the Kaduri saga suspected that *Israel Today* might have been pressured to take down its Internet account of the event.

In response to the uproar, I contacted officials at *Israel Today* in early 2013, when I first verified the missing Internet story. They assured me that the original April 30, 2007, article would soon be reposted and that the entire website had only recently been removed and was merely undergoing an upgrade. I was also assured that *Israel Today* was categorically standing by its original article.[46]

Adjusted Reappearance

Sometime later, the article was indeed reinstated on the website. However, the newly posted piece showed a different original posting date: May 30, 2007. The title had also been changed to a somewhat less sensational version: "The Rabbi, the Note and the Messiah."

Additionally, the editor's note at the top of that reposted page claims: "*This is a reprint* of a cover story that first appeared in the April 2007 issue of *Israel Today Magazine*." While that statement might be technically accurate concerning the magazine article, it did not account for the fact that the reprinted Internet article had been significantly adjusted as compared to the original.

Oddly, the reinstated Internet version did not contain the section with the heading that had been initially titled "The Rabbi's Followers React." The comments about the "many" Kaduri manuscripts, the "signs of the angel," the "cross symbols," and the observation about damaging "the revered old sage's name" had mysteriously vanished.

Because of this suspicious anomaly, I again contacted a key figure within the *Israel Today* organization and requested information regarding the noticeable omissions. The next day, I received the following response:

> Please note that the definitive publication of this story was in our print magazine. The iterations that appeared on our website, including that first appearance, were all just "republications" of the original article. Depending on who was in charge of posting the story to the website, different parts might have been left out, since in the magazine layout some were in separate "boxes" and not a single "story" if my memory serves. The note regarding the [differing] publication date is likely just a mistake by whomever was posting to the website, since this would have been different people in both cases.
>
> As far as I am aware, there has never been any effort to retract or hide certain parts of the original story. Our website is very much secondary to our print magazine, and not all content from the magazine is republished there in full.
>
> The website version of any article also appearing in our print magazine is NOT definitive. The original version in the magazine is the definitive version.
>
> Whatever appeared in our print magazine regarding this story, including the original title ("The Rabbi, the Note and the Messiah"), remains *Israel Today*'s official position. What was printed in our magazine is what *Israel Today* had to report and say on the matter. Period. End of story. Our website is very much a promo-

tional platform for the magazine. Sometimes articles are republished online in full, sometimes in part, and often not at all.[47]

A few days after receiving the above response, the same representative of *Israel Today* emailed me a copy of the entire original magazine article. Noticeably absent was the subject matter concerning the cross symbols, the angel, and the potential of "damaging" Rabbi Kaduri's name. When I asked for an explanation of this lingering incongruity, I received no reply. Communication from *Israel Today* abruptly ceased. I was beginning to feel that I might have hit upon something.

It was Messianic Zev Porat who offered up the key for the most probable answer to this mystery. His reasoning is sound and once again demonstrates the dramatic depth of the Orthodox elite's attempted cover-up of the truth of Kaduri's Messiah revelation.

9

The Aleph and the Tav

This is what the LORD says—Israel's King and Redeemer, the LORD Almighty: *I am the first and I am the last*; apart from me there is no God.
—Isaiah 44:6, emphasis added

[Jesus said,] I am the Alpha and the Omega, the First and the Last, the Beginning and the End.
—Revelation 22:13

Messianic Rabbi Zev Porat revealed:

> This is an amazing thing, about the disappearance of the cross symbols from *Israel Today's* story! Kaduri's yeshiva students have been telling me about something that matches this very thing. In fact, they are still talking about it today. And in light of the missing information from the second printing of the Internet article, what the students are telling me now makes perfect sense.

He continued:

> The students tell me that Rabbi Kaduri had been teaching them about the Hebrew letters—the Aleph (א) and Tav (ת). As you probably know, these are the first and the last letters of the Hebrew alphabet. According to the New Testament language of

Greek, Yeshua called Himself the Alpha and the Omega. But in the Hebrew, it is *the Aleph and the Tav.* The Tav is especially interesting because in the most ancient pictographic representations, the Tav was designated by a symbol that looks exactly like the sign of the cross. Its meaning is *the mark*, or the sign.[48]

On the other hand, the Aleph, the first letter of the Hebrew alphabet, was represented by the ancient pictographic form of an ox head. That particular symbol meant *the leader, or the One who is most powerful.* In the most ancient times the Aleph represented God Himself—and was pronounced *El.*[49]

The figure of the ox head also stood for *the sacrifice.* The ox was used in ancient Hebrew worship as the Peace Offering and the Fellowship Offering.[50]

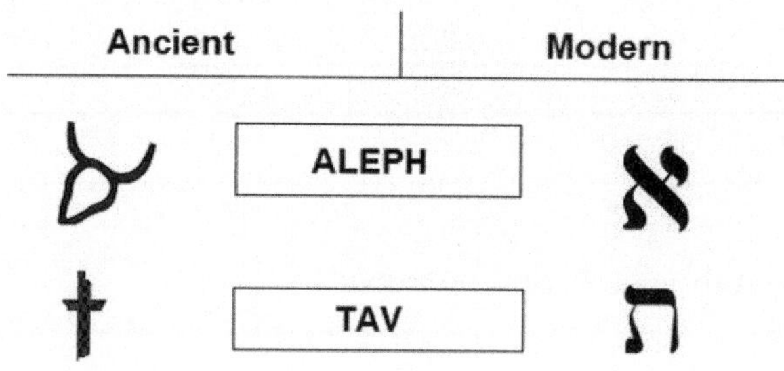

Rabbi Porat continued:

Based upon the information in that *Israel Today* article, and what Kaduri's students are telling me, I believe those cross symbols were *Tav depictions* that Rabbi Kaduri was drawing on his documents. I think he was preparing the world for his eventual Messiah note—declaring that Yeshua is the Aleph and the Tav—and that the sign of the cross, *the Tav*, is further proof that Yeshua is the Messiah—the King of kings, the most powerful One, who became our ultimate sacrifice for sin, bringing us peace with God. Yeshua is *the mark* of God's plan of salvation![51]

Zev further elaborated:

The fact that *Israel Today* published the information about the cross symbols is further verification that what Kaduri's students have been telling me is true. Since they ultimately backed off of that part of the original article, to me, it might be an indication that they received persecution for printing this amazing part of the story. It appears that the reprinted Internet story may have been changed for this very reason. We probably will never know the absolute truth of the matter. However, the pressure to shut down this story, or at least these particularly revealing elements of it, is real.

I have used this information about the ancient Hebrew alphabet in our ministry's witnessing outreach in Israel on many occasions. Teaching these symbols and their meanings to today's Jewish people is such a powerful way to open their eyes to the truth of Yeshua as Messiah.

In fact, it is so effective that not too long ago I actually had two very prominent Israeli rabbis contact me about what I was doing. They literally pleaded with me to *please not teach* these ancient symbols to Jews in my outreach presentations. They claimed that it might "confuse" the people. One of the rabbis contacted me by email, the other one called me on the phone. It's an amazing thing that for thousands of years these symbols were not confusing at all—that is, until after Jesus was crucified on a cross and fulfilled every prophecy of the coming Messiah.

After speaking with those concerned rabbis, it became very apparent to me that this one tremendous truth alone, *the ancient Hebrew pictographs*, was having a much larger impact in witnessing to the Jewish people about Yeshua than I had imagined. I politely told them that I would continue to use the teaching—after all, it is a historical fact of our own language, dating back thousands of years. Why should our people not know these eternal truths? But, I can tell you—the rabbis clearly don't want this truth taught anymore, because it points directly to *Yeshua Ha' Mashiach.*[52]

Changing the Alphabet

"What's really amazing about all this, though," Zev asserted, "is that Israel is the only nation that has ever eliminated its own alphabet,[53] especially the teaching of the ideographic meanings, and the symbols for each of the letters."

He explained:

Before Yeshua was crucified, the rabbis didn't understand the sign of the cross as being directly related to Messiah. However, *after* the crucifixion, they *all* saw it! They stopped teaching about the symbols that represented each Hebrew letter within a few decades of the crucifixion of Yeshua because they knew it matched Yeshua's Aleph/Tav statements. Rabbi Kaduri was resurrecting the teaching of these ideograms with his students! This is what the students themselves are telling me. The cross symbols match perfectly with what *Israel Today* had originally reported—then eventually omitted—and they match with what his former students are now saying.

I also know from spending many hours with Kaduri's former students that he did not teach them the full gospel, especially the part about the resurrection. Kaduri probably did not yet understand those elements of the gospel message. However, these are the foundational truths that I am now teaching the students when I am with them.

More than likely, Rabbi Kaduri was leaving pieces of a puzzle, preparing the Jewish world for the earth-shattering bombshell of his Yeshua revelation. We know that the cross is the biggest symbol by which Yeshua is known today, throughout the world. We also know that the angel Gabriel appeared to Mary to tell her that she would fulfill the prophecy of Isaiah 7:14 (Luke 1:26–38). Think about it! *The angel* of the Lord and the *cross signs*—in Kaduri's own handwriting! This is absolutely amazing!

The Foundational Truth

Regardless of the mystery surrounding the suspiciously missing material from *Israel Today's* Internet article, each of that news organization's Internet postings of the Kaduri story relates that Rabbi Kaduri's note did indeed reveal the name of the true Messiah.[54]

Nevertheless, the mysterious disappearance of the information in that second Internet article caused some followers of this important story to grow increasingly apprehensive. After all, Aviel Schneider, the author of that article, had already admitted to being "urged not to publish" the original piece from the very beginning[55] and had been told by Kaduri's own son, a prominent and powerful rabbi, that the story "should have never come out."[56]

Let's wade in a little deeper to find out what the uproar is really all about. The truth may not be quite as obvious as one might think.

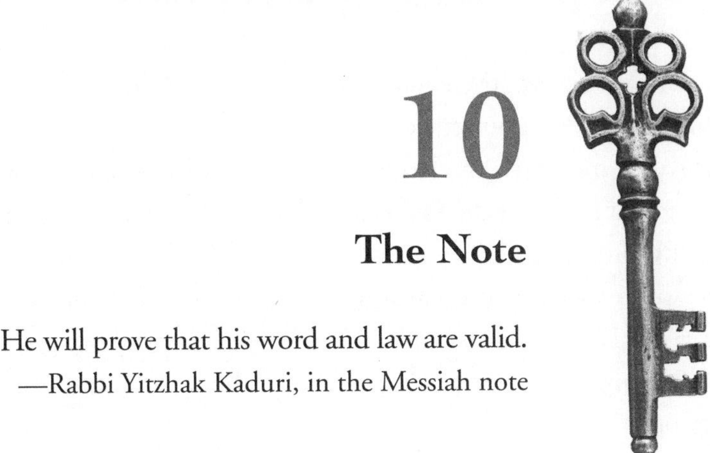

10

The Note

He will prove that his word and law are valid.
—Rabbi Yitzhak Kaduri, in the Messiah note

The following words were written in Rabbi Kaduri's Messiah note (the words are translated into English, but it was, of course, originally penned in Hebrew—the only language Rabbi Yitzhak Kaduri spoke):

> Concerning the letter abbreviation of the Messiah's name, *He will lift the people and prove that his word and law are valid.* This I have signed in the month of mercy.[57] (Emphasis added)

It is uncertain who initially deciphered the code or precisely when that decryption process occurred. However, it was only after the note had been displayed for several weeks on Kaduri's website that the original, promised message was finally revealed.

The key to its unlocking had been there all along. Rabbi Kaduri had inserted the clue, hidden in plain sight, in the very first portion of the first sentence: "Concerning the letter abbreviation of the Messiah's name."

The Encryption Code

To the non-Jewish eye, the key might not have been that obvious. However, this veiled clue pointed to an ancient Hebrew custom of using an acrostic-styled method ("the letter abbreviation of His name") of emphasizing words or letters of the Hebrew alphabet. The first letter of a word in a paragraph or passage served as the *marker* for that selection.

Acrostics of this nature are found in the book of Psalms—chapters 25, 34, 37, 111, 112, 119, and 145. The well-known passage Proverbs 31:10–31 is also an acrostic. This method is likewise found in Lamentations chapters 1–4.

Psalm 119 is the most elaborate example of the technique, with the initial letter of the first word of each paragraph representing each successive letter of the entire Hebrew alphabet, beginning with the first letter, the *Aleph*.[58]

These examples from Scripture are not necessarily meant to reveal a hidden code; rather, they represent a Hebrew literary practice. However, in Kaduri's case, it is apparent that he meant for the acrostic procedure to apply only to a certain portion of his note, to decrypt a hidden message: the name of the true Messiah.

The Rendering

Rabbi Kaduri's secret key portion of the note was immediately followed by a selection of six Hebrew words. Those words effectively translate in English to: "He will lift the people and prove that his word and law are valid." This was the conspicuously separated portion of the note that was to be used to decipher the Messiah's name.

When the first letters of each of those Hebrew words are strung together—from right to left, as the Hebrew language is properly read, and with the appropriate vowel sounds included—they spell out the word *Yehoshua*. This is the older, long-form rendering of the Hebrew word *Yeshua*—or, as most English-speaking people pronounce the name, *Jesus*.[59]

בענין הר"ת על משיח
ירים העם ויוכיח
שדברו ותורתו עומדים
באתי על החתום בחודש הרחמים התשס"ה
יצחק כדורי

Rabbi Kaduri's handwritten note

There it was! Displayed before the eyes of the world! Once it was properly decrypted, Rabbi Kaduri's message finally revealed what he had promised his followers: the name of the true Messiah.

But there was one monumental problem. To the Orthodox Jew, that name was an abomination. For the last two thousand years, this had been the very name the Jews had passionately tried to discredit. Now, their most famous Orthodox rabbi was telling them that this name was, in fact, the one that should be revered above all others. How were they going to deal with this theological nuclear explosion?

Nothing to See Here!

One of the first attempts to explain away Kaduri's revelation of Jesus as Messiah was to claim that *Yehoshua* is merely a common Hebrew name for a male, translating to "Joshua." The detractors argued that this name therefore could have been meant to identify any number of men in Israel; it didn't have to be connected to the Yeshua of the New Testament at all.

This may sound like a reasonable explanation, except for three important facts. First, only one faith system in the entire human existence declares a Savior/Messiah by the specific Hebrew name of *Yehoshua/Yeshua*. When that name is uttered in conjunction with the term "Messiah," practically everyone on the planet knows exactly who is being referenced—Jesus of Nazareth.

Further, *Yeshua* is the Hebrew word that most every Jewish believer in Jesus as Messiah uses when speaking His name. Rabbi Kaduri promised his followers that this was exactly what he would provide through the message of his note—the precise name of the *true Messiah*.

Finally, regardless of how common the name might be in Hebrew, *Yehoshua/Yeshua* means "God saves," "God is salvation," or simply "salvation."[60] One cannot get past the first page of the New Testament without running right into this stark Hebrew truth:

> She will give birth to a son, and you are to give him the name Jesus [*Yehoshua/Yeshua*], because *he will save* his people from their sins. (Matthew 1:21, emphasis added)

For the last two thousand years, Yeshua has been universally known to be directly connected to the Messiah represented in the New Testament. Certainly, Rabbi Kaduri was keenly aware of this truth, and we can be assured that the current Orthodox naysayers know it as well.

But there's another important reason the detractors' argument falls flat.

11

The Despised One

Surely he took up our pain and bore our suffering,
yet we considered him punished by God,
stricken by him, and afflicted.
—Isaiah 53:4

Most Christians are surprised when they first learn that a number of Orthodox Jewish people use derogatory names when referring to *Yehoshua/Yeshua* of the New Testament.

From a very young age, many are taught to despise the name of Jesus and the Christian faith in general, as well as the New Testament documents. Likewise, if a Jewish person embraces Jesus as Messiah, he or she is considered to have converted to Christianity and is no longer deemed Jewish.[61] That's how despicable the name of Jesus is to Jews who are solidly Orthodox. Therefore, over many centuries, the name Yeshua/Jesus has undergone several Jewish "adjustments" to ensure that the name is not spoken with any degree of respect or reverence.

Yeshu

Among the Jews who reject Yeshua as Messiah, He is often referred to as *Yeshu*. That name can be particularly deceptive, because to the English-speaking person, it simply sounds like a shortened form of Yeshua—perhaps even a term of endearment, almost a child-like pronunciation. Some researchers insist that this is indeed the meaning of the term.[62] However, the weightier facts simply don't support that position.

The word Yeshu is widely known, even among Orthodox Jews of today, to be a long-held, traditional acronym for the Hebrew expression, *yemach shemo vezichro*, which means, "May his name and memory be obliterated."[63] Of course, this expression doesn't even come close to a term of endearment.

Sometimes, a lengthier expression is used when speaking of the New Testament Jesus: *Yeshu HaNotzri* (*yemach hanotzri shemo vezichro)*—the second word of that phrase meaning "the Nazarene." This longer rendering expresses the disparaging thought: "May the name and memory of the Nazarene be obliterated."[64]

In the only two references to Jesus in the Talmud,[65] His name is rendered *Yeshu.*[66] This is unique in both the Aramaic and Hebrew languages from the early medieval period until today. The term is reserved solely for Jesus of Nazareth. Many scholars regard the two Yeshu texts in the Talmud (Sanhedrin 43a and 107b) to be later amendments, not original to the earliest of the Talmudic texts.[67]

Not a Good Jewish Name

Dr. Kai Kjaer-Hansen penned a peer-reviewed work titled, "An Introduction to the Names Yehoshua/Joshua, Yeshua, Jesus and Yeshu." That paper outlined the thrust of his larger doctoral dissertation. An excerpt sums up his overall findings:

> On the basis of such [all that is presented to this point in the paper] and other observations I conclude that generally speaking the Yeshu form is not a good Jewish name and that it can hardly be considered a neutral name in a Jewish context in its written form.

> While the oral form may have been the normal pronunciation of Yeshua in a few places in Galilee, the form Yeshu did not only undergo a change of value in its written form but also in its oral form if, as I presume, **non-Galileans sneered at it.**
>
> Suffice it here to say that in several versions [of the Toledoth Yeshu literature[68]] Jesus is given the name Yeshua or Yehoshua at his birth. **After his mother has declared him a bastard, the rabbis, according to this literature, dictate a change of name to Yeshu.**[69] (Emphasis and bracketed words added)

Messianic Rabbi Matt Rosenberg of Seattle, Washington, and the Restoration Synagogue concur:

> Sometimes the name Yeshu is used by non-Messianic Jews to describe Yeshua. But these names do not mean the same thing. The name "Yeshu" is actually an acronym for the formula (Y'mach Sh'mo V'Zichro) meaning "may his name and memory be obliterated." When non-Messianic Jews use this name, it is an intentionally derogatory name for Yeshua. They treat Yeshua like he is the Voldemort of Judaism—as in "You-Know-Who" or "He-Who-Must-Not-Be-Named."[70]

Messianic Rabbi Zev Porat adds:

> Using the derogatory name Yeshu is indeed an ancient practice of avoiding the pronunciation of the more common name Yehoshua, especially as that name might be connected to the Jesus Christ of the New Testament. I guarantee that almost every Jew, especially here in Israel, knows this fact—regardless of those who try to claim it's not really a slight upon Yeshua's name. I come from a long line of rabbinic family tradition, going back well before Israel was reborn in 1948. I have been familiar with this term, and its well-known derogatory meaning, all my life.[71]

The Son of Panther

The matter is rather indisputable at this point. The proper name Yeshua, or Yehoshua, is fervently avoided by an Orthodox person who wishes to refer to the Christian Messiah. Yet, Yehoshua was the very name Rabbi Kaduri encoded in his note. This alone stands as especially convincing evidence that Rabbi Kaduri knew what he was doing when his note was arranged to reveal the name of Messiah as Yehoshua/Yeshua.

Other ancient Jewish writings reveal yet another disparaging substitute title for Yeshua. It is meant as an even more pronounced insult: *Yeshu ben Pantera* (sometimes *Pandera*). This Hebrew expression translates to "Yeshu *son of Pantera*." *Pantera* is said by the Jews to be the name of Mary's Roman lover. *Pantera* is the Latin/Roman word for "panther," and is a particularly vile and suggestive insult aimed at the Christian understanding of the virgin birth narrative.[72]

Pantera, sometimes called *Stada* as a nickname, is said to have been a Roman soldier. In other words, Yeshua, to the Orthodox Jews, is merely the product of Mary's love relationship with a despised Roman soldier—or worse, she was raped by the soldier.[73]

More than two dozen derogatory nicknames for Jesus make their way into various Jewish writings and spoken communication. If readers do not know this cultural practice of the Orthodox Jews, especially if they don't speak or read the Hebrew language, they will miss the disparaging references to Yeshua. One of the most popular examples of the phenomenon is the Hebrew phrase *otho ha'ish*—meaning "that man," "that certain person," or "so-and-so."[74]

Element of Proof

The purpose for introducing the preceding information is so the reader might understand the historical context concerning the innate disdain for the name of Yeshua among today's Orthodox. This is no small consideration as we attempt to grasp the heated aftershocks of the Rabbi Kaduri revelation.

However, in all fairness to the Jew who does not understand genuine Yeshua-centered biblical Christianity, I would ask the reader to consider the atrocities the Jews have suffered throughout history—in the "name of Jesus." The Inquisition, the Holocaust, and other forms of horrific persecution of the Jewish people were often carried forth under the banner of a twisted and zealous Christianity. In view of this, a fair-minded individual could understand why a Jewish person might hold a deep-seated loathing for the only faith system on the planet that worships a supposed Jewish Messiah, yet one that has killed millions of Jews around the world in the name of that Messiah.[75]

We are left with a profound consideration: Why in the world would Rabbi Kaduri dare identify Yehoshua/Yeshua as the *real* Messiah? A move like that would appear to be insanity on Kaduri's part—unless, of course, Kaduri did have a divine encounter with Yeshua that would change his life, ministry, and legacy—forever.

The ones who had the most to lose in the wake of the Kaduri note tsunami must have thought: *This must be stopped! We cannot allow this revelation to stand!* Predictably, several would-be champions of the cause enthusiastically stepped forward in an attempt to bring the story to a screeching halt.

Powerful voices with large microphones were getting involved.

It had started.

This was war.

12

Proven False

Then they scoffed, "He's just the carpenter's son,
and we know Mary, his mother, and his brothers—
James, Joseph, Simon, and Judas."
—Matthew 13:55, NLT

Not all who heard the story of Kaduri's note were convinced that it was genuine, much less that it revealed what a number of people were claiming.

One of the most widely publicized naysayers is Rabbi Tovia Singer, the director of the counter-missionary (anti-Christian) organization, Outreach Judaism, located in Israel.

Rabbi Singer's website states that for almost ten years, he was "the host of one of Israel's most compelling radio talk shows... *The Tovia Singer Show.* [Singer] is [now] a powerful and provocative voice of reason on Israel National Radio on Channel 7 in Israel."[76]

Rabbi Singer has used his radio show's popularity and renowned media persona to disparage the revelation of Rabbi Kaduri's Messiah note. For example, in 2015, Rabbi Singer was interviewed in a *Breaking Israel News* (*BIN*) article titled: "Rabbi Kaduri 'Jesus as Messiah' Claim Proven as False."

In that article, Rabbi Singer was asked why he was just then becoming interested in the matter of Kaduri's Messiah disclosure, even though the note had first appeared eight years earlier, in 2007. Rabbi Singer responded:

> I do a show where people can call in with any question about the Tanakh [the Jewish Bible]. This popped up from a caller. I spontaneously addressed it on air. I'm glad I did because curiosity was growing about this topic.[77]

Notice that a full eight years after the first appearance of the Kaduri note, Rabbi Singer admits that "curiosity was growing."

Embedded in that *BIN* article was a video wherein Rabbi Singer addressed his foremost concerns about the Kaduri note. His trepidations were stated as follows:

1. Singer insisted that the note was an outright forgery.
2. Singer asserted that the note simply does not say what many people claim it says.
3. Singer further claimed no one, not even Kaduri family members, knew about the note.

Let's address each of Rabbi Singer's concerns, in order.

The Note Is a Forgery

Remember, Rabbi Kaduri stood before his own Yom Kippur congregation in 2005 and spoke openly about the note he had written and how he had turned it over to his ministry officials for safekeeping. He also publicly disclosed that the note was to be placed on his own website one year after his death. These facts are well documented.

Sure enough, in January 2007, a note was indeed posted on his website and widely hailed as the long-awaited revelation. This claim was also made by the article on Kaduri's website that had accompanied the note. Numerous screenshots of the note and the article were captured and posted all over the Internet, thus cataloging forever that it was posted by his ministry, as instructed by Kaduri.

Furthermore, the note was taken down only *after* it was decoded and the name Yehoshua/Yeshua appeared as the coded name of Messiah. Before that revelation was made public, there were no claims *from anyone* of it being a forgery. Apparently, there was not even a suspicion that the note might be a forgery. The words "forgery" and "fake" were used only after the note's real message was deciphered.

The Note Doesn't Say Yeshua/Jesus

In that *Breaking News Israel* interview, Rabbi Singer argued that Kaduri's note does not say what Christians think. Singer flatly contradicts that claim within the context of his own argument.

Here is what I mean: Rabbi Singer admits that the note's coded message spells out the name "Yehoshua." Considering the grammatical and historical truth of that word's equivalence to "Yeshua," this proves what many have maintained all along.

Following is Rabbi Singer's argument:

> [Singer] **confirmed** that the first letter of each of the Hebrew words in **the cryptic message spells Yehoshua**, the Hebrew name of Joshua, the disciple of Moses. **It does not spell Yeshua**, which is the name messianic groups use for Jesus.
>
> Although others addressed this, no one made the most important point: **The note does not say that Jesus is the messiah.**[78] (Emphasis added)

Yehoshua/Yeshua

The truth concerning the comparison of Yehoshua and Yeshua is altogether different than what Rabbi Singer expressed. As you will see, the note *does* say that Jesus is the Messiah.

Consider the following scholarly evidence. Dr. James Price, professor of Hebrew and Old Testament at Temple Baptist Seminary, served as a section editor (historical books) for the highly popular Holman Christian Standard Bible translation. He holds a PhD in Hebrew and was the executive editor of the NKJV Old Testament, as well as the chairman of the Executive Review Committee of that translation.[79]

Especially note the sections I have highlighted in bold:

> [Therefore] it can be concluded that in post-exilic times of the Biblical era, **the names Yeshua and Yehoshua were regarded as equivalent** [in the Hebrew Bible]....
>
> As far as the Talmud is concerned, it is evident that the old uncensored editions of **the Talmud associated Jesus [Yeshua] of Nazareth with the name Joshua [Yehoshua]**. This is demonstrated by the following passage: Sotah 47a.

Dr. Price concludes his article with this straightforward confirmation:

> From this evidence it can be concluded that in post-exilic Bible times the names Yehoshua and Yeshua were regarded as equivalent names of the same person.[80]

But There's More

From a scholarly article that quotes the *Jewish New Testament Commentary* and the *Lexicon of Jewish Names in Late Antiquity*, we are again assured that Yeshua was indeed a common alternative form of the name "Yehoshua."

> The Hebrew Bible uses Yehoshuah (יהושע), and later form Yeshua (ישוע), for Joshua, which means "Yah is Salvation." Tal Ilan's Lexicon of Jewish Names in Late Antiquity (2002), notes Yehoshuah (יהושע), **and later Yeshua** among many names containing Yah derived from Yahweh.[81]

This assertion is true in later books of the Hebrew Bible as well as among Jews of the Second Temple period. The name Yehoshua/Yeshua corresponds to the Greek spelling *Iesous,* from which, through the Latin *Iesus,* comes the English spelling "Jesus." In short, *Yehoshua* in Hebrew is equivalent to *Jesus* in English.

The Prime Minister Agrees

For still another authentic Hebrew attestation to the meaning and understanding of the word Yehoshua, consider the following.

In an opening chapter of this book, you'll remember that I mentioned Israeli Prime Minister Benjamin Netanyahu and his awareness of the Kaduri story. My acquaintance who introduced my first Kaduri book to the prime minister related the following after his meeting with Netanyahu:

> [Prime Minister Netanyahu] and I sat down privately for about fifteen minutes. I told him about your book and the Rabbi and the name of the Messiah. When I said, "His name is Yehoshua" Netanyahu murmured, "Jesus"! And I agreed.

Apparently, it's rather common knowledge in Israel—from the prime minister right down to the man on the street—that Rabbi Kaduri's Yehoshua revelation indisputably translates in the Hebrew mind as "Jesus."

Additional Attestation

Messianic Rabbi Zev Porat explains:

> Here's the truth of the matter. The difference between Yehoshua and Yeshua would be a little like the difference between Steven and Steve, or Joshua and Josh. In other words, they each signify the very same name. But in Hebrew, the difference goes much

> deeper than even that. Yehoshua is the word for "savior." Yeshua is the word for "salvation."
>
> So Yehoshua would effectively mean "Yeshua is our savior." It all depends upon the context of its use. Yehoshua could also mean "He will save" or "He saved." Again, it depends upon the context in which the word is used. But there's no doubt about it, Yehoshua and Yeshua are the same word, conveying the same overall meaning.... Yeshua is the savior of humanity and He was sent from Yahweh.
>
> I believe this may be the very reason that Rabbi Kaduri used the word Yehoshua in his note, because he wanted to be clear that he was speaking of Jesus/Yeshua the savior. He wanted to be clear that his note was not about a "different Yeshua," it was meant to specifically reveal the name of *Yeshua Ha' Mashiach.*

Surely Rabbi Kaduri knew these basic Hebrew truths when he penned his Messiah note. How could he not? And if Kaduri knew it, how could Rabbi Singer not have known this fact as well? But like it or not, Kaduri's note *did* "say" that Jesus is the Messiah. Ironically, it seems we can ultimately agree with Rabbi Tovia Singer—this truly is "the most important point" of the entire Kaduri saga.

No One Knew about the Note

There's another incredulous claim Rabbi Singer made in that article. He insisted that not a single person among Kaduri's family or students knew anything about the note:

> I think that the mysterious "note from the grave" feature sparked enormous curiosity. Given that the note said nothing that endorsed Christianity, I asked a number of people who studied

> under the great sage. I asked family members. **Uniformly, no one knew anything about this note.**[82] (Emphasis added)

Of course, allowing for Rabbi Singer's powerful voice and influence among the Jewish people, and further considering that he was already on record as attempting to suppress the spreading of Kaduri's revelation, it is no wonder that Singer was unable to find anyone who knew anything about the note.

How unlikely would it be, given the enormous curiosity about the note, that not a soul within Kaduri's own family would know anything about it? How did the family and Rabbi Singer account for Kaduri's own son, David, giving the previously mentioned interview to *Israel Today*, in which David Kaduri admitted that his father had written the note and that it had been posted on the Kaduri ministry website?[83]

As a former law enforcement officer, I can attest to being faced with the same problem when trying to convince people to tell me what they really knew about a particular matter under investigation. If people think they might incur some sort of reprisal for the information they possess, they suddenly seem to have a "memory lapse."

Nonetheless, Rabbi Tovia Singer was not the only important and persuasive rabbinical personality to lash out against the Kaduri Messiah revelation. Rabbi Kaduri's story was also making waves among the Jewish Orthodox all the way across the Atlantic Ocean—in Monsey, New York.

13

It's a Scam

Many testified falsely against him,
but their statements did not agree.
—Mark 14:56

Rabbi Yosef Mizrachi[84] is another influential voice that attempted to delegitimize the Kaduri story. On November 14, 2014, one year after the original book on the Kaduri Messiah note was released, a video featuring Mizrachi was posted on the Internet.[85]

In that video, Mizrachi attempts to explain away Rabbi Kaduri's note. Like Rabbi Singer, Mizrachi admits that he still receives a great deal of correspondence and questions regarding Kaduri's revelation. Following are his transcribed words from that interview. Knowing what you now know, Yosef Mizrachi's obfuscations will be easy to spot:

> I get a lot of emails [from people] who are **fooled by the Christians**. They ask me, "Rabbi, we hear that Rabbi Kaduri before he passed away…he gave a letter to his son and before he passed away he said to his son to open this letter a year later and when his son opened the letter he found out that the Messiah will be 'JC.' How can it be that a Jew wrote such a thing?"
>
> Right away I knew it was a scam. Christians are the masters of lies. [They] invent all kinds of lies. So I said, let me go

and check that nonsense story—where it came from. First of all, Rabbi Kaduri never left anything. Somebody made up that story.... There's a lot of naïve people. Whatever you feed them, they believe.

The Christians made [a] **mistake** with **their regular ignorance.** What was their mistake? They presented supposedly a letter from Rabbi Kaduri—and it says over there that the Mashiach would be...**Yehoshua—not Yeshua!**' How do Christians call "JC"? Yeshua! **It's a different name!**

So, **even if the letter was true,** even if he left it to his son and he told him the name of the Messiah would be Yehoshua—**what does it have to do with Yeshua**—with "JC"?

The fact that a Jew would think that an orthodox big rabbi would write that Mashiach would be "JC" shows how naïve people are—it's crazy how people would think such a thing.

So, the answer is that it never happened. And **even if the story was real**—according to *their* story, it says Yehoshua. That's what they claim. They didn't claim Yeshua, **they made a mistake, as usual.** They always try to claim they have something from God, but in the end, we check it and we find they have a lot of human error.[86] (Emphasis in bold added)

Notice that besides the generalized vitriolic attacks upon the integrity of Christians in general, Mizrachi resorts to the same scholastically disproven argument used by Rabbi Singer—that the name "Yehoshua" is not the same as "Yeshua."

Getting It Straight

Regarding the existence of the note in the first place, we must ask: *So, which is it?*

Rabbi Singer admits the note existed. He also admits it was posted and translated as "Yehoshua." Yet, Rabbi Yosef Mizrachi insists the note never existed in the first place and that the entire story is a Christian lie. However, apparently to cover himself—just in case, he says—*if it did exist,* the Christians simply *made a mistake.*

The remaining questions are equally profound. Does Mizrachi really believe that the note and the entire story never happened, when the note was published for several months on Kaduri's website for all the world to see—and, presumably, it was posted by Kaduri's own webmaster?[87]

By now, the facts are clear. To quash the truth about Rabbi Kaduri's revelation of Yeshua as Messiah, the Orthodox elite were willing to resort to just about any argument that seemed to stick against the wall.

Unfortunately, Mizrachi and Singer are only two examples of the greater misinformation machine the Israeli Jews are up against when researching the Rabbi Kaduri phenomenon. Thus, the need for the book you are now reading.

Zev Porat weighed in on the matter of these two rabbis:

> Both Rabbi Yosef Mizrachi and Rabbi Tovia Singer have made numerous public attempts to keep Messiah of Israel Ministries from telling the Rabbi Yitzhak Kaduri story. They have both disparagingly referred to our ministry by name, and my use of the Rabbi Kaduri story in witnessing to Jews.
>
> I have offered, many times, to come on Rabbi Tovia Singer's show to have a friendly and live discussion of the facts of this matter. He has never responded to a single offer I have made to him. The same goes for Rabbi Mizrachi. Since they know that I am a well-known voice in Israel regarding the Rabbi Kaduri story, it is very telling that they refuse to openly discuss the phenomenon with me. If I am wrong, surely the facts would prove it, wouldn't they? What do they have to fear? Unless they know they are wrong.
>
> The attempted cover-up of this true story runs very deep. But Yeshua is having the victory in spite of all the concealment measures. Our ministry is continually inundated with calls, emails,

and letters from Jews all over Israel who want to know about everything they can get their hands on concerning the Kaduri Messiah note.

The Myth

There simply was no "Christian lie" involved with the Kaduri note. The imaginary "trickster Christians" did not write the note, nor did they deviously publish it on Kaduri's website. Rabbi Kaduri wrote it and left it with his ministry officials, just like he said he would. Furthermore, his own ministry organization published the note, proudly displaying it before the world until the message was decoded.

In the next chapter you will see for yourself what the problem really is. There is a powerful and shocking reason the rabbis and the other Orthodox elite didn't want anyone to make the connection between Rabbi Kaduri's revelation and Yeshua; it's something they hoped no one would understand.

But now, we'll finally unravel that biblical mystery.

What's in a Name?

But I trust in your unfailing love;
my heart rejoices in your salvation.
—Psalm 13:5

The following illustrates the foundation of the uproar over Rabbi Kaduri's note and its Yeshua revelation:

Almost every Hebrew-speaking person on the planet who reads the Tanakh knows something that a large number of English-speaking Christians do not. They understand that the name of Jesus, in Hebrew, is written all over the Old Testament, and it's not written in "code." It's in the surface text.

This secret is one reason the Kaduri note, in the mind of the Orthodox Jewish leaders, *had to be* discredited. It is also why many Orthodox Jews insist on referring to Yeshua as "Yeshu," the often-derogatory substitute name we uncovered a few chapters back.

The Insurmountable Conundrum

Among the Kaduri note detractors, many would have us believe that the name Yehoshua/Yeshua could be "any common person" ("Joshua"). However, if these detractors had a say in the matter, they would much prefer that Kaduri had revealed any Hebrew name *but* that particular "common" name.

Messianic Rabbi Zev Porat explains:

> The name "Yehoshua," or "Yeshua," is a very distinctive Hebrew word. It translates as "salvation." Therefore, every time someone speaks the word "salvation" in the Hebrew language they are actually saying "Yeshua"—or, as the word is commonly pronounced in English—"Jesus." And this just happens to be the name that everyone in the world recognizes as the Messiah that is disclosed through the New Testament.[88]
>
> So, in this beautiful and Heaven-anointed way, Jesus/Yeshua is all over the Bible! And when this truth is revealed, using the Tanakh, many doorways to salvation in Yeshua are opened to the Jewish people. As a matter of fact, I frequently use this great biblical truth in witnessing to my Jewish brethren. They are shocked when they see it for the very first time.

Yeshua Is Everywhere!

More than seven dozen times, from Exodus to Zechariah, the word "Yeshua" appears—right in the middle of God's Old Testament promises.

In the English translations, we see the word as "salvation." But, as previously stated, in the Hebrew text, the word is *yeshua*, or a direct *form* of the word, depending upon the other contextual qualifiers.[89] Herein lies the problem with Rabbi Kaduri's revelation of the name of the true Messiah.

Let me illustrate. As we examine several passages that use the word *yeshua* ("salvation"), we will substitute the English word "Jesus" to illustrate what the Hebrew reader beholds when confronted with this truth.[90]

Following is one of the Tanakh's earliest appearances of Yeshua (with emphasis added):

> The Lord is my strength and my song; he has become **my Jesus. He is my God**, and I will praise him, my father's God, **and I will exalt him**. (Exodus 15:2)

From the Psalms:

> But I trust in your unfailing love; my heart rejoices in **your Jesus.** (Psalm 13:5)

> The Lord is my light and **my Jesus**—whom shall I fear? The Lord is the stronghold of my life—of whom shall I be afraid? (Psalm 27:1)

> My soul finds rest in God alone; **my Jesus** comes from him. He alone is my rock and **my Jesus**; he is my fortress, I will never be shaken. (Psalm 62:1–2)

More than three dozen other passages from the Psalms are just like the preceding examples. But, additional instances are also found elsewhere in the Old Testament. And they are just as striking.

From the prophet Isaiah:

> Surely God is **my Jesus**; I will trust and not be afraid. The Lord, the Lord, is my strength and my song; **he has become my Jesus.** With joy you **will draw water from the wells of Jesus.** (Isaiah 12:2–3)[91]

> I will also make you a light for the Gentiles, that **my Jesus** may reach to the ends of the earth. (Isaiah 49:6)

> In the time of my favor I will answer you, and **in the day of Jesus** I will help you. (Isaiah 49:8)

> The LORD has made proclamation to the ends of the earth: "Say to Daughter Zion, 'See, **your Jesus comes**! See, his reward is with him, and his recompense accompanies him.'" (Isaiah 62:11)

> Turn to me and **be given Jesus (*yasha*),**[92] all you ends of the earth; for I am God, and there is no other. By myself I have sworn, my mouth has uttered in all integrity a word that will not be revoked: Before me every knee will bow; by me every tongue will swear. (Isaiah 45:22–23; also see Romans 14:11; Philippians 2:10).

From the prophet Jonah:

> But I, with a song of thanksgiving, will sacrifice to you. What I have vowed I will make good. **Jesus comes from the Lord.** (Jonah 2:9)

From the prophet Zechariah we find this striking use of the Hebrew word *yasha* (OT #3467),[93] meaning "having salvation":

> Rejoice greatly, O daughter of Zion; shout, O daughter of Jerusalem: behold, thy King cometh unto thee: he is just, and **having Jesus**; lowly, and riding upon an ass, and upon a colt the foal of an ass. (Zechariah 9:9, KJV)

From beginning to end, Yeshua/Jesus is right there in the Old Testament, and quite dramatically so. In each of the dozens of times the name is found, His name can be tied directly to the New Testament fulfillments and promises in *Yeshua Ha' Mashiach*—Jesus the Messiah.

The Amidah Prayer

The Hebrew Amidah Prayer[94] is the central prayer of the Jewish liturgy. This prayer, among others, is found in the *siddur*, the traditional Jewish prayer book. In Hebrew, the prayer is called *Tefilat HaAmiday*—"The Standing Prayer." The original prayer constituted eighteen blessings. Today, nineteen blessings are used.

Blessing number 15 of the Amidah Prayer is titled as a prayer "For the Messianic King." Where the word "salvation" is spoken in Hebrew (*yeshua*), I will again substitute the English form, "Jesus":

> Speedily cause the offspring of your servant David to flourish, and let him be exalted by your saving power, for we wait all day long for **your Jesus**. Blessed are you, O Lord, **who causes Jesus to flourish.**

Kaduri Knew

No doubt, you now understand one of the most monumental problems with Rabbi Kaduri's Messiah revelation. His ministry officials understood it as well, and so do the current Orthodox rabbis, the Sanhedrin, and the Jewish anti-missionary organizations in Israel.

Messianic Rabbi Porat confirms, "This is what the Hebrew eye sees when looking at these Scriptures. This is why the name 'Jesus' or 'Yeshua' is so controversial among the Orthodox Jews. This is why they are so afraid of Rabbi Kaduri's revelation. This is why most Orthodox Jews are constantly told not to read the Scriptures for themselves, but to depend upon the teachings and interpretations of the rabbis."

Rabbi Yitzhak Kaduri knew all of this, too. There's no way he didn't know. That is why thirteen of his personal students are now professing believers in *Yeshua Ha' Mashiach*. They are his lasting evidence and legacy, and their testimonies strongly attest that "Kaduri knew."

What Remains?

If Kaduri's note was indeed genuine, and if its existence was widely known because of Kaduri's Yom Kippur announcement, and if the name in the note's code really was Yeshua/Jesus, and if Kaduri's own students still testify that their aged rabbi was teaching them that Yeshua is Messiah, what valid options are left for the detractors as they continue to attempt to discredit this story?

A popular defense frequently brought forward is that Kaduri had become, in his later years, a senile old man; therefore, he didn't even know what he was saying.

However, that assessment does not appear to come even close to the truth.

15

A Crazy Man?

If we are "out of our mind," as some say, it is for God; if we are in our right mind, it is for you.
—2 Corinthians 5:13

When faced with such an insurmountable wall of evidence concerning the credibility of the Kaduri note, a number of its detractors resort to another tactic. They argue that sometime shortly before his death, Rabbi Kaduri simply lost his mind.

However, enormous hurdles must be crossed before that outlandish argument can rightfully be made.

Kaduri had his Messiah vision on November 4, 2003, only two years before his October 2005 synagogue announcement.[95] Kaduri was recognized by a plethora of the political elite as well as by his own rabbinical peers as a sharp, dependable, and highly intelligent rabbi—right up to his death. The argument that he eventually became a crazy old man simply doesn't hold water. This is an embarrassingly inconvenient truth for the disparagers of Kaduri's Messiah note.[96]

Messianic Rabbi Porat offered his firsthand knowledge of the claims that Rabbi Kaduri had become addle-minded: "It is absolutely true that some in Israel try to describe Rabbi Kaduri's revelation of Yeshua by saying that he had become an old man whose mind was slipping. They say he couldn't have known what he was talking about regarding Yeshua."

Zev continued:

> However, it's interesting to note that even up to the last six months of Kaduri's life he was often seen on television and in the halls of the Knesset. He was seen and heard giving instructions, recommendations, and prayers to other leading rabbis as well as to Aryeh Deri, Israeli Minister of Interior and main liaison to Israel's nascent Sanhedrin Council. No one in Israel can deny these facts. And these public appearances were long after he announced that he had met Messiah through a vision or dream.
>
> In the last few months of his life, Rabbi Kaduri even gave advice to the basketball coach, Pini Gershon, of the Maccabi Tel Aviv sports club. At almost every game they played, Gershon sought a blessing from Rabbi Kaduri. This was a much-publicized fact. Would this basketball coach continually seek blessings from a crazy old man who was mumbling and fumbling around—a man who had lost his mind? I think not!

No More Kabbalah

Then Zev offered this surprising piece of insider information: "The only thing that some of the Orthodox Jews might have considered strange or mentally unstable about Kaduri in the last eight months of his life was that Kaduri was not teaching Kabbalah anymore."

Zev continued:

> Rabbi Kaduri was still pronouncing his blessings, and prayers, but not from the traditional Kabbalistic approach. This might have confused some of the Orthodox. This might be a reason they would think he was getting senile. But nothing could be further from the truth. We now understand, of course, that this was because Kaduri was a true believer in Yeshua near the very end of his life. He was obviously beginning to back away from Kabbalah.

As an example of Kaduri's mental state at the time of his death, consider the following words, written in January 2014, in memorandum of Rabbi Kaduri—eight years after his death.

> It is said that [Rabbi Kaduri] memorized the entire Talmud (over 6200 pages of dense text in some 63 volumes), together with its commentaries, along with a multitude of other works. He wrote several mystical texts of his own, which were never published, as Rav Kaduri did not want them getting into the wrong hands. He went on to become the head *mekubal* ("Kabbalist") among Israel's rabbis.[97]

Notice that not a single word intimates that somehow Rabbi Kaduri had lost even an inkling of his mental acuity at the time of his death. And there was certainly no indication that he had become a "crazy old man" between his reported vision of 2003 and his synagogue announcement of 2005. Don't forget, we still have to take into account the testimony of over a dozen of his former students. Those witnesses affirm that Kaduri was teaching that Yeshua is Messiah when the rest of the Jewish world was calling Kaduri the greatest of all the rabbis in Israel.

In light of the insurmountable evidence of the veracity of Rabbi Kaduri's note, the Jewish elite began to step up their defensive measures. The story had to be terminated. It simply could not be allowed to endure.

But *Yahweh* had other plans.

16

Protecting the Legacy

What you have said in the dark will be heard in the daylight, and what you have whispered in the ear in the inner rooms will be proclaimed from the roofs.
—Luke 12:3

Upon the exposure of the note's decrypted message, Kaduri's ministry organization circled the wagons. They quickly determined that the phenomenon had to be crushed. Other influential voices were recruited to join the attempted shutdown.

Aviel Schneider, the author of the original *Israel Today* story, claimed that the officials at Kaduri's yeshiva urged him not to publish the story. Kaduri's own son, David, one of the top ministry officials, initially insisted it was "impossible" that the note had actually been written by his father, Rabbi Yitzhak Kaduri.[98]

As it turned out, the Kaduri note did, in fact, receive negligible coverage in the global media. In Israel, only the Hebrew websites News First Class and Kaduri.net cited the Messiah note. Both of those reports deemed it to be authentic. The Hebrew daily publication, *Ma'ariv,* ran a story on the Kaduri message, but categorically labeled it as a forgery, without any forensic evidence to support that claim.[99]

Jewish readers of those articles left comments declaring, "So this means Rabbi Kaduri was a Christian?" and "The Christians are dancing and celebrating."[100]

Apparently, there was no misunderstanding among the Jews regarding the meaning and impact of Rabbi Kaduri's note—or what the word "Yehoshua" really meant. Indeed, what little reporting that was actually done on the topic was fairly unnerving to Orthodox and secular Jews alike.

The Kaduri Ministry Organization

Rabbi Yitzhak Kaduri's son, David, who was 80 years old at the time of his father's passing, claimed the note posted on Kaduri's ministry website was somehow a fake. Yet, there has never been a credible explanation from the organization as to how that "fake" could have been so prominently and proudly displayed at Kaduri.net in the first place.

Interestingly enough, an ultra-Orthodox *Arutz Sheva Israel National Radio* show host, Yehoshuah Meiri, admits to being Kaduri.net's webmaster. Presumably, he would have been responsible for content that made it to Kaduri's website, including the now-infamous Messiah note. And, surely, if he didn't put the note there, he would have noticed almost immediately that a "fake" article and note had appeared. Yet, I am not aware that such a claim as this was ever made by Kaduri's organization.

Mr. Meiri attests:

> The Kaduri.net website, which I operate, is the official website of Rav Yitzhak Kaduri. In the website, there is an explicit letter of approbation signed by Rabbi Kaduri for the website and my activities.[101]

But, David Kaduri was next in line to take over his father's highly influential ministry organization. The legacy of the entire Kaduri ministry was now riding upon the disclosure of Yitzhak Kaduri's Messiah revelation. Upon original inquiry of *Israel Today* concerning the note, David Kaduri summarily claimed, "It's not his writing."[102]

David proceeded to cart out a stack of eighty-year-old documents bearing his father's signature. He presented these papers in an effort to somehow prove that the handwriting on the recent note was not the same as the handwriting of eighty years ago; therefore, it could not have been his father's. This, of course, was an extremely unconvincing argument—and forensically untenable at the face of it—but it was one that David Kaduri insisted upon presenting as irrefutable evidence that the note was a forgery. Apparently, David offered no explanation for how the fake note could have been posted on the website.[103]

However, David Kaduri did acknowledge that in the last months of his father's life, the aged Yitzhak Kaduri spoke incessantly about his latest visions of Messiah. "My father has met the Messiah in a vision," David Kaduri confirmed. "And [he] told us that [Messiah] would come soon."[104]

"I have had personal conversations with the late Rabbi David, and know others who did as well," Messianic Rabbi Zev Porat told me. "David Kaduri was continually questioned about your original book, Carl. Jews in Israel want to know if the account is true. They want more information on the matter. Rabbi David Kaduri told them the book was untrue. David Kaduri continually tried to suppress the story of his father's Messiah note."

Zev continued, "Rabbi David Kaduri, before his 2015 death, had a huge influence upon the anti-missionary organization Yad L'Achim.[105] This is an organization that attempts to keep Jews in Israel from believing in Yeshua as Messiah. Yad L'Achim is still frantically trying to debunk the Kaduri Messiah story. They seem to be fixated upon it, almost above anything else."

Zev further revealed that Yad L'Achim's aggressive tactics appear to be dramatically backfiring.

"Carl, I can't tell you how many witnessing opportunities are opening for our ministry because of the curiosity that has been stoked by Yad L'Achim's continual protests over the story, and their lack of concrete answers and proof to discredit it," Zev said, and continued:

Their routine answer to the Jews who are seeking the truth of the matter seems only to be "Don't read that book!" or "Pay no attention to that note—it's a fake!" But they don't know how to prove their accusations. And many of the Jews know this. That is why they are suspicious of Yad L'Achim's protestations.

To this day, Yad L'Achim and the Kaduri Ministry leaders encourage the Jews in Israel to stay away from the Yitzhak Kaduri Messiah-story and to especially stay away from my ministry.

He then added:

One thing I've learned in my life from growing up in a rabbinic family in Israel...you don't tell a Jew what they "can't" or "shouldn't do!" All they are doing by trying to cover up this well-documented story is creating a deeper desire for many Jews to seek me out, and to study Kaduri's story even further. And I am more than happy to oblige them!

Then Zev shared this tidbit of personal insight:

Carl, I truly believe that many in Israel, even among the Orthodox elite, *know* this story is true. They just don't know what to do with it. It's an overpowering story that won't go away. They can't shut it down. It's like we're right back in New Testament days when Yeshua first walked among the Jews in the Holy Land and confounded their leaders. No matter how hard they tried to trap Him, they couldn't stop Him!

To accept Yeshua as Messiah would mean that their whole way of Orthodox life would be turned on its head. Power, position, prestige, and riches would all have to be sacrificed in order to bow down to this amazing revelation. It's simply too much for many of them to even consider.

I find it truly ironic that very important leaders hung on

almost every word Kaduri uttered, and every vision that he had, except this particular vision. But now, the Jewish leaders would rather go down fighting than to even give a moment's consideration to the possibility that Rabbi Yitzhak Kaduri actually spoke the truth in this final vision as well.

We must pray for the Jews in Israel. This is a strong spiritual battle they are in, especially in these prophetic times.

The Gatekeeper Passes

Sadly, Rabbi David Kaduri died in March 2015 as a result of traumatic head injuries he sustained a few months prior, when he had slipped and fallen on the steps of Yeshiva Nachalat Yitzchak. He was delivering the evening prayer when the accident occurred.[106]

The rabbi was 88 years old when he passed away. Even though he maintained until the very last that the infamous Messiah note was a fake, he never plausibly explained how that fraudulent note could have made it to the website. Nor did he ever explain how it could be that, prior to the manifestation of the Yehoshua revelation, the note's authenticity had not been questioned by anyone. In fact, at first, the note was celebrated by Kaduri's organization, hailed as the genuine article…until the name of Jesus was found encoded within the text. Then *everything* changed…

Part Three

THE DIVINE PERSPECTIVE

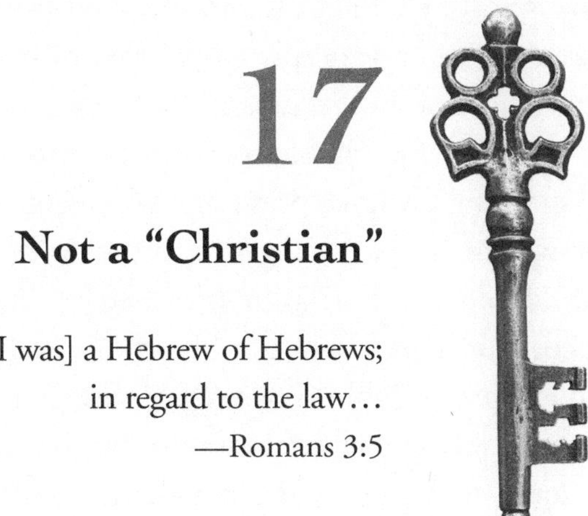

17

Not a "Christian"

[I was] a Hebrew of Hebrews;
in regard to the law…
—Romans 3:5

Let me be clear. I am not attempting to be the late Rabbi Kaduri's apologist. Nor am I his public-relations liaison to the evangelical Christian community. I have no desire to make this story into anything more than what it is already documented to be.

However, the irrefutable fact remains: Kaduri's *note from beyond the grave* identifies Yehoshua/Yeshua as the true, coming Messiah. Those familiar with the New Testament and the gospel message of Jesus Christ know that regarding the ultimate revelation of Kaduri's note, the elderly rabbi nailed it.

Calling It as It Is

We must also understand that Rabbi Kaduri probably could not have cared less concerning the traditional Christian world's thoughts about his revelation.

That statement might surprise some readers. But, by his own understanding of the word, Kaduri's revelation wasn't meant for the Christians. It was specifically intended for his people—*the Jews*—beginning with those living in Israel. Rabbi Kaduri believed the world was in its prophesied last days. He was deeply committed to making certain the Jewish people were told of the real Messiah before it's too late.

Let us admit what should by now be obvious: Rabbi Kaduri was not a Latin-speaking Catholic priest or a white-collared Protestant minister. Neither was he a fiery evangelical preacher banging on a pulpit and holding a Bible in the air as he preached. Rather, Kaduri was an aged, renowned, hard-core Lubavitch Hasidic,[107] and a deeply Kabbalistic,[108] Sephardic[109] Jewish rabbi. His ministry among those of the Orthodox Jewish faith was globally famous for its widely distributed amulets, prayer cloths, talismans, and other charms of blessing. To this day, one can still find authentic *Kaduri items* of this nature for sale all over the Internet.

If you are not familiar with Judaism, I know that's a mouthful of rather confusing information. But once we get the preconceived images out of our head, we can begin to get a clearer picture of Kaduri's mind and his deeply entrenched desire to speak to the Jewish soul—*in the Jewish way.*

New Testament Context

By the way, as a point of biblical context, consider that the beloved Apostle Paul was also a thoroughly Jewish rabbi as well. Paul was a teacher (rabbi) of the Law before he had his own Messiah revelation, and he was a teacher of the Law *after* his conversion—except that after he met Messiah Yehoshua, Paul took the Jewish Scriptures and went into the Jewish synagogues. There he proved that Jesus was the genuine Messiah for whom the Jews had long been waiting (Acts 17:3). Paul knew that the message of salvation in Messiah Yeshua had to ultimately be delivered to the Gentiles as well (Isaiah 49:1–15; Acts 13:47). This was his specific calling.

Kaduri did something similar regarding the Jews of his day, at least within the confines of his yeshiva and his synagogue, and with a specific group of his students. Of course, the Apostle Paul lived for many years on the other side of his Messianic vision. After years of preparation, Paul finally began his ministry with which most Christians are now familiar.[110] Kaduri, on the other hand, lived only a couple of years after his vision, and then the Messiah note was finally revealed as his prolific, global witness.

However, while Paul eventually went to the Gentiles with the gospel of Yeshua—as God had directed him—he almost always went to the Jews and their synagogues *first.* There's a reason for that. That was where Paul was most at home. His heart was, first and foremost, for his own people, and, secondly, it was for the Gentiles (Romans 9:2–4). How often we forget that. In our minds, we sometimes want to dress Paul up in a suit and tie and stick him in a church behind stained-glass windows while leading a rousing rendition of "Amazing Grace."

Observe Paul's personal testimony to the early Church:

> [I was] circumcised on the eighth day, of the people of Israel, of the tribe of Benjamin, a Hebrew of Hebrews; in regard to the law, a Pharisee; as for zeal, persecuting the church; as for righteousness based on the law, faultless. (Philippians 3:5–6)

First Called Christians

We shouldn't become overly concerned that Kaduri and the select few of his students who believe in Yeshua as Messiah would not immediately call themselves "Christians." As stated before, the average Jewish understanding of that moniker is considerably different than that of most Westernized Christians of today.

Also, we must not forget that practically the entire early Church was made up of Jews for the first several decades of its existence. Among them were many priests and teachers of the Law, as well as synagogue officials and rabbis (John 12:42; Acts 6:7, 18:8).

The Early Church

Here's another shocker to most modern Christians. In the same way the thoroughly Jewish Yitzhak Kaduri would not have even thought to call himself a "Christian," *neither did the members of the early Church.*

When the early believers were first called "Christians" at Antioch (Acts 11:26), the term had been invented by their detractors, Jews as well as Romans, as an expression of ridicule (Acts 26:28). The early disciples of Yeshua would not begin to wear that name with any kind of honor until many decades later.

Several renowned commentaries address this. Especially notice the words emphasized in bold type.

Ellicott's Commentary:

> The Emperor Julian (Misopog., p. 344) notes the tendency to invent nicknames, as a form of satire, as characteristic of the population of Antioch in his time, **and the same tone of [contempt] seems to have prevailed on the first appearance of the new faith.**
>
> As used in the New Testament, we note (1) that the disciples never use [**the name "Christian"**] **of themselves. They keep to such terms as the "brethren" (Acts 15:1), and the "saints" (Acts 9:13), and "those of the way" (Acts 9:2).** (2) That the hostile Jews use the more scornful term of "Nazarenes" (Acts 24:5). (3) That the term [Christians] is used as a neutral and sufficiently respectful word by Agrippa in Acts 26:23, and at a somewhat later date, when it had obviously gained a wider currency, as that which brought with it the danger of suffering and persecution (1 Peter 4:16).
>
> It was natural that a name first given by outsiders should soon be accepted by believers as a title in which to glory.[111]

Expositor's Greek Testament:

> **In the New Testament the Christians always named themselves [disciples, brothers, saints, believers, etc.], but on no occasion "Christians,"** whilst the Jews not only refused to recognize that Jesus had any claim to be the Christ, but also called His followers [the Nazarene sect, or cult] (Acts 24:5).[112]

Vincent's New Testament Word Studies:

> [The term "Christian" is found] only three times in the New Testament, **and never as a name used by Christians** themselves, but as a nickname or **a term of reproach.**[113]

The designation "Christian" for the earliest believers in Yeshua is used only two other times in the New Testament after the use of it in Acts 11. It is found in Acts 26:28, where King Agrippa tells Paul that "you almost persuade me to become a Christian," and in 1 Peter 4:16, where the apostle is trying to comfort the persecuted believers, who are "suffering for being Christians."

Of these two instances, *Ellicott's Commentary for English Readers* says:

> Peter purposely uses the name [here in 1 Peter 4:16] which was a name of derision among the heathens. It is not, as yet, one by which the believers would usually describe themselves. It only occurs twice other in the New Testament—in Acts 11:26, where we are told of the invention of the nickname, and in Acts 26:28, where Agrippa catches it up with insolent scorn.... So contemptible was the name that "Well-bred people avoided pronouncing the name, or, when forced to do so, made a kind of apology."[114]

The *Cambridge Bible for Schools and Colleges* confirms that the term "Christian" only later became a label of honor among the early believers in Yeshua as Messiah:

> The words now before us [1 Peter 4:16] probably did much to stamp it on the history of the Church. Men dared not disown it. They came to exult in it. Somewhat later on they came to find in it…a new significance.[115]

Assigning Labels

The bottom line is this: Rabbi Yitzhak Kaduri was not interested in the title "Christian," nor was he interested in "becoming a Christian." Those descriptions would mean something entirely different to him than they do for us.

However, in the purest form of the meaning of the word, Rabbi Kaduri could truly be known as a Christian as well, as could any other Jew who is born again by believing that *Yeshua Ha' Mashiach* is Lord (Romans 10:9). In reality, the designation simply means "follower of Yeshua as Christ—or Messiah." However, to this day, it is still difficult for Jews to grasp the concept of being called Christian, at least in the way they have been raised to understand the title.

Therefore, I am not interested in "converting" a Jew to a "concept" so I can somehow feel he or she is finally "one of us." Neither am I interested in forcing Jews to call themselves by a title they do not yet fully understand just so that I can feel better about my witness to them. More than likely, that understanding will come with time, as it did with the early Jewish church.

I am most interested in helping the Jewish person understand that Yeshua/Jesus truly is the "One" for whom he or she has been waiting all along. I am interested in that person becoming a "completed Jew"—a Messianic Jew, one who fully believes and trusts that Yehoshua is indeed the true, coming Messiah/Savior…*Yeshua Ha' Mashiach*…just like Rabbi Kaduri revealed in his note.

18

Revealing Mysteries

The mystery that has been kept hidden for ages and generations, but is now disclosed to the saints.
—Colossians 1:26

Let me show you a mystery.

Surprising to many Christians are the New Testament hints that indicate the Apostle Paul himself may have been influenced by Kabbalah.

Don't panic! Highly renowned scholars support this. Besides, that revelation shouldn't come as a surprise now, especially when we consider that Paul was thoroughly steeped in Jewish mystical Orthodoxy prior to his Damascus Road conversion experience—just like Rabbi Yitzhak Kaduri.

For example, Paul frequently speaks of the "mysteries" of God and the things that have been "kept hidden" and are "now revealed." He employs these terms often throughout his writings to the early Church.[116]

The Hebrew word *Kabbalah* simply means "to receive." However, in the context of the Jewish mysticism practice of Kabbalah, the word more specifically means: "A received mystical teaching or a revelation that was previously hidden—by implication —the revelation was received directly from God Himself."[117]

Dr. Alfred Edersheim's[118] renowned scholarly work titled *Brief Outline of Ancient Jewish Theological Literature: Sketches of Jewish Social Life* dramatically underscores Kabbalah's influence among the people of Jesus' day:

> **There can be no doubt, that so early as the time of our Lord a series of doctrines and speculations prevailed** which were kept secret from the multitude, and even from ordinary students, probably from fear of leading them into heresy.
>
> **This class of study bears the general name of the "Kabbalah,"** and, as even the term (from "kabal," to "receive," or "hand down") implies, represents the spiritual traditions handed down from earliest times
>
> The "Kabbalah" grouped itself chiefly around the history of the creation, and the mystery of God's Presence and Kingdom in the world.[119] (Emphasis added)

As another attestation of Kabbalah's potential influence upon Paul and the larger New Testament audience of the early centuries, consider the following description provided by the Christian Research Institute (CRI):

> Kabbalah is the name of an occult philosophy and theosophy that developed among Jews in Babylonia, and later Italy, Provence, and Spain, between the sixth and thirteenth centuries A.D.
>
> **At first** [Kabbalah] **was used by the mainstream of Judaism**, but eventually it became identified with those who believed that the Kabbalah was an esoteric, occultic tradition that **explained the true meaning of the Hebrew Scriptures, which was kept hidden from the masses and only made known to those who were spiritually ready to receive it.**[120] (Emphasis added)

Now compare Dr. Edersheim's analysis and the CRI's straightforward description of Kabbalah with the following biblical truths declared by the Apostle Paul. Especially note the words that are highlighted:

> And [God] **made known** to us **the mystery of his will** according to his good pleasure, which he purposed in Christ (Ephesians 1:9)
>
> The mystery made known to me by revelation, as I have already written briefly. In reading this, then, you will be able to understand my insight into the mystery of Christ, which was not made known to men in other generations as it has now been revealed by the Spirit to God's holy apostles and prophets. (Ephesians 3:3–5)
>
> And **to make plain** to everyone the administration of **this mystery**, which **for ages past was kept hidden in God**, who created all things. His intent was that now, through the church, **the manifold wisdom of God should be made known** to the rulers and authorities in the heavenly realms. (Ephesians 3:9–10).
>
> I have become its servant by the commission God gave me to present to you **the word of God in its fullness—the mystery that has been kept hidden for ages and generations**, but is **now disclosed** to the saints. To them God has **chosen to make known** among the Gentiles **the glorious riches of this mystery**, which is Christ in you, the hope of glory. (Colossians 1:25–27)

The Kabbalistic influence upon Paul's language and the early Church is difficult to overlook. Most of today's Christian readers of the Jewish Scriptures completely miss the distinctive Kabbalistic language contained therein. But it's there.

Kabbalah and the New Testament

Even though Paul did not practice Kabbalah as we now understand it, and with all of its blatantly occultic overtones, he still used Kabbalistic terminology that would resonate with the Orthodox mind. It would have been completely natural for Paul to have done so, just as it was for Rabbi Kaduri, because this was the mindset and language of the largest part of their audiences.

This is the reason, in today's churches of Western civilizations, one seldom hears preaching from the pulpit that derives from a distinctly Jewish context. Our audience is primarily Western or Western influenced, so, unfortunately, the message of the Jewish Scripture is often given only from a Western perspective.

In connecting as closely as possible with the Jewish attitude of his day, Paul's goal was to link those Jews with the truth of salvation through *Yeshua Ha' Mashiach*. Observe his admission of this:

> To the Jews I became like a Jew, to win the Jews. To those under the law I became like one under the law (though I myself am not under the law), so as to win those under the law. To those not having the law I became like one not having the law (though I am not free from God's law but am under Christ's law), so as to win those not having the law.... I have become all things to all people so that by all possible means I might save some. I do all this for the sake of the gospel that I may share in its blessings. (1 Corinthians 9:20–23)

Eyes to See

Revealing mysteries from God through esoteric means is first extolled in the Old Testament. A full one thousand years before the time of Christ, Psalm 78:2 speaks of revealing Yahweh's "hidden things" through parables (cryptic stories and riddles that contain concealed spiritual messages): "I will open my mouth with a parable; I will utter hidden things, things from of old."

In relation to how Yeshua would conduct His own ministry among the Jews, He quoted Psalm 78 in Matthew 13:35. Accordingly, Jesus declared that He would only reveal to His closest disciples "the mysteries of the kingdom," but to the masses He would mostly speak in parables (Mark 4:11; Matthew 13:10–11; Luke 8:10). This was done, Jesus said, so that only "those with eyes to see—will see."

These facts are no small consideration as we develop the cultural and historical *context* necessary to gain a better understanding of the Kaduri account and the similar manner in which he spoke to his followers.

19

Charms, Amulets, and Superstition

So that even handkerchiefs and aprons that had touched him were taken to the sick...
—Acts 19:12

There is yet another interesting piece of biblical evidence of Kabbalah's influence upon the people of New Testament times:

> God did extraordinary miracles through Paul, so that even handkerchiefs and aprons that had touched him were taken to the sick, and their illnesses were cured and the evil spirits left them. (Acts 19:11–12)

As difficult as it may be for most Christians to accept, the traditional Jewish Kabbalistic influences of amulets, prayer cloths, charms, and other physical and non-physical items, often seen as divine talismans of healing and blessing, were rampant in New Testament times. Even more surprising to modern-day Christian readers of the Bible, those Kabbalistic beliefs were sometimes accommodated by the ministers of the early Church, including Jesus Himself.

For example, in addition to receiving Paul's prayer cloths, the New Testament also speaks of Jews who wanted to "touch the hem of Jesus' garment" for healing, as well as those wanting to be in a position so that Peter's "shadow" might "pass over them" as a cure for their diseases (Matthew 9:20–21, 14:35–36; Mark 6:56; Luke 8:46; and Acts 5:15).

We know that today's Kabbalistic practices have been widely perverted as far as purely scriptural understanding is concerned. Nonetheless, the deeply ingrained nature of much of Kabbalah's ancient practices is indeed present in the New Testament documents. Many of the most conservative and respected Christian scholars have known this for ages. The reason you've probably never heard these truths before, especially from a Sunday morning pulpit, is that the American Christian mind doesn't process them very well. As examples, consider the following commentary entries.

Expositor's Greek Testament:

> The carrying of the [prayer cloths] would only illustrate *the superstitious practices which showed how often, in the homes of culture, quackery was also found*, and the Evangelist gives them no word of commendation.
>
> On the other hand we must remember that…even in the means employed we may perhaps *see a possible appeal to the populace,* who would recognize that *these charms and amulets in which they put such confidence* [thoroughly Kabbalistic practices]. But in this *accommodation to special forms of ignorance* we are never allowed to forget that God is the source of all power and might.[121] (Emphasis and bracketed words added)

Concerning the instance of "Peter's shadow" in Acts 5:15, *Expositor's Greek Commentary* says:

> There is nothing to show that St. Luke endorses the enthusiastic superstition of the people. Luke does not distinctly assert that cures were wrought by the shadow of Peter.[122]

Robertson's Word Pictures (NT) similarly says:

> There was, of course, no virtue or power in Peter's shadow. That was faith with superstition, of course, just as similar cases in the Gospels occur (Matthew 9:20; Mark 6:56; John 9:5) and the use of Paul's handkerchief (Acts 19:12). God honors even superstitious faith if it is real faith in him. Few people are wholly devoid of superstition.[123]

Beginning with Acts 5:15 and the topic of Peter's shadow, *Barnes' Notes on the Bible* addresses all the New Testament examples previously mentioned:

> They "imagined" that if they could "anyhow" come under his influence they might be healed. The sacred writer does not say, however, that any "were" healed in this way, nor that they were commanded to do this. He simply states the "impression" which was on the minds of the people that it "might be." Whether they were healed by this, it is left for us merely to conjecture.
>
> An instance somewhat similar is recorded in Acts 19:12, where it is expressly said, however, that the sick were healed by contact with "handkerchiefs" and "aprons" that were brought from the body of Paul. Compare also Matthew 9:21–22, where the woman said respecting Jesus "If I may but touch his garment I shall be whole."[124]

Specifically regarding the woman who wanted to "touch the hem of His garment," note how the scholars unequivocally acknowledge the New Testament accommodation to the Jewish Orthodox and Kabbalistic culture:

Pulpit Commentary:

> Observe that she is "saved" **in spite of her superstition**; God "pitieth the blind that would gladly see."[125] (Emphasis added)

Matthew Henry's Concise Commentary:

The variety of methods Christ took in working his miracles, perhaps was because of the different frames and tempers of mind, which those were in who came to him, and which He who searches the heart perfectly knew.[126] (Emphasis added)

Ellicott's Commentary for English Readers:

Yet weak as the faith was, **it was accepted**, and **outward things were endowed with a "virtue"** which was not their own. So afterwards, where **a like belief prevailed**, the "handkerchiefs and aprons" that were brought from St. Paul's flesh **became means of healing** (Acts 19:12).[127] (Emphasis added)

If you are at all shocked by what you have discovered in this chapter, just wait until you read the next one.

The context you are learning about through this study will immeasurably enhance your ability to see the New Testament Scripture through Jewish eyes, as it was meant to be understood from the beginning, thus giving you a much deeper insight into the mind and world of Rabbi Yitzhak Kaduri.

20

The Number of His Name

Let the person who has insight calculate the number
of the beast, for it is the number of a man.
—Revelation 13:18

Another Kabbalistic element is found in a familiar passage of Scripture. Have a look at the following verse from Revelation 13, and especially note the highlighted portions:

> [The beast] also forced all people, great and small, rich and poor, free and slave, **to receive a mark** on their right hands or on their foreheads, so that they could not buy or sell unless they had the mark, **which is the name of the beast or the number of its name. This calls for wisdom.** Let **the person who has insight calculate the number** of the beast, **for it is the number** of a man. **That number is 666.** (Revelation 13:16–18)

The numbering of words and names by using the Hebrew alphabet and each letter's numeric value are all part of an ancient Kabbalistic practice known as *Gematria,*[128] which is still a widely practiced element of Kabbalah to this day. Many reputable scholars see this passage in Revelation as a direct reference to this ancient Orthodox practice among the Jews.

Have a look at a few scholarly attestations of this fact, again noting the highlighted portions:

Cambridge Bible for Schools and Colleges:

> In Hebrew and in Greek, letters were used for numerals, **every letter having its own proper significance as a number**. Among **the Jews (and to some extent among early Christians**, especially heretics) this suggested the possibility of **finding numbers mystically corresponding** to any word: the numerical value of all the letters might be added together, and the sum would represent the word. This process was called by the Jews ***Gematria***. It remains true that **a Jew of St John's time** would probably mean, by "the number of a name," the number formed by ***Gematria*** from its letters.[129]

Vincent's Word Studies in the New Testament:

> The method of mystic numbering obtained alike among pagan Greeks, Gnostics, **Christian Fathers**, and **Jewish Kabbalists**. The Gnostics affixed to their **gems and amulets** [a certain mystic word], under the idea of some virtue attaching to its number, 365, as being that of the days of the solar cycle. Barnabas and Clement of Alexandria [early Christian Church fathers] speak of the virtue of the number 318 as being that of IHT, the **common abbreviation for Jesus crucified.**
>
> In the pseudo-Sybilline verses, **written by Christians**, about the end, probably of the second century, are found versified enigmas **giving the number and requiring the name.**
>
> The translation of one of these on the word *Jesus* is as follows: "He will come upon earth clothed with flesh like mortal men. **His name contains** four vowels and two consonants: two of the former being sounded together. And I will declare the entire number. **For the name will exhibit to incredulous men** eight units, eight

tens, and eight hundreds." [In other words, Jesus' name is represented by the Gematria value of 888.][130]

Benson Commentary:

It was **a practice among the ancients to denote names by numbers** [Gematria]. It has likewise been the usual method in all God's dispensations, for **the Holy Spirit to accommodate his expressions to the customs, fashions, and manners of the several ages.**

Since then **this art and mystery of numbers was so much used among the ancients**, it is less wonderful that the beast also should have his number; and there was this additional reason for this obscure manner of characterizing him in the time of St. John, that **no other manner would have been safe.**[131]

If you have never studied the Jewish "mystery" literature's influence upon biblical texts, you might think that I am stretching the point. But nothing could be farther from the truth.

For example, Dr. Alfred Edersheim says of Kabbalah's influence in the New Testament:

Much that is found in Kabbalistic writings approximates so closely to the higher truths of Christianity, that, despite the errors, superstitions, and follies that mingle with it, **we cannot fail to recognize the continuance and the remains of those deeper facts of Divine revelation, which must have formed the substance of prophetic teaching under the Old Testament**, and have been understood, or at least hoped for, by those who were under the guidance of the Holy Spirit.[132]

Dr. Edersheim also speaks to how the Jewish writers would often use Gematria to conveniently conceal an otherwise controversial translation of a passage of Scripture.

> **The "Gematria"—allowed the interpreter to find out the numerical value of the letters in a word and to substitute for a word one or more which had the same numerical value.**
>
> Thus, if in Numbers 12:1 we read that Moses was married to an "Ethiopian woman" (in the original, "Cushith"), Onkelos [author of the Targum Onkelos] substitutes instead of this, by "Gematria," the words, "of fair appearance"—the numerical value both of Cushith and of the words "of fair appearance" being equally 736.
>
> By this substitution the objectionable idea of Moses' marrying an Ethiopian was at the same time removed.[133]

Apparently, Gematria has been attached to certain matters of biblical understanding and interpretation among the Orthodox Jews for a very long time.

Context and Perspective

Please do not misunderstand: I am not suggesting that traditionally understood Kabbalistic practices are *promoted* by the New Testament. Nor am I implying that it is acceptable to use Kabbalah within today's true biblical faith. In fact, several aspects of ancient Kabbalah—occult-like rituals to bring good luck, death curses, summoning of angels, mystical incantations, abject numerology, divination of the future, and communicating with the dead, etc.—are expressly forbidden throughout Scripture.

Rather, I am merely pointing out the obvious historic and biblical connections often missed entirely by today's Westernized Christian Church—namely, that influences upon the Orthodox Jewish populace of Jesus' day concerning certain Kabbalistic practices and ideas were quite pronounced. Those influences are still among Jews to this day—and they were especially so in the life and ministry of Rabbi Yitzhak Kaduri and his millions of followers.

If modern Christians so desire, they can call Kaduri a heretic for accommodating the belief system of the culture in which he moved and ministered—the only belief system with which he was familiar. However, those people would also have to come very close to making that same charge against Jesus Himself, as well as against Peter and Paul, if that standard were applied equally. Therefore, we should tread carefully and contextually before handing out categorical pronouncements of heresy.

To the Jew First

Let me emphasize again this important point: Rabbi Kaduri was a *Kabbalistic* Jewish rabbi for almost ninety years of his life. Kabbalah was as natural to him as breathing.

This does not make the practice biblically correct, but it does help us understand the frame of mind from which he operated for most of his life. Our more contextual understanding should now help answer the question, "Why would Yeshua choose to reveal Himself through a Kabbalistic rabbi?"

In truth, the question might answer itself more easily if it was rephrased: *Why would Yeshua use modern Israel's most honored and celebrated rabbi as the vehicle through whom He would reveal Himself as Israel's true Messiah, especially in these profoundly prophetic last days?* As I said, the question answers itself. God's plan of using Rabbi Kaduri was perfect—as always.

21

The Two Messiahs

We have found the one Moses wrote about in the Law, and about whom the prophets also wrote—Jesus of Nazareth, **the son of Joseph.**
—John 1:45 (Emphasis added)

All the people were astonished and said, "Could this be the **Son of David?**"
—Matthew 12:23 (Emphasis added)

To offer additional illumination about the Jewish mind, which is so deeply influenced by the Talmud and Kabbalah, it is supremely important that we explore and understand the Jewish concept of the "Two Messiahs." Many of today's Hebrews are still looking for *Messiah, Son of Joseph*, as well as the ultimate Messiah—*Messiah, Son of David.*

If you haven't heard of this distinctly Jewish teaching, you're in for some enlightenment. Admittedly, this topic can get a bit complex. However, I'll keep the explanation as fundamental as possible. There are plenty of additional sources available for your own research should you desire to undertake a deeper study.[134]

Son of Joseph and Son of David

A significant number of Orthodox Jews have been immersed in the traditional teaching that there will first appear a Messiah figure in the last days—a figure known as *Messiah ben* ("son of") *Joseph.* In general, they believe this will be a mere man—perhaps a renowned political or military figure. He is usually depicted as one who suffers greatly at the hands of his own people, but who eventually "comes back from the dead" (either literally or figuratively, depending on the school of thought), and then is ultimately triumphant among his people and rises as a great Messianic leader.

Many Christians think Jews reject the idea of a resurrected Messiah. However, several sects of the Jewish faith system teach that Messiah ben Joseph will be physically resurrected from the dead. The rabbis teach that he will be anointed by God to battle the enemies of Israel and then lead Israel and the Jews to a place of strength and righteousness so that the ultimate Messiah—the true Savior of Israel—can finally appear.

That second Messiah figure is known as *Messiah ben* ("son of") *David*, and he is the one who will finally establish the longed-for Messianic Kingdom on Earth. The Talmud states that when Messiah ben David finds Messiah ben Joseph slain, he will ask the Lord of the Universe for Messiah ben Joseph to receive "the gift of life."[135]

In July 2018, speaking to an Israeli-based media source, Orthodox Rabbi Yosef Berger explained the concept of the Two Messiahs from the Orthodox, "mystical" view:

> In the Zohar [an ancient Kabbalistic reference source], it is written that before the Messiah from the House of David appears, there will first be the Messiah from the house of Joseph. The Messiah from the house of David will be a specific person but the Messiah from the house of Joseph will be a process, focusing on the return to Israel. But the Zohar goes on to say that before the Messiah from the House of David will be revealed, a hidden righteous man will be essential in helping prepare the way for him to be revealed.[136]

In short, the Orthodox of Israel are perpetually looking for a "Savior figure," one who will work through a Messianic "process"—a Messiah who will lead the nation toward the ultimate political/spiritual restoration of the glory days of Israel, complete with a king from the line of David. Many biblical scholars believe this very fact makes the Jewish people vulnerable regarding the acceptance of false messiahs.

Jesus even warned His Jewish disciples about the pervasive spirit among the Jews that is characterized by continually searching for a Messiah figure—especially in the very last days, before His return:

> At that time if anyone says to you, "Look, here is the Messiah!" or, "There he is!" do not believe it. For false messiahs and false prophets will appear and perform great signs and wonders to deceive, if possible, even the elect. See, I have told you ahead of time. (Matthew 24:23–25)

Nevertheless, the *Messiah ben Joseph* spirit is frequently in play in the minds of most Orthodox Jews, especially those living in Israel. Kaduri knew this as well as anyone.

This is a strange concept in the ears of most westernized, New Testament Christians. Regardless, it is a vital part of the Orthodox Jewish psyche. Without understanding this, the student of the Kaduri story will often miss the bigger picture.

The "Two Messiahs"—Fulfilled?

You have probably already noticed that Yeshua/Jesus does fulfill even the Orthodox Jewish concept of the Messiah phenomenon, almost to a tee. To the born-again Christian and the completed Messianic Jew, it is frustrating that today's unbelieving Jewish people cannot see the truth right before them.

To the believer, it is apparent that Jesus Christ was both "the son of Joseph," and the "son of David" in one singular Messiah figure. Yeshua fulfilled the biblically prophesied expectations as well as the Orthodox and Talmudic Jewish expectations of Messiah.[137]

This is the reason the New Testament writers (all Jewish[138]) went to such great lengths to present these two facts over and over. And this is why the New Testament so plainly presents Jesus as both human and divine in the same person. It is why the New Testament genealogies show Jesus' lineage as a literal "son of Joseph" and also a descendent or "son" "of David." The writers expounded upon these concepts and others that were related to them precisely because they were writing primarily to the first-century Jews.

Professor of theology, W. F. Adeney, illuminates our study:

> CHRIST WILL COME IN GLORY. He ascended in triumph; He will return in triumph. In the prophets we have visions of glory and humiliation associated with the Messiah, and **the Rabbis expected two Messiahs, one suffering and the other conquering.** We now see that **one man can be both in successive periods. Christ fulfils prophecy by degrees.** Had the whole of Christ's career fallen in the days of Tiberius the Jews might properly have rejected Him. We look for the final fulfilment of prophecy to the future glory of Christ.[139]

Burden for the Jews

The New Testament writers wanted their unbelieving brethren to see that Yeshua/Jesus met even their own Orthodox expectations, and that Yeshua is the long-awaited Messiah ben David who will soon return as the reigning King of Kings and Lord of Lords.

Observe the heartfelt and passionate words of the Apostle Paul, a "Hebrew of Hebrews," as he mourns over his own people:

> I speak the truth in Christ—I am not lying, my conscience confirms it through the Holy Spirit—I have great sorrow and unceasing anguish in my heart. For I could wish that I myself were cursed and cut off from Christ for the sake of my people, those of my own race, the people of Israel. Theirs is the adoption

> to sonship; theirs the divine glory, the covenants, the receiving of the law, the temple worship and the promises. Theirs are the patriarchs, and from them is traced the human ancestry of the Messiah, who is God over all, forever praised! Amen. (Romans 9:1–5)

Kaduri Connection

Let me say it again: *Kaduri was thoroughly Jewish, in every definable way.* When we finally come to terms with this and see the Israeli world through his eyes, the clearer and more understandable this incredible story becomes.

22

Messiah Fever in Israel

So if someone tells you, "Look, the Messiah is out in the desert," don't bother to go and look. Or, "Look, he is hiding here," don't believe it!
—Matthew 24:26, NLT

The previous chapter explains why the name of a well-known Israeli rabbi will often appear in an international headline pointing to a popular political figure and saying something like, "*This* man might be Israel's Messiah!"

When that happens, you now know that these rabbis are speaking of *Messiah ben Joseph,* the human figure who will eventually usher in the true Messiah to Israel. In truth, they are referring to a Heaven-sent "father-figure savior," a political or military man who will help pave the way for the ultimate Messiah by protecting Israel from its enemies and turning Israel's corporate heart back to God.

For this to make biblical sense, we must not think of the word "messiah" in the Christian manner of it referring to our ultimate Savior, Jesus Christ. Rather, we must think as a Jew who is looking for a great leader, one who is strong and unafraid of the powers of the world that continually rise up against Israel.

Usually this Messiah ben Joseph is an Israeli citizen. The belief in a coming—and perhaps even *resurrected* Messiah—is still a phenomenon in the Orthodox population of Israel. Consider these words from a 1998 *New York Times* article titled, "Messiah Fervor for Late Rabbi Divides Many Lubavitchers."

> Four years after the death of Rabbi Menachem Mendel Schneerson,[140] the charismatic Hasidic leader, his Lubavitch movement finds itself embarrassed by a persistent group of his followers, mostly in Brooklyn, who stubbornly proclaim the rabbi as the Moshiach, or Messiah, and eagerly await his resurrection.[141]

A dozen years later, in 2010, *Haaretz* of Israel reported on the issue again. The article was titled, "Was the Lubavitcher Rebbe Really the Messiah?" Following is an excerpt from that article:

> [Rabbi Menachem Mendel Schneerson's] followers identified him, at least potentially, as the long-expected messiah, and were sure he saw himself in that light....
>
> Many Lubavitchers—how many is a matter of dispute—continue today to view him as the messiah who either is not actually dead or will return from the dead. The notion of a resurrected messiah, uncomfortably reminiscent of Christianity, has led some Jewish critics to pronounce Chabad messianists to be heretics.[142]

Then, in 2018, the *Los Angeles Times* once again reported on the Rabbi Schneerson Messiah-resurrection expectation among certain Orthodox Jews: "The controversial belief of many in Chabad is that Schneerson is the Messiah, and some expect his resurrection soon."[143]

Make no mistake: For certain vocal segments of the Orthodox Jewish faith, the resurrected Messiah ben Joseph expectation is ever present.

An American President?

Israel's Messiah figure, or the one who will ultimately hasten His arrival, doesn't necessarily have to be an Israeli. As long as there is a bona fide connection to Israel, the true Messiah ben Joseph or his predecessor can apparently come from almost anywhere.

Several striking examples of this belief can be found in widely documented rabbinical statements concerning President Donald Trump, especially during the first couple of years of his first term (2017–2018).

The Jerusalem Post:

Under the headline, "'Trump's Election Heralds Coming of Messiah' says [Interior Minister] Deri," Israel's Messiah fever began with Donald Trump's November 2016 election as United States President:

> [Shas chairman and Interior Minister Arye Deri said] If such a miracle can happen, we have already reached the days of the Messiah. Therefore, we are really in the era of the birth pangs of the Messiah when everything has been flipped to the good of the Jewish people.[144]

Breaking News Israel:

> "I have known for months that Donald Trump would win the elections," Rabbi Berger told *Breaking Israel News.* "The Gematria (numerology) of [Trump's] name is *Moshiach* (Messiah). He is connected to the Messianic process which is happening right now. When he promised to move the American Embassy to Jerusalem, he attached himself to the power of *Moshiach,* which gave him the boost he needed."
>
> "All of the academics and the media, who create their own world with evil words, they worked against Trump," continued

Rabbi Weiss. "They tried to create a man-made reality in which Trump could not win. In the end, it did not work. Hashem is moving us towards a greater Jerusalem, and anyone who goes against that, is destined to fail."[145]

Israel Today:

Rabbi Berger cited a medieval rabbinical source which predicted that while the first two temples were built by Israel, the third would be built by the "descendants of Edom," a phrase that in some later rabbinical literature is a euphemism for the Christian world.

"No leader in history has recognized Jerusalem as the capital of the Jews and Israel. [Trump] has already created a great *tikkun* (reparation) for the Christians through his unprecedented relationship with Jerusalem. Trump is the representative of Edom who will perform that final historic reparation for his entire nation by building the Temple."[146]

Newsweek:

Even American mainstream media got in on the prophetic action when, in December 2017, *Newsweek* teased the question with this headline, "Will Trump Hasten the Arrival of the Messiah? Jews and Evangelicals Think So."

In the wake of President Donald Trump's controversial decision to recognize Jerusalem as the capital of Israel, some Jewish activists argued that the U.S. president was being guided by God to restore Jewish control of sacred sites.

Activists lobbying for the construction of a Jewish Temple in Jerusalem said Trump was playing a similar role to the Persian emperor Cyrus the Great, who allowed the Jews to return to Israel from exile.[147]

As the Messiah ben Joseph-type enthusiasm over the Donald Trump presidency spread like wildfire in Israel, not all of the Orthodox were happy about it. While acknowledging the Messianic overtones that Trump appeared to display to the Jewish mind, the generally Orthodox publication *Haaretz* had deeper concerns.

Haaretz:

> "The prophets' words of prophecy are coming forth from the Bible and becoming facts right before our eyes," said Likud lawmaker and prominent Temple Mount movement figure Yehuda Glick, appearing on Israel Channel 10 television Wednesday evening as Israel awaited Trump's expected announcement on Jerusalem.
>
> But just whose Messiah is Trump hastening? Is it the fundamentalist Israeli vision of a return to a Jewish kingdom and priesthood reminiscent of the Old Testament? Or is it the Evangelical belief in the return of Jesus Christ and the conversion of all the Jews to born-again Christian doctrine and faith?[148]

Since Israel's fervor for consistently seeking after their Jewish Messiah is ever before them, perhaps we are now on the trail of discerning the proper context concerning some of the oddest things about Messiah that Kaduri ever uttered.

23

Quagmire and Context

The words of the mouth are deep waters, but the fountain of wisdom is a rushing stream.
—Proverbs 18:4

The amazing story of Rabbi Yitzhak Kaduri is not without several apparent theological dilemmas. Remember, I said from the outset that this journey was complex.

However, now that we've tackled the topic of the Two Messiahs and how the Orthodox mind works in regard to this concept, some of the most protested of Kaduri's Messiah prophecies will make more sense. Remember, the Kaduri Yeshua note was meant primarily for the Jews living in these prophetic last days.

Rabbi Yitzhak Kaduri is infamously known, especially among conservative Christian circles, for having made what, at first reading, appeared to be several outlandishly unbiblical statements.

The most disconcerting of these claims was made concerning his reported "revelations" regarding the eventual appearance of Israel's Messiah. Because of that, some Christian researchers summarily dismiss the veracity of Rabbi Kaduri's Yeshua revelation as well. They often say something like: "If that note is indeed authentic, then the 'Yeshua/Messiah' that

Kaduri speaks of must be a *false one*—it might even be that his vision was of the antichrist himself."

I understand the angst of the traditional Christian. But with the understanding you now possess, especially in relation to the Orthodox, Two-Messiah concept, I believe the contextual framework of Kaduri's statements will be seen in its proper light.

Hard Sayings

First, have a look at six of the most publicized examples of the difficult sayings of Rabbi Kaduri concerning Israel's Messiah.

1. It is hard for many good people in the society to understand the person of the Messiah. The leadership and order of a Messiah of flesh and blood is hard to accept for many in the nation. As leader, the Messiah will not hold any office, but will be among the people and use the media to communicate. His reign will be pure and without personal or political desire. During his dominion, only righteousness and truth will reign.[149]

2. Will all believe in the Messiah right away? No, in the beginning some of us will believe in him and some not. It will be easier for non-religious people to follow the Messiah than for Orthodox people.[150]

3. The revelation of the Messiah will be fulfilled in two stages: First, he will actively confirm his position as Messiah without knowing himself that he is the Messiah. Then he will reveal himself to some Jews, not necessarily to wise Torah scholars. It can be even simple people. Only then he will reveal himself to the whole nation. The people will wonder and say: "What,

that's the Messiah?" Many have known his name but have not believed that he is the Messiah.[151]

4. With the help of [God], the soul of the Mashiach has attached itself to a person in Israel.[152]

5. When he comes, the Messiah will rescue Jerusalem from foreign religions that want to rule the city. They will not succeed for they will fight against one another.[153]

6. The Mashiach is already in Israel. Whatever people are sure will not happen, is liable to happen, and whatever we are certain will happen may disappoint us. But in the end, there will be peace throughout the world.[154]

The Light Comes On

Do you see it now? In light of what we have learned, the following clarify Kaduri's six proclamations:

1. Actually, this needs very little interpretation. Kaduri's claim that many "good people" would have a hard time understanding the person of Messiah certainly applies today—especially of Yeshua, whom Kaduri ultimately identified as the Messiah. His "good people" statement is reminiscent of the biblical declaration that even a "good person" needs to be born again by believing in the true Messiah.

It is easy to see the veracity of everything Kaduri claims in this particular statement, even including the part about "communicating through the media." However, you now understand that Kaduri is most likely referring to the Messiah ben Joseph figure and not the ultimate Messiah ben David. Since the first is "just a man" who is a political or military leader, then of course he would communicate through the media. With today's social media platforms and global Internet and cell-phone capabilities, we can understand exactly how this prophetic utterance might work.

2. This statement can be taken as being completely accurate just as stated. This is especially correct if Kaduri is speaking of Yeshua Himself, whom the Jews would consider, in that context, to be Messiah ben David (Luke 18:38; Matthew 21:9).

3. Here, Kaduri says the Messiah revelation comes in two stages. Again, he is most likely speaking of the Two-Messiah concept. The first portion of his statement is related to the political/military figure upon whom Israel is waiting. But the last sentence, "Many have known his name but have not believed that he is the Messiah," is most likely Kaduri's hint toward the stunning revelation he would eventually make regarding Yeshua. It is a fact that the Jews "know His name." The problem is that, until now, they have refused to believe that Yeshua is the Messiah, and they have actually spurned His name. Kaduri's message is currently being used of Yahweh to change that paradigm.

4. This declaration goes directly to the Jewish teaching of Messiah ben Joseph. Apparently, Kaduri believed that the precursor to the ultimate Messiah was already in Israel. This statement was supposedly made at Kaduri's 2005 Yom Kippur service.[155] If that is so, it indicates that even though Kaduri had received in a vision that Yeshua was the "true" Messiah (ben David), he also thought Messiah ben Joseph would be filled with the Spirit of Yeshua, and was now in Israel, ready to usher in the days of Messiah ben David.

- Even the Orthodox publication that reported the alleged statement of Kaduri explains the proclamation in a similar manner:

> That the above-mentioned "attaching" of a righteous soul to a person of Israel makes the recipient a candidate for Mashiach,

> [ben Joseph] but **not yet the actual Mashiach** [ben David].[156] (Brackets and emphasis added)

5. This can also be taken at face value and as absolute truth—especially if the declaration was made in relation to Yeshua as the ultimate Messiah.

6. Again, the first part of this statement goes to the Jewish belief that a Messiah ben Joseph figure, a political savior for Israel, is frequently expected to be "among" them. But the last sentence of his statement would only apply to Messiah ben David, ultimately Yeshua, in bringing final peace upon the planet.

"Thinking like a Jew" regarding the Two Messiahs will carry a long way in understanding Kaduri's mind, as well as the minds of those listening to him. Addressing the Hebrew thought process in the Jewish Orthodox way was Rabbi Kaduri's foremost consideration. He knew the Jewish psyche better than any other Orthodox leader of his time. This is one of the reasons he was so vastly adored by such a huge group of Israel's Orthodox population—which might explain another "odd" thing the elderly rabbi did just before he passed away.

24

The Preaching Rabbi

The mystery that has been kept hidden for ages and generations, but is now disclosed to the Lord's people.... Which is Christ in you, the hope of glory.
—Colossians 1:26–27

As we look back to Rabbi Kaduri's Yom Kippur service in October 2005, I want to let you in on some additional inside scoop. After writing my first book about Rabbi Kaduri, I was just getting to know Messianic Rabbi Zev Porat through phone calls and emails, and I was amazed by several things he related to me.

The Question

After Zev finished reading the Rabbi Kaduri book, he called me at home and asked, "Concerning your chapter about Rabbi Kaduri's Yom Kippur synagogue service in October 2005, *were you actually at that service*? Were you in Israel during that time?"

My first thought was, *Oh no! I got something dreadfully wrong in that chapter, and Zev is getting ready to tell me how incorrect my account of the service really was!*

With a bit of hesitation, I answered. "No, Zev. I wasn't there," I said. "I simply read the few printed accounts about it, those I could find on the Internet, then summarized them in a dramatic fictional setting. I put a footnote on that chapter indicating it was only a fictional account and that it was based on the reported stories of the actual event."

Zev replied, "The reason I asked you is that *I do know* what happened that night. I know how it felt, how people reacted, and what the rabbi actually said—and how he acted. I asked you that question, Carl, because your account of it is exactly as it happened—according to people I know who were actually there! It's as though you had been transported there in your mind and spirit. It is as though the Lord showed you that night. That chapter was incredible! You captured the actual emotions of that event, perfectly."

The Revelation

"But, what you probably *don't know*," Zev continued, "is that Rabbi Kaduri did several things that night that are so 'un-Jewish!' First of all, he literally *preached a message*. Rabbis don't usually 'preach' in a synagogue service, especially on a feast day like Yom Kippur. Instead, there is a very strict and formalized ritual that is followed. So, for Kaduri to actually deliver a message was quite an untraditional thing to do. What Kaduri did is usually frowned upon by the congregants as well as other rabbis."

"I had no idea," I told Zev. "What did he preach about?"

"That's just it," Zev answered. "You're not going to believe this. Kaduri preached several gospel truths. But not in the way you might be thinking. He didn't reveal Yeshua's real name on that night. Of course, his note revealed that later on. But he did preach the gospel in a 'code'—like in a parable."

Zev continued:

> Kaduri told his people about the need for personal repentance, and to have a personal connection to the Messiah who was coming for our salvation. He said that the forgiveness of individual

sins can only come by the atonement of blood! To say that in a synagogue, on Yom Kippur, is a Levitical stoning offense, and certainly against the rabbinic teachings! But no one laid a hand on Rabbi Kaduri that afternoon. He was under the protection of Yahweh.

Kaduri also predicted that many of the Jews would not actually believe the one who really was the Messiah, when they discovered his name. Kaduri said they would ask, "What! Is this really Him?"

National Will

Zev went on:

> These are amazing things for a Jewish rabbi to say! Because Jews don't believe in the need for a strict personal repentance alone, or a personal Messiah. They believe in a national repentance and a national savior. That is why the rabbis are teaching the people that they must follow the Law and be good citizens, so that Messiah will finally come—but only when we are "good enough" as a people. It is kind of a "national repentance" or a "national will" that is required for messiah to come—in the Jewish way of thinking.

The Jewish mindset of a national will Zev speaks of is confirmed by Rabbi Pinchas Winston in a *Breaking News Israel* article in June 2016.

A renowned Kabbalistic Orthodox rabbi, Winston hosts the *Ask the Rabbi* radio show for Arutz Sheva, Israel National Radio, and has given formal lectures in the United States, Canada, and England. The rabbi teaches weekly classes in Jerusalem and Ramat Bet Shemesh.[157]

The article in which Rabbi Winston addresses the national will of Israel is titled "Why Hasn't the Messiah Revealed Himself?" Notice especially the highlighted portions of the following excerpt from that article:

In a voice filled with passion for the topic, Rabbi Winston declared, "And now we're **approaching the Final Redemption.** Without question. **Moshiach is around the corner… Without question he's here already.** I don't know how old he is, where he's sitting, what he's doing, what he's learning. **But he's here.** He's not going to be born tomorrow. **We're just too close to the end.** Way too close to the end. **He has to be here right now!**

"**So why hasn't he revealed himself?** Why are we still fighting? Why are we still struggling? Why are we still suffering? Why is there still terrorism?"

His conclusion is that, at this time, the Jewish people "lack the national will for geula [redemption]." That's something he's intent on changing.[158]

Closely echoing Rabbi Winston's sentiments are those of Orthodox Rabbi Shraga Simmons in an article he wrote for Aish.com:[159]

The world is in desperate need of Messianic redemption [*geula*]. To the extent that we are aware of the problems of society, is the extent **we will yearn for** redemption. As the Talmud says, one of the first questions **asked of a Jew** on Judgment Day is: "**Did you yearn for the arrival** of the Messiah?"

How can we hasten the coming of the Messiah? The best way is to love all humanity generously, to keep the mitzvoth [commandments] of the Torah (as best we can), and to encourage others to do so as well.

Despite the gloom, the world does seem headed toward redemption. One apparent sign is that the Jewish people have returned to the Land of Israel and made it bloom again. Additionally, a major movement is afoot of young Jews **returning to Torah tradition.**

The Messiah can come any day, and **it all depends on our actions.** God is ready when we are. For as King David says:

> "Redemption will come today—if you hearken to His voice."[160] (Brackets and emphasis added)

To those unfamiliar with these Orthodox beliefs concerning the Jewish requirements for Messiah to come, the revelation can be quite eye-opening. In short, the Orthodox Jewish person is hoping that Israel as a whole, with his or her individual part in it, can eventually become "good enough" so that Messiah will finally come.

Now you can understand how Rabbi Kaduri's 2015 Yom Kippur "sermon" was such a shocking departure from the traditional Orthodox message.

25

The Isaiah 53 Factor

> Like one from whom people hide their faces,
> He was despised, and we held him in low esteem.
> —Isaiah 53:3

In further correspondence with me on the topic of Rabbi Kaduri's 2005 Yom Kippur service, Rabbi Zev Porat continued:

> On top of all of this, when Kaduri spoke of how the Jews would say "Is this really him?" or "Is this really the one?" or "How can this be? Is this really the Messiah?"—that gets very close to saying that Isaiah 53 is really about the Messiah. And most Jews are taught that this passage is not about Messiah.

Zev explained:

> In fact, most of the rabbis tell their followers that Isaiah 53 is about the prophet himself, or it is about Israel. But they usually discourage their followers from reading Isaiah 53, or they don't tell their congregation about that passage at all – because they know it sounds a lot like the Yeshua of the hated New Testament.

Despised and Rejected

Following are the first six verses of Isaiah 53. This passage is probably familiar to most readers. Notice, however, how these verses echo much of what Rabbi Kaduri preached on that Yom Kippur evening in his synagogue in October 2005:

1 Who has believed our message
    And to whom has the arm of the LORD been revealed?
2 He grew up before him like a tender shoot,
    And like a root out of dry ground.
He had no beauty or majesty to attract us to him,
    Nothing in his appearance that we should desire him.
3 He was despised and rejected by mankind,
    A man of suffering, and familiar with pain.
Like one from whom people hide their faces
    He was despised, and we held him in low esteem.
4 Surely he took up our pain
    And bore our suffering,
Yet we considered him punished by God,
    Stricken by him, and afflicted.
5 But he was pierced for our transgressions,
    He was crushed for our iniquities;
The punishment that brought us peace was on him,
    And by his wounds we are healed.
6 We all, like sheep, have gone astray,
    Each of us has turned to our own way;
And the LORD has laid on him
    The iniquity of us all. (Isaiah 53:1–6)

I could hardly believe what I was hearing as Zev continued to speak. He was ecstatic about what Kaduri had done, and was even more thrilled that I had put much of it in writing. This, he told me, was the type of material he needed to get Kaduri's message into the hands of his fellow Israeli Jews.

Verification

As I continued to research the Kaduri Yom Kippur message, I discovered further confirmation of what Messianic Rabbi Zev Porat had originally related to me. Posted on a website called Nazarene Judaism: The Original Jewish Followers of Yeshua is an article titled, "The Profound Revelation of Rabbi Kaduri."

The writer of that piece appears to understand the Hebrew language, as well as the Kabbalistic aspects of much of the Orthodox Jewish mindset. As one reads through the eighteen points of interpretation of Rabbi Kaduri's sermon, it is apparent that the writer saw many of the elements of Kaduri's message that Rabbi Zev understood as well, right down to the Isaiah 53 connection.

Under points 14 and 18, we find the writer's English interpretation of what he reportedly observed on Kaduri's website. The references to Isaiah 53, found in the parentheses and bracketed words, are the writer's original notes of clarification. I have only italicized to emphasize the writer's representation of Kaduri's own words.

14.) *His true test will not be His ability to perform miracles, but the very essence of His being and His actions. He will act as a simple Jew. His entire will is to do the will of Elohim, and Elohim gives Him help. He is very humble, He has no stately form or majesty that we should look upon Him, nor appearance that we should be attracted to Him* (Isaiah 53:2).

[In modern Rabbinic Judaism, this chapter is usually applied in relationship to Israel and not to Messiah.]

18.) *When He is revealed many will wonder: What, is it He? Who has believed our report, and to whom has the arm of the Lord been revealed? As for His generation, who considered?* (Isaiah 53:1, 8).

And I will pour upon the House of David and the dweller of Jerusalem a spirit of grace and supplication, so that they will look upon Me whom they have pierced and they will mourn for Him as the mourning for an only son, and they will weep bitterly over Him like the bitter weeping over a firstborn (Zechariah 12:10).

[Again, in modern Rabbinic Judaism, Isaiah 53 is usually applied in relationship to Israel and not to Messiah.][161]

The Example of Paul

Kaduri's 2005 "gospel message" was not the first time the Messiah had been disclosed in a synagogue service. The Apostle Paul did the same thing, albeit much less cryptically. Consider the following account from Acts 17:2–8:

> **As was his custom, Paul went into the synagogue, and on three Sabbath days he reasoned with them from the Scriptures, explaining and proving that the Messiah had to suffer and rise from the dead. "This Jesus I am proclaiming to you is the Messiah," he said.** Some of the Jews were persuaded and joined Paul and Silas, as did a large number of God-fearing Greeks and quite a few prominent women.
>
> **But other Jews were jealous; so they rounded up some bad characters from the marketplace, formed a mob and started a riot in the city.** They rushed to Jason's house in search of Paul and Silas in order to bring them out to the crowd. **But when they did not find them, they dragged Jason and some other believers before the city officials, shouting: "These men who have caused trouble all over the world** have now come here, and Jason has welcomed them into his house. They are all defying Caesar's decrees, saying that there is another king, **one called Jesus."** When they heard this, the crowd and the city officials were thrown into turmoil. (Emphasis added)

For his efforts, Paul was imprisoned several times through the conspiratorial arrangements of his own rabbinical peers who were in concert with the Roman authorities. Apparently, not much has changed since the very beginning.[162]

From God's Throne

"Here is the main truth that people need to see," Zev Porat explained, then continued:

> On that night, in October 2005, Rabbi Kaduri set the stage for his people to receive the message of his Messiah note. Not only that, but when they finally were made aware of the message, and after it was decoded, they would plainly know that *Yeshua* is the Messiah that Kaduri spoke of in that Yom Kippur celebration service. They would also know that Yeshua is the Messiah of Isaiah 53. The approach of using the encrypted note was absolutely brilliant!
>
> I believe the whole thing that Rabbi Kaduri did had to have been orchestrated by the Holy Spirit, and that his wisdom to do what he did came directly from the Throne of God.

However, as powerful as Kaduri's sermon and Messiah note were, there was still something even more powerful that he did.

He left witnesses.

26

Secret Disciples?

His parents said this because they were afraid of the Jewish leaders, who already had decided that anyone who acknowledged that Jesus was the Messiah would be put out of the synagogue.
—John 9:22

As stated in the opening pages of this book, Rabbi Kaduri's story and the impact it's having upon Israel is complicated. In the 108 amazing, war-torn, mystical, and tumultuous years of his life and the overall religious climate in that part of the world, how could it not be?

I am prayerful that at this point in our journey, at least a number of your initial doubts have been satisfactorily answered. However, a few often-asked questions have not yet been fully addressed.

How Can They Be "Secret" Disciples?

Following is one of the most frequently asked questions that I receive:

How can it be that Rabbi Kaduri—and even some of his yeshiva students, as well as other Jews in Israel who claim to be believers in Yeshua—are so secretive about their faith? Isn't that proof of their insincerity of belief? Why can't they just boldly declare their faith—like we do?

Christians living in the United States are still relatively free from intense persecution centered upon our faith in Yeshua/Jesus. Because of this, it is sometimes difficult to process when we hear of people in other parts of the world claiming to have been born again, yet are seemingly hesitant to share that testimony in an open display of boldness.

Often, Christians who voice this objection quote the following passages of Scripture:

> Whoever is ashamed of me and my words, the Son of Man will be ashamed of them when he comes in his glory and in the glory of the Father and of the holy angels. (Luke 9:26)

> Whoever acknowledges me before others, I will also acknowledge before my Father in heaven. But whoever disowns me before others, I will disown before my Father in heaven. (Matthew 10:32–33)

But there are several problems with the free-handed quoting of those Scriptures and others like them. In the first place, Zev and I know of no sincere Jewish believers who are truly "ashamed" of their belief in Yeshua. Some may ultimately prove to be so, but they certainly are not the norm.

Secondly, most of the true Jewish believers are indeed "acknowledging" their faith. That is precisely why so many are being intensely persecuted. To be sure, they are not standing on a street corner holding a sign that says: "I'm a believer in Yeshua!" or "Kaduri was right!" Neither are they marching into their synagogues or family reunions, grabbing microphones and screaming: "Hey everybody, listen up! I believe in Yeshua/Jesus as Messiah!" Those scenarios may not be happening, but a number of the Yeshua believers *are* sharing their faith in the best way they know how within their cultural context.

Also, many Jewish believers are seeking places where they can be discipled as they make the life-altering transition. They frequently begin their new life in Yeshua by sharing their faith with their spouses, very close friends, or other Jews they know who are also on the verge of believing.

Even then, "opening up" about a newfound faith in Yeshua can often have devastating effects.

The problem, it seems, is that most American Christians don't have a clue about what it really costs a Jew in Israel to "convert" to Christianity. Before we are too quick to judge our brothers and sisters in Christ who are living in Israel, consider the following perspective.

Startling Insight from the Inside

Rabbi Porat gives the following anecdote as insight into our examination. "Not too long ago, our ministry team was witnessing to an Orthodox man that lived in the highly Orthodox city of Bnei Brak, just east of Tel Aviv." This man, Zev explained, "had finally professed his belief in Yeshua as Messiah and Savior.

"But what makes this situation most interesting," Zev related, "is that he was actually a yeshiva teacher, *a rabbi*, who was teaching the students to be rabbis. The large yeshiva where he taught is located in Jerusalem. He commuted from Bnei Brak to Jerusalem every day to go to his teaching position there."

Zev continued:

> The man has five children. His wife is a housewife and takes care of the children and household matters. He is the sole financial provider for the family.
>
> For the first year of his newfound faith in Yeshua, he continued his teaching job in the yeshiva. But eventually he became deeply convicted that he couldn't continue to teach. He came to realize that the teaching of the strictly Orthodox Jewish ways were not valid. They didn't line up with his faith in Yeshua. So, he eventually left his teaching position at the yeshiva.
>
> This is where the story takes a tough turn.
>
> Somehow, a group of hardcore Orthodox Jews found out that this man had become a believer in Yeshua. His wife was not a

believer, but he was consistently witnessing to her about his biblical discoveries and his new journey of faith in Jesus. They weren't keeping it a super-close secret, but they weren't broadcasting it yet, either. That's when the persecution started.

The tormentors actually painted the door to his house in red paint. They "marked the family" for the whole town to see. He knew this was a serious threat and a method of singling out his family for severe, and potentially dangerous, measures of persecution. His wife and children were terrified. That's when he reached out for help.

Rabbi Porat said the man called him in desperation, "Zev, I don't know what to do. I've got to get my family out of here. This is getting serious."

Zev and his ministry team went into immediate action. He contacted other believers and they started raising money to help the man, his wife, and their children get out of the town. The house in which he was living was a rental home.

They took a team of people with a large van to the man's home at 11:30 at night to secretly load up his family and their possessions. They whisked him to safety under the cover of darkness, smuggling the man and his family out of his own home to a faraway city so that they might be assured of a reasonable degree of safety and anonymity.

To keep the family's serious persecutors from tracking them down, they had to rent their new house and register all of the utility bills under someone else's name. All of this was arranged by Zev's ministry, and had to be done simply because this Israeli Jew professed that Yeshua is Messiah.

"This is just one of many stories like it that we deal with all the time," Zev told me. "These are the kind of things that new believers in Yeshua living in Israel have to go through. Other situations are not as bad. But some are even worse—much worse."

Zev asked, "Can you imagine what people living in your city might do, if this is how they had to continually live, simply because of their faith in Jesus? And these are the so-called secret believers in Israel. In reality, they are not being secretive at all, they are simply trying to be smart. They are protecting their lives, and their family's lives—so they can continue to be effective witnesses for many years to come."

The understanding that Zev offers presents a very different perspective on the matter, doesn't it? Let us therefore commit to pray for our brothers and sisters living in the prophetically returned land of Israel who are now trying to faithfully live out their newfound faith in Jesus Christ.

27

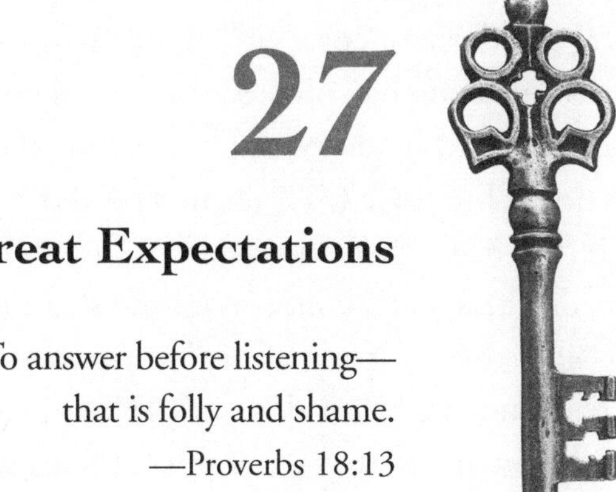

Great Expectations

To answer before listening—
that is folly and shame.
—Proverbs 18:13

What about the note itself?

Why did Rabbi Kaduri not share the contents of that note at a much earlier date—why would he hide the revelation? Why would he wait until a full year after his death to reveal it, and what's significant about that time period? Also, since there's so much controversy over the legitimacy of the note, why didn't anyone run a forensic test on it to determine if it was a fake or the real thing?

These are all great questions that are frequently asked. Let's tackle the answers here.

Why Hide the Note?

If the note is real and Kaduri believed that Yeshua (of New Testament fame) is the Messiah of Israel, why didn't he just come out and admit it? Why didn't he make his claim public right after he had received the revelation? Why conceal it?

First of all, Rabbi Kaduri did not "hide" his disclosure. As a matter of fact, he put the revelation in a note! In his own handwriting. Then he addressed the existence of the note with his synagogue congregation. This way, there could be no "cover-up" of the matter. Too many witnesses knew he had written it and had ordered the note to be eventually exposed to the world. Admittedly, he delayed the revealing of that note until a full year after his death, but there is a brilliantly powerful reason he did that as well. We'll address that in just a moment.

Also, don't forget: Kaduri was indeed sharing his revelation with other people. More than a dozen of his former yeshiva students testify to that today. The students heard the truth from Kaduri long before his death and long before the note was published on his website.

Rabbi Zev Porat, who has personally spoken with a number of Kaduri's believing students, explains, "If Kaduri had come out immediately claiming that Yeshua was the real Messiah, the people would not have believed him—some might have even tried to kill him—and they certainly would have never published his claim *anywhere*."

He continued:

> The ruling elite would've buried the story and shut him down. It's as simple as that, and Kaduri knew it. Look what they're doing now! Can you imagine what they would have done had Kaduri not left that note? His "revelation," because of his prominence, would've meant nothing to the world, it would have gone nowhere. I can promise you this!
>
> But, to put the revelation in a note, to turn it into a "mystery" of sorts, is exactly the way his followers would have gladly received it. It would have been what they would have expected from their rabbi. So, he obliged them, thus creating a great expectancy. It was an expectancy that eventually resulted in his note's message reaching the world! The fact that you are reading about it now attests to this fact. You could not have known of this revelation if Kaduri had revealed it immediately, in the open, right after his vision. It would not have seen the light of the day, as far as the rest of the world would have been concerned.

Why One Year Later?

Why did Kaduri wait a year? Why not open it and post it immediately after his death? Or, maybe he could have instructed that it be posted just a few weeks or a few months after his passing. Why wait a full year?

"It's something very Jewish," says Zev. "Even secular Jews understand what was done, and why."

He continued:

> It's an Orthodox Jewish custom, in some circles, that when someone passes away in your family, you don't do anything that would be remotely disrespectful towards that person's memory—for one full year. That would include things like attending parties, participating in lively joyous music and dancing, or even attending weddings and other celebratory festivities.
>
> If Rabbi Kaduri had left instructions for the note to have been opened before the one-year mourning period was up, his followers and family probably would not have respected the note. If one understands the culture, you realize it would not have been acceptable to have a note of this magnitude to be revealed any earlier than one year after his death.

Where's the Handwriting Analysis?

Here's another important and frequently asked question:

Since there was so much dispute from Kaduri's ministry officials regarding the authenticity of the note, especially from his son, David Kaduri, why didn't they just offer up the note for a handwriting analysis? Why not have the note forensically examined to determine whether or not it was authentic? Wouldn't something like that have quickly settled the matter?

Yes. It would have. That's just it. This is exactly why Zev and I, and many others who are familiar with the intricacies of the story, believe an analysis was not made of the note. The officials in Kaduri's ministry didn't do it simply because they *knew* the note was genuine. Remember, it was in their custody for a year, according to Rabbi Kaduri's publicly stated instructions. Also remember that the note was indeed posted on his website for all the world to see, and it was widely lauded by the Kaduri ministry as the genuine thing—until, that is, the note was finally decoded.

You're probably asking, *Well, then, what happened to the note? Where is it now? Why don't we get a forensic examination of it and be done with the matter?*

Great questions!

You won't believe the answer.

28

A Stunning Admission

> Carl, as a Jew, I am ashamed of what they did next.
>
> —Barry Farber, syndicated radio talk show host[163]

On January 17, 2014, just a few months after the release of my first book on the Kaduri story, I was interviewed on the CRN Talk Radio Network by internationally renowned host Barry Farber. What he revealed in that interview was earth-shattering.

But before we get into what he said, let's find out more about Barry Farber. Mr. Farber was born into an Orthodox family. He has made several dozen trips to Israel and is intensely involved in several Israeli charity organizations. He has thus developed numerous important contacts within the Israeli religious and political environs.

In 2002, *Talkers* magazine ranked Mr. Farber as the ninth-greatest radio talk-show host of all time.[164] He has written articles for the *New York Times*, *Reader's Digest*, the *Washington Post*, and the *Saturday Review*, and is proficient in five languages—Mandarin Chinese, Russian, Spanish, French, and Italian—besides his native English. Mr. Farber also has extensive knowledge of a couple dozen more languages.

Suffice it to say, Barry Farber is not a dull man. He knows his stuff, and when he speaks authoritatively on a topic, people listen. On the night of my interview, that's exactly what he did.

Barry Farber Spills the Beans

In that January 2014 CRN interview with Mr. Farber, he revealed a stunning piece of information about the Kaduri story previously unknown to me. Six minutes into the interview, he passionately unloaded the following word-for-word revelation:

> Carl, as a Jew, I am ashamed of what they [Kaduri's organization] did next. They censored that [note]; they **dropped it into sulfuric acid** and poured it into the Dead Sea. They took it off of his website. **It was a massive cover-up.**
>
> **….I am correct that they did a cover-up job. They didn't want anybody to know that this famous Orthodox rabbi had pinpointed Jesus Christ as the identity of the Messiah!** I mean the entire Jewish religion is based upon the fact that Jesus was not divine! …
>
> **My Jewish religion is not shaken by this story. My journalistic religion is excited by it**, but my Jewish religion is not shaken by this at all. I don't know why they went to such extremes to cover up the rabbi's prophecy.…
>
> I mean, wow! Carl Gallups just grabbed a half-nelson on this story! …He *owns* this story…keep your hands off it, you may comment, you may question, but this story belongs to Carl Gallups.[165] (Brackets and emphasis added)

When we were off air, during a commercial break, Mr. Farber told me that he, indeed, possessed "insider" knowledge concerning the note's destruction. He claimed that this was information he had cultivated from talking with some of his important contacts within the Israeli Jewish community. He said they had told him of how the Kaduri note met its end through a Kabbalistic "curse" ritual and had been destroyed forever.

As a former law enforcement officer, having conducted and successfully solved several of my own criminal investigations, I've seen that the intentional destruction of key evidence in a case usually is a sign of guilt: It most often means someone is trying to hide something. An innocent person simply doesn't destroy the one piece of crucial evidence that might prove he or she is telling the truth.

The only logical reason to destroy the note was that the organization's leaders knew it was indeed the genuine article and didn't want it to be subjected to a forensic investigation, thus forever proving its authenticity. They probably thought that if proof was ever brought forth to the Jewish community in Israel, the devastating impact would reverberate around the globe.

If Mr. Farber's account is accurate, we will never be able to forensically examine the original Kaduri note. However, because of the way the story continues to spread around the world, that examination appears to be nonessential to the ultimate carrying out of Yahweh's plan. In my estimation, the note's peculiar demise only adds to the intrigue of the entire affair and to the added appearance of the potential guilt of the parties who scream the loudest that it was only a fake.

Added Mystery

There's still more intrigue. That radio program was archived on Mr. Farber's CRN website for a few days, then it simply disappeared. Have you noticed a pattern yet? It seems that an awful lot of information on the Kaduri case initially reported in mainstream media sources winds up disappearing like a shadow melting into a darkened corner.

To be sure, Farber's statement was powerful and controversial, and it lent much-needed insight into the overall Kaduri account. Furthermore, Farber's unmitigated endorsement of my journalistic integrity probably was not greatly appreciated among certain important people listening to that evening's interview. I can only speculate why the broadcast was eventually removed from the website's archives. In fact, I have a pretty good idea why it happened.

For several years, I kept watch on Farber's podcast site. As far as I could discern, my interview was the only one removed during that timeframe. Knowing what I now know and what I have experienced concerning the entire Kaduri story, this doesn't surprise me in the least.

In case Mr. Farber is reading this book, if he would like to repost that show, I have a recording of it in my possession. Like so many other photos, videos, and articles posted to the Internet, it has not "disappeared."

What about Sharon's Death?

Kaduri told his synagogue congregation on that October 2005 afternoon that his Messiah revelation also included the information that Messiah would not appear until after the current prime minister at that time, Ariel Sharon, had died.

As revealed in an earlier chapter, Sharon suffered a stroke just a few weeks later, on January 4, 2006, and was admitted in a comatose state to the Hadassah Hospital in Jerusalem. He then underwent a seven-hour surgery, the first of several grueling surgical procedures. Ariel Sharon never regained consciousness.

After spending four months in Hadassah, Sharon was ultimately transferred to the Chaim Sheba Medical Centre at Tel Hashomer in Tel Aviv. He remained there, in "serious but stable condition," until his death on January 11, 2014—eight years and seven days from when he first suffered his stroke. He was 85 years old when he passed away.

Some who have closely followed the Kaduri story have asked how Sharon's death plays into the *exact* timing of Messiah's coming. The answer is: *It doesn't.*

Kaduri did not set an "exact time" to be associated with Sharon's death—only that the Messiah would not return until *after* Sharon had passed. Remember, when Kaduri made that claim, Ariel Sharon was still the active, seemingly healthy, prime minister of Israel. As for the "Sharon portion" of Kaduri's prophecy, the rabbi was correct: Messiah *did not come before* Sharon passed away. Of course, Kaduri was also correct concerning the name of the true Messiah.

Some might wonder why Kaduri's vision included Sharon's death as an element of the Messiah prophecy. The answer is fairly straightforward: If Kaduri's prophecy was genuinely from the Lord, then Sharon's death was meant to be a marker, not a date-setting mechanism.

Setting a marker for the ultimate fulfillment of a prophecy is not an entirely uncommon practice connected with biblical prophecy (see Daniel 9:25; Matthew 2:1–2, 24:15; Luke 21:20).

Sharon's death could well be a prophetic marker indicating that the return of the Lord is very near. At the time of the publication of this book, it has only been five short years since Ariel Sharon passed away, a mere nanosecond in the prophetic scheme of things.

Of course, this part of the Kaduri prophecy might have intended to accommodate the Jewish understanding that Messiah ben Joseph had to first pave the way before Messiah ben David, the ultimate Messiah, would appear.

Some in Israel even held up Ariel Sharon as a potential Messiah ben Joseph candidate. For example, on the day of Ariel Sharon's death, the *Times of Israel* reported that Gush Emunim, the religious arm of the Gaza settlement movement, viewed Sharon as "Messiah's donkey," or the beast upon which their salvation would arrive.[166]

Two years after that first report, the *Times of Israel* further stated: "Above all, Sharon possessed an absolute belief that he was historically *destined to save the Jewish people*. He didn't 'think' or 'believe' that—he just knew it."[167]

Those of the Jewish faith who were aware of these Orthodox attitudes and descriptions regarding Ariel Sharon would most likely interpret his passing as potentially ominous. This would be especially true in light of Rabbi Kaduri's specific attachment of Sharon's name to his Messiah prophecy.

Now, let's have a look at the back stories of the two rabbis of whom we speak the most in this intriguing saga—Rabbi Yitzhak Kaduri and Messianic Rabbi Zev Porat. The way their lives and testimonies are directly connected is uncanny.

What you'll read in the next section is one of my favorite parts of this whole story…

Part Four

THE DIVINE CHANGES

29

Out of Ur

Terah took his son Abram, his grandson Lot son of Haran, and his daughter-in-law Sarai, the wife of his son Abram, and together they set out from Ur of the Chaldeans to go to Canaan.

—Genesis 11:31

Where did our main character Yitzhak Kaduri come from...this 108-year-old, world-rattling rabbi? What is his life's story?

Kaduri, whose birth name was Yitzhak Diba, was raised in Baghdad, Iraq, about 220 miles north of the ancient biblical city of Ur, which is now located very near the site of modern Nasiriyah—Iraq's fourth-largest city. Of course, Ur was the city from where Abraham had made a similar trek to what would eventually become the land of Israel almost four thousand years before Yitzhak was born.

Yitzhak, whose birth name was Yitzhak Diba, was probably born in the late 1800s to live a life that would span the entire twentieth century, part of the one before it, and a portion of the one after that. His father was Katchouri Diba ben Aziza, a rabbi and a trader in exotic spices.

While he was still in his teens, Yitzhak Diba developed a strong attraction to the Orthodox Jewish practice of Kabbalah. He immersed himself in his studies, trying to unravel the deepest mysteries of the universe while most of his friends went on with the normal lives of turn-of-the-twentieth-century Iraqi teens.

Yitzhak was eventually accepted as a student of the renowned Kabbalist Rabbi Yosef Chaim of Baghdad, Iraq, where he formally studied Kabbalah at the Zilka Yeshiva. Rabbi Chaim was the man who would pronounce a prophetic vision over a 13-year-old Yitzhak, assuring the serious-minded teenager that he would receive a revelation of the identity of the true Messiah before he died.[168]

Amazingly, it has also been long-reported that Rabbi Chaim additionally assured Yitzhak, when he was just 16 years old, that he would have an unusually "long life." As time has now proven, both of Rabbi Chaim's prophecies were correct.[169]

War Hero

During the developing years of World War I, the Ottoman Empire was conscripting the Jews of Baghdad into its military ranks. The news spread through the Jewish communities that the Ottomans were going to raid the yeshiva in Baghdad—where Yitzhak was a student.

Young yeshiva scholars were quickly recruited. The yeshiva officials were looking for those who would be willing to go into hiding within the city to preserve the Holy Scriptures as well as the sacred writings of Kabbalah. The volunteers were told they would be expected to skirt from location to location to try to evade authorities. They were to remain in hiding, guarding their precious treasures with their lives, for the duration of the war.

Only four young men volunteered for the life-threatening duty. Yitzhak Diba was one of them. After the war was over, he was hailed as a hero for successfully completing his sacred assignment. His admirers proclaimed that God's hand was upon him. They were certain that the young man was destined for greatness. If they had only known…

Changes and Destiny

In 1923, twenty-five years *before* the nation of Israel would prophetically resurrect from the dead, fulfilling a 2,700-year-old biblical prophecy,

Yitzhak left Baghdad and journeyed to the British Mandate of Palestine. This move was undertaken on the advice of various leading elders of Baghdad.[170]

It was in this new home that Yitzhak changed his last name from Diba, of his father's family, to Kaduri, which is Hebrew for "sphere." The concept of the sphere is deeply connected to the mystical practice of Kabbalah. The Ten Spheres of Kabbalah are a system of instruction and discipline that assist the learned and committed searcher in discovering the deepest secrets of God and His creation. Kabbalah's mystical spheres would become Kaduri's life pursuit, reflected in the changing of his name.[171]

By 1933, young Rabbi Kaduri humbly and quietly operated his own consulting rooms in the Old City of Jerusalem. There, he taught patrons how to predict the future by unraveling secret texts hidden in the Psalms, or how to beckon the aid of angels to help overcome personal problems. In his lifetime, Kaduri published no religious articles or books for public consumption. What he did write, he confined to the halls of his yeshiva, and only for the private use of his personal students.[172]

However, he would eventually rise to become not only modern Israel's most well-known Kabbalistic Orthodox rabbi, but also the planet's oldest living rabbi. Furthermore, because this aged man lived his last years in the age of the Internet, he used it to his ministry's greatest advantage. He had a following of millions around the globe.

As it turned out, Rabbi Kaduri would indeed live to see the prophetic rebirth of Israel and would come to know every major political and military figure from the nation's inception right up to his death in 2007. He would even be officially credited with affecting the outcome of several of Israel's most important elections.

His first wife, Rabbanit Sara, died in 1989. Kaduri remarried in 1993 to Rabbanit Dorit, a *baalat teshuva.*[173] She was just over half his age.

In January 2006, Rabbi Kaduri was hospitalized with pneumonia in the Bikur Holim Hospital in Jerusalem. He died around 10 p.m. on January 28, 2006, and was said to have been attentive and articulate until his last day.[174] After his death, Kaduri's 80-year-old son, David, took the reins of the Kaduri ministry, an organization with a huge global following as well as with a highly influential power-base among Israel's Orthodox elite.

Jewish Iraqis Today

The historic journey of the Jews in the land of Iraq goes back almost four thousand years—all the way to the biblical patriarch Abraham of Ur. That trek is also deeply connected to the Babylonian monarch Nebuchadnezzar, who sent the Jewish people into exile there more than 2,500 years ago.

When the nation of Israel was reborn in 1948, violent uprisings against the Jews living in Iraq caused tens of thousands of them to flee to the new Jewish homeland. Many more have been leaving Iraq ever since, especially in light of the Gulf War of 1990 and the Arab Spring uprisings of 2011.

In 1947, just one year before Israel's birth, the population of the Iraqi-Jewish community was calculated to be close to 150,000. As of May 2018, their numbers in Iraq had dwindled to single digits.[175]

> As Sunni and Shi'ite militias slaughter one another across the city, in the heart of terror-ridden Baghdad **there are eight residents** hiding a dangerous secret.
>
> Eight Baghdadi Jews are believed to be the last Jews in Iraq, a community that once numbered well over 130,000 and was one of the oldest Jewish Diaspora communities in the world.
>
> Today the remnants of Iraq's Jewish community live in constant fear as terrorism rages throughout Baghdad and Islamic extremism is on the rise.[176] (Emphasis added)

Between 1950 and 1952, close to 125,000 Iraqi Jews were airlifted into Israel. Every one of them was required to relinquish their Iraqi citizenship.

In Israel, near the shores of the Mediterranean Sea, stands the Babylonian Jewry Heritage Centre. Inscribed on the entry gate are the mournful words, "The Jewish community in Iraq is no more." Today in Israel, there are about six hundred thousand Iraqi Jews out of a total national population of close to 8.8 million.[177]

Such is the historical journey of the Jews of Iraqi heritage who are living in Israel today. This was the heritage of Rabbi Yitzhak Kaduri, the most venerated Orthodox rabbi in Israel's modern history to date.

Divine Connections

There can be no doubt: Rabbi Yitzhak Kaduri's legacy to the world—as wildly popular as he was—will forever be overshadowed by the mystery of his Yeshua note.

But that note ultimately revealed its Heaven-directed connections through the life of yet another Israeli-born Jew. As it turns out, this man was apparently destined, through a deep family rabbinic legacy and subsequent connections to Kaduri himself, to become a monumental part of the Kaduri story. This man was also slated by family heritage to be an Orthodox Israeli rabbi of very important stature.

You have been introduced to him throughout this story. His name is Zev Porat.

Following is his fascinating personal journey of faith.

30

To Be a Rabbi

Crispus, the synagogue leader, and his entire household believed in the Lord; and many of the Corinthians who heard Paul believed and were baptized.
—Acts 28:8

Rabbi Zev Porat's life is directly linked to every one of the major players in Rabbi Kaduri's story, and in surprising ways that have yet to be disclosed.

I asked Zev to provide me with an account of his personal journey and of his connections to the Kaduri story in his own words. I have heard him share his testimony on several occasions, and it is riveting. This is the first time it has appeared in print. In the next several chapters, you will be treated to an abbreviated, but amazing, autobiography of Zev Porat's life, conversion, and ministry calling.

Zev's Story: A Journey of the Supernatural

I was born in Israel to a family of rabbis.

My father, grandfather, and great-grandfather were well-known and highly respected Orthodox rabbis.[178] My great-grandfather, Rabbi Abraham Porat, was what is known as a "Dayan" among the rabbis—a judge serving in the official rabbinic courts of Israel.

My grandfather, Rabbi Pinhas Porat, was a Holocaust survivor. His entire family was exterminated in the Nazi gas chambers when he was a teenager. As a young man, he fled the horrifically unthinkable persecution and eventually landed in Belarus. There, he met and married the woman who would later become my grandmother.

By mid-1946, my grandfather finally made it to the land of Israel. In 1948, at Israel's re-birth, he became one of the distinguished leaders of Israel's Orthodox Rabbinate, the ruling elite among the rabbis.

Growing up as an Orthodox boy in a deeply Orthodox family, I still never felt the personal presence of the God of Abraham, Isaac, and Jacob. I seemed to feel nothing but bondage to an ingrained form of mere religiosity and deep-seated tradition. I grew increasingly miserable with my "religion."

Anytime I asked questions of my elders as to why I didn't feel the presence of God in my life, the answer was given in relation to the Jewish Sabbath requirements.

My problem, they said, was because I did not celebrate the Sabbath consistently enough. They told me that I didn't understand it properly and that I should study Sabbath law even more than I had done. I later discovered this attitude was exactly what Jesus spoke about—"They glorify the Sabbath more than the Sabbath maker" (Matthew 12:1–8; Mark 2:23–28; and Luke 6:1–5). Because of this struggle, there was something missing in the depths of my soul.

As a boy, I primarily lived and studied in Israel. However, a few times a year we would travel to the United States where my father held a double position as a rabbi of a synagogue and a rabbi of a big school in California. When he went to the United States, I would go with him. So, I grew up going to school in America as well as in Israel. As a result of this arrangement, I grew up speaking Hebrew and English fluently.

I never really wanted to be a rabbi, but I was repeatedly told that I must continue the family tradition. I fought that idea with a vengeance. I didn't understand why being a rabbi had to be my lot in life. I felt no calling from God, whatsoever, to pursue that "predetermined" path.

Looking back, I now understand that God did actually have a calling on my life. However, He was not going to allow me to succeed in the path of becoming a rabbi. He knew the connections I would establish. He knew the ministry He had for me. Eventually my life would be set apart to take Yeshua to the Jews of Israel. However, the Holy Spirit worked for decades in my life before I finally became a believer in *Yeshua Ha' Mashiach*.

Generation to Generation

My father passed away while he was ministering in California. His body was flown back to Israel to be buried in a rabbinic cemetery called Ponevezh—also the home of a prominent yeshiva in Bnei Brak. Ponevezh is the most venerated rabbinic cemetery in Israel. Only the most renowned Israeli rabbis are buried there. This is where my father and grandfather are buried. This is the rabbinic legacy of my family.

At that point in my life, my grandfather became like a father to me. He wanted me to continue the family tradition and become a great rabbi in Israel. He wanted me to study in Ponevezh Yeshiva so that I could become an authorized Sanhedrin rabbi—one who could be a part of the Sanhedrin.[179] To my dismay, my life had been planned out—*by my family*—and by tradition. So, I finally began my yeshiva studies. I was going to be a rabbi.

A Young Adult

Because of the authority and power my grandfather possessed among the Israeli elite, he was able to have me drafted into the Israeli army—with special privileges. He pulled his powerful strings to make certain it was officially *arranged* that I was to be given a pass—a few times a week—so that I could complete my studies in the yeshiva while still serving in the army.

While fulfilling my duty to the IDF (Israel Defense Forces), I eventually completed my yeshiva studies as well and became an authorized

Sanhedrin rabbi. However, years later, after becoming a believer in Yeshua, I returned that certification. I have no need for it now. I have only one true Rabbi—*Yeshua Jesus*.

When I completed my Israeli army commitment, because of my army management skills and because I spoke Hebrew and English fluently, I obtained a very good job in a German medical company called Granulox, located in HaZore'a, Israel. While at Granulox, I managed thirty-seven employees. I was earning five times the national average salary in Israel. I had a new car and all my bills were paid, but I still wasn't happy. In fact, I grew more miserable with my life. I was still running from God.

I am now ashamed to say that I began to drink heavily. I went to bars, I got into fights and I was arrested by the police—and I actually assaulted the police officer who came to break up one of my fighting episodes. After that arrest, I was taken before the judge. The judge asked me if I was sorry for what I did. I told him, "Take off these handcuffs and I'll beat *you* up too!" My anger knew no boundaries in those days.

Believe it or not, even after assaulting a police officer and threatening a judge, I didn't go to jail. Apparently, it was determined that news of the arrest of the grandson of a foremost Sanhedrin rabbi, and a certified Sanhedrin rabbi myself, probably didn't need to be splashed all over the headlines of the newspapers. But, most important, I now understand that God had a calling on my life even then. He graciously protected me.

However, from a strictly earthly standpoint, my grandfather cleaned up the mess and got me out of jail. He and the other officials over whom he held sway were able to keep the story out of the media.

At that point, I found an extra job, in addition to the one I held at Granulox. But I desired even more money. I wanted more fine gold jewelry, a fancier and more expensive car, and much nicer clothing. I sought my happiness in wealth and in the "shiny" things of the world. Still—I was empty in my soul.

The extra job I secured was that of working as a clerk in a very nice hotel. One day, a woman walked into that hotel. She was in Israel with a group from China. She and her group were participating in a food expo that was being held at our hotel. At the time, she was also a nonbeliever in Yeshua and was from a Buddhist background.

That woman stayed in Israel after that expo, with a little urging from me. We were married ten months later. I didn't know it at the time, but God Himself had selected her as my future ministry partner for the kingdom of Yeshua.

Nevertheless, during the early years of my marriage I was still seeking peace with God—and not finding it…

31

Desperation

Then one of the synagogue leaders,
named Jairus, came, and when
he saw Jesus, he fell at his feet.
—Mark 5:22

Zev continues his story:

My anxious quest to uncover my "Jewish answers" continued. I was spiritually miserable, and that condition was eating at me daily.

I started searching the Internet for the solutions that my family of distinguished rabbis couldn't seem to adequately provide. A man from the United States named Todd found me in an Internet chat room. He found out I was in Israel and that I had studied in yeshiva to be a rabbi. Todd began to explain the gospel of Yeshua to me. For a total of four years—almost on a daily basis—Todd took time to reveal Yeshua to me, through the Old Testament. In the earlier days of that process, I became convicted and angry. I rejected what Todd was trying to do. Every fiber of my Jewish upbringing screamed out against what Todd was telling me, mainly because the truths he revealed pointed directly to the New Testament account of Yeshua as Messiah.

"Don't speak to me about such things!" I insisted. "I'm a Jew. I don't want to hear the New Testament!"

Then I finally demanded, "Just leave me alone, I am running away from God! I have no need for Him in my life."

Yes. I actually told him that *I was running away from God.* Truer words could not have been spoken.

But Todd lovingly persisted. After two solid years of listening to this man from America explaining that Yeshua is Messiah—and doing this from the Old Testament—I truly became miserable. I was under intense conviction, and I just couldn't shake it. I couldn't hide from God's presence no matter how hard I tried.

The Holy Spirit of God started waking me up in the middle of the night. I began to see what I can only now describe as *visions*. The Bible verses I had been studying on the Internet—Isaiah 53, Micah 5:2, Jeremiah 23, Psalm 22, and many others—continually resonated in my mind. I couldn't sleep. I actually *saw* those verses coming to life in my visions. I thought I was going crazy.

I kept hearing what I now know to be the voice of Satan saying, "Yeshua is the Messiah of the Gentiles! He is not the Jewish Messiah! Stay away from Him! Go the other way! Pay no attention to this teaching! You are Jewish—that's all you need!"

Digging in the Word of God

I finally decided to start my own "Jewish" investigation into this matter. After all, I had been trained to be a rabbi. I came from a family of rabbis. I had dozens of rabbi friends and connections. This Yeshua "thing" should be easy enough to disprove—especially with the "army" of distinguished Jewish rabbis I could bring to the fray.

In the beginning of my search, I was particularly interested in Micah 5:2, because it spoke of the birth of a king/messiah in Bethlehem.

In Hebrew, the words in that passage say, "His days are *before the foundation of the world*." But how could this be? How could anyone, except God Himself, be a king and also be described as being from "before the foundations of the world?" I decided to ask the rabbis. Surely they would know the answer to this mystery.

I was in for a shock. Over the next two years, I counseled with thirty-two different rabbis and my grandfather as well. I asked these thirty-three rabbis about Micah 5:2, and the apparent theological dilemma that passage presented.

I received twenty-six different answers from those holy men, and none of them was completely satisfactory. This indicated to me that even the "all-knowing" rabbis were thoroughly confused on the subject as well; they were just as confounded by the depth of it as I was.

The Vision

Then, near the conclusion of that study, I was awakened one morning at 3 a.m. I heard the voice of God. He spoke to me from a shiny cloud. Looking back, I believe it was the same glory through which God revealed Himself to the children of Israel as they were coming out of Egypt. It was His Shekinah Glory!

In that revelation, God called out my name in Hebrew. He spoke it two times. "Zev! Zev!"

I was stunned. Then God spoke again, "Zev, Isaiah 53, which you have been studying so diligently—*this* is the Messiah of Israel. This is *Yeshua.*"

I felt a jolt of electricity go through my body. At that moment, I fell to my knees beside my bed, weeping, and I called out for Yeshua to save me and to receive me as His own. At that moment I was born again.

It took me a few days to process my experience. All that week, I shared with my wife about my supernatural encounter with Yahweh. I was determined to share the gospel of Yeshua with my Buddhist wife so that she also might believe. Upon hearing all that I had to say, and after a full week of exploring the Scriptures together, my wife renounced her Buddhist beliefs and called upon Yeshua to save her.

The previously "dark" spiritual house of our home in Israel became the *House of Light*—for both of us. We became the "one new man" spoken of in Ephesians 2:14–18. How miraculous! A Jew and a Gentile were now together as one. We became not only a husband and wife, united with Christ, but we were also a brother and a sister in Yeshua—*to the glory of Yeshua Ha' Mashiach.*

Tough Times

During the first two years of our newfound faith, my wife and I were severely persecuted. My family disowned me. My friends abandoned me. My employers forbade me from sharing my faith in Yeshua. The entire Orthodox culture rejected me. I was cursed, spit upon, and reviled almost everywhere I went. Yeshua's sanctification process of "humbling Zev" had begun.

Our livelihood began to shrivel up. I was fired from my place of lucrative employment. The company's owner said I could not share my faith in Yeshua, even away from the job. I refused to acquiesce to his demand in this regard. I knew the consequences, and eventually, I paid the price.

We wound up being homeless. We lived out of our car and in a tent that we would set up each night on the beach at the Mediterranean Sea. We lived like this for three and a half months. The reason? Only because of our faith in Yeshua as Messiah. I had committed the "unpardonable" Jewish sin. I had become a follower of Yeshua—the most detested name on the planet. I was considered an utter disgrace.

The Test

One day, our family lawyer called me on my cell phone. I was at my "beach home" when he called. He told me that he needed to see me in his office for some very important business. We loaded up our "mobile" home as quickly as possible, and we were off in a flash. The news he needed to tell me crushed me. He said, "Zev, your grandfather has died."

The lawyer explained that my renowned and very important rabbi grandfather had become extremely wealthy over his lifetime. In cash and property, he was worth many millions of dollars. The lawyer told me that my grandfather had left me forty million dollars in tangible assets. It was all mine. We were going to be taken care of *for life.*

Could this really be? Could it be that my wife and I were going to be able to move off the beach and into a nice home and become instant millionaires? Could it actually be that all our financial woes were really over? Well, as it turned out, the matter was not quite that simple.

The lawyer, after announcing my grandfather's financial intentions for my life, looked at me from the other side of his desk and said, "Zev, there is only one condition to all of this." I could feel the other shoe was about to drop.

He continued, "You must renounce this crazy stuff about Yeshua. You are embarrassing your family and your Jewish tradition. Live a good Jewish life and all this wealth will be yours. If you do not agree to that, you'll receive absolutely nothing."

It did not take me long to decide my response. I told the lawyer that I would never renounce Yeshua. The lawyer was completely befuddled. My response was unbelievable to him. I got the feeling that he might have been willing to sell his soul to the devil if the shoe had been on the other foot. He was beginning to get angry with me.

"Zev," he snapped, "*Look.* Just sign the paper. I'm not a rabbi, I'm a lawyer. I don't care what you do with your life or your religious beliefs. Just sign the paper and take the money so my job can be done. Your financial concerns will immediately end. You will be set for life."

My head was spinning. I couldn't believe what I was hearing.

"Later," he continued, "when all this dies down, you can always go back to your Yeshua stuff. You can even do it now—secretly. Who will know?"

I told him, "*I will know*. The Lord will know. And I will not put my name to a document that renounces Yeshua as Messiah. I won't do it. You can keep the money."

With that, we walked out of his office. We went back to our tent on the beach. We turned our back on our "wilderness temptation" moment. We had passed the test. But for now, we were still homeless.

By the way, the first night or so of living in a tent on the Mediterranean Sea was really quite romantic. But once reality set in that this would probably be our home for a very long time, the romantic aspect began to ease away. There are only so many nights you can spend in a tent with drunks and crabs continually trying to get into your "house." It gets old very quickly.

Messiah of Israel Ministries Is Born

However, through a long sequence of events, the details of which I will not bore you with, we began to slowly pull our lives back together. The first job I found where the boss didn't care about my faith was as a dishwasher for a little restaurant run by an Arab.

From *riches to rags*—we were now living that story. We lived very meagerly for a long time, and although we never shied from sharing our faith in Yeshua, we became a bit more guarded concerning with whom, when, and where we shared that faith. But Yeshua honored us and He was growing us in the Word and in our marriage and faith.

As time passed, we were able to slowly recoup a more normal style of life. Our humble dwelling of "beachfront property" was finally in our past. This is when the Lord allowed us to start our official ministry outreach to the Jewish people of Israel. Thus began Messiah of Israel Ministries.[180]

Now, these many years later, to the glory of Yeshua, we are preaching the gospel all over the world. We are primarily in Israel, Europe, China, and the United States. The Lord has opened up television interviews, radio interviews, Internet video-casting, websites, joint ministry efforts with other like believers, print media articles, conference preaching, and guest preaching in churches.

As we began that ministry, still undergoing intense persecution for our faith, we never dreamed that soon our lives would be intricately connected to a name I had heard all my life, growing up in my rabbinic home.

It was the revered name of Israel's most venerated Kabbalistic Orthodox rabbi: Yitzhak Kaduri.

At that moment, the idea that we would soon be caught up in the spiritual battleground and the Orthodox firestorm of the *Kaduri Revival*[181] was inconceivable.

32

The Heavenly Collision

Crispus, the synagogue leader, and his
entire household believed in the Lord;
and many of the Corinthians who heard
Paul believed and were baptized.
—Acts 18:8

Zev's story continues:

I am often asked: How is it that I, Zev Porat, am directly connected to the Rabbi Yitzhak Kaduri affair? Some ask me, "What gives you any authority in this matter? Why is it that you are so eagerly determined to make certain the world knows the truth of this story?"

Those are fair questions. However, the answers are quite unbelievable. It is a story I have seldom shared in great detail. That's why I am now putting it in writing, for all the world to see.

As I have already related, my family and my friends were of the *rabbi class* of Jews; we were deeply connected to very important people, both in Israel and in the United States. It is in that specific context of culture, society, and relationship where God's divine associations began to shape my life and future ministry.

Yitzhak Kaduri

To this day, what many people do *not* know is that both my grandfather and my great-grandfather were very good friends with the renowned

Rabbi Kaduri. They all knew each other personally and moved in the same circle of important people.

Not only did they frequently speak *with* Rabbi Kaduri, but, among our family and friends, they also spoke *about* him and his ministry endeavors. I grew up knowing Rabbi Kaduri's name as a household name and as someone who was a beloved friend of our rabbinic family. At the time, I took this relationship for granted. It was simply a well-established fact of our deep family connections among important and powerful people. As a kid, I had no idea what those relationships would later mean to me.

Growing up hearing Kaduri's name in our house, I could not have imagined that one day I also would believe in Yeshua as Messiah. And never in my wildest dreams could I have known that Rabbi Kaduri would not only have the same revelation, but that he would also teach that truth to a group of his yeshiva students—and then leave the divine disclosure in a handwritten note posted on his personal website for all the world to see!

The divine collision of those two events was undeniably life changing for me. My Yeshua revelation was now directly linked with Rabbi Kaduri's Yeshua revelation! Now, this great rabbi and I would, together, take the message to the Jews of Israel and around the world, the message that Yeshua/Jesus is Messiah and Lord of all! Only Yahweh could do something like this. Obviously, it was His master plan from the beginning.[182]

Ariel Sharon

An even greater shock to me was when I eventually discovered that Rabbi Kaduri had also publicly linked Israel's Prime Minister Ariel Sharon to the Messiah prophecy.

Ariel Sharon had also been a close, personal friend of my family through the prestigious positions of power held by my father and grandfather. My grandmother often delighted in telling me of the time that my father first brought Ariel Sharon to their home. On that particular occasion, Ariel Sharon had slept in my grandfather's house as a personal friend and guest of our family.

Both Kaduri and Sharon were an intricate part of my family's history and legacy. Soon, I would be more deeply connected to them than anyone could have known.

The Note Was Unveiled

When word got out that Rabbi Kaduri, in 2005, had announced that Prime Minister Sharon was attached to his Messiah vision, and then in 2006 when Kaduri passed away and left the Messiah note to be posted a year later, the Orthodox rabbinic community was set on edge.

I was flabbergasted when I discovered that Rabbi Kaduri had coded the message in his note that Yeshua was the true Messiah! The revelation shocked the Jewish world. They were in a panic. All of a sudden, the most famous rabbi in Israel was saying the same thing I had been saying. Kaduri had made the same proclamation for which I had been severely persecuted! I was ecstatic. This was unbelievable!

So, I quickly started trying to tell everyone I could what Rabbi Kaduri had said, but the Orthodox leaders had almost instantly established a powerful and intricately woven movement to shut the story down. Their centerpiece message was: *It's a lie! The note's a fake! Pay no attention to this story! We are your rabbis. We know what we are talking about.* Their appeal worked.

I tried telling my fellow Jews about the note. But they already believed it was a lie. I showed them pictures of it from the Internet posting. They had already been brainwashed. They flatly told me, "It's a forgery!"

But, I knew better. I knew how all this went down. I knew how the process worked. I was familiar with the intricate working of the rabbinical elite, the movers and shakers of Israel's political and informational world. I had grown up in it. I was one of its deepest benefactors. I was directly related to some of its most powerful members and families. I had seen its wheels grinding from the inside.

I was convinced that the note was the genuine article. But, I was getting nowhere when I tried to share it with other Jews in Israel. I began to make the topic of the note a regular subject of my prayer life. I believed that the amazing connections to my life were simply too supernatural for this story to die. I knew that somehow, Yahweh was going to intervene. Somehow, this story had to be verified and shared with the world. I never dreamed I would become one of the main conduits of Rabbi Kaduri's note.

By early 2011, after almost four years of consistent prayer over the matter, I began to use the Kaduri note again in my public ministry endeavors. I had been using it very discreetly before then. But few cared to see it. They were already convinced that the entire ordeal was one big, fabricated lie.

But, by the summer of 2011, there was a divine breakthrough. Something happened that could have only been orchestrated at the Throne of God.

Divine Encounter

It was a warm evening. I was stopped at a red light in downtown Tel Aviv, making my way home from a ministry encounter that had begun earlier that evening.

A bearded Orthodox Jew in his mid-sixties came up to my car while I was at that red light. He seemed to almost appear from *nowhere.*

He knocked on my window. He looked to be holding a stack of pamphlets in his hand. I normally do not roll my window down for such attempts at solicitation, especially at night. But, on this night, I felt an unexplainable feeling to give the man a hearing. I rolled down the window. The man offered me a flyer *with Rabbi Kaduri's picture on it!*

I told him, "Look. I really can't accept this, but I feel I must take it, anyway." I reached for his flyer.

As he was handing me his paper, the man asked me, "Why did you feel you can't accept it?"

I said, "Because I believe that Yeshua is the true Messiah."

The man leaned in a little closer, he looked right into my eyes and said, "So do I!"

I couldn't believe what I just heard! Did he know about Kaduri's Messiah vision? How could it be that he just walked up to my car late at night at a red light in downtown Tel Aviv to speak to *me* about Kaduri and Yeshua? This was overwhelming. I had to know more.

I told him to meet me under the streetlight at the curb. I pulled my car over and got out to speak with the man. That's when he revealed to me that he was a student at Kaduri's yeshiva. He told me, in no uncertain terms, that Kaduri had been guardedly teaching that Yeshua was the true Messiah to a select group of his students.

We stood there that night for several hours. He had many questions about Yeshua. I spent most of that time discipling him and showing him biblical truth. He was hungry to know more about Yeshua, now that his beloved rabbi was gone.

He did not yet understand about the resurrection of Yeshua. I took him through the Scriptures and explained how to be truly born again. Right there, late that night, on that Tel Aviv street corner, the man from "nowhere" prayed and received personal salvation through Jesus Christ.

33

The Students

Then a man named Jairus, a synagogue
leader, came and fell at Jesus' feet,
pleading with him to come to his house.
—Luke 8:41

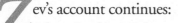

Zev's account continues:

After that late-night meeting in Tel Aviv, that former Kaduri student, now a born-again believer in Yeshua as Messiah, began to introduce me to several more of the rabbi's yeshiva students. They also knew about Yeshua/Jesus. The Kaduri message was, at that time, starting to become popular again because of the Internet. It seemed the time was now right. It appeared that Yahweh was up to something big.

One by one, the students began to contact me. They knew that Yeshua was Messiah, they said. They knew this because their rabbi, Yitzhak Kaduri, had told them so! They knew it because Rabbi Kaduri had connected this truth with the Old Testament Scriptures.

I had been right all along. Now I had the evidence I needed; this was not a *fake note.* This was not a movement of deception. This was real. And the Orthodox rabbis *knew it. They* were the ones involved in a "conspiracy," not me—and not the believers who understood the truth. It was time to act. It was time to get serious about this. This truth could no longer stay covered up.

Three of those Kaduri yeshiva students agreed to give their testimony of salvation in Yeshua and their eyewitness accounts of Kaduri's teaching. They agreed to have their words on video.

In Need of a Miracle

For the next two years, I shared these videos and testimonies everywhere. But still, very few believed. The damage that had been leveled by the rabbinical elite and the anti-missionary organizations in Israel had already been done. There was an almost insurmountable wall of unbelief and media blackout that had been erected throughout Israel.

Then, in late 2013, I earnestly prayed, "Lord, the Jews are not accepting this message. I need some more divine intervention!"

Shortly thereafter, the Lord led me to Jerusalem. I went to the Kotel (Western Wall) to pray for the Jewish people of Israel. I left there having a peace in my heart that the Lord had heard me and that He would somehow answer that prayer.

Soon, I got an email from someone I had never met before. The senders identified themselves as Chuck and Tami Mohler from the United States. They told me they were currently in Israel and wanted to meet me.

I seldom meet with strangers that I have no relationship with. I have to be very careful about those kinds of things—especially with the threats and persecution my wife and I are continually exposed to. But, I couldn't shake their plea. They told me they had something earth-shattering to share with me and something to give me. We made the appointment. We met the Mohlers at a restaurant in downtown Tel Aviv. When we sat down at the table, Chuck pulled out a book and said, "Have you ever seen this before?"

The book was titled *The Rabbi Who Found Messiah: The Story of Yitzhak Kaduri*. It was written by a man in America named Carl Gallups. Chuck and Tami told me they had met Carl personally and that he was a genuine man of God.

I read the book and studied it from front to back to make certain the information in it was correct. I was overwhelmed. This was just what I had been praying for.

Heaven's Train Ride

Shortly after that meeting, I was on the train to Haifa. I was reading the *Rabbi* book. I was almost finished with it, and had already reached the conclusion that the book was anointed by Yahweh and could be powerfully used in my ministry endeavors.

Sitting across from me on that train were two IDF soldiers. I could tell they were looking at the book. Kaduri's face was prominently displayed on the front cover; it was a face recognized by almost every Jew in Israel.

One of the soldiers asked me, "What is this? Did Kaduri write that book?" I told them that Rabbi Kaduri did not write the book, but that he did write a note saying he believed in Yeshua as Messiah. I turned to the page in the book where a picture of Kaduri's note was located. Now, over half the passengers on the train were listening to everything I was saying. They were drawn like magnets!

That was when I understood. This book was anointed. I started using it with the Jews. Since the Jews frequently take at face value everything the rabbis say, how could they simply dismiss what was in this book? I found that the book first drew them to Kaduri, then to the note, then to the Word of God. Many Jews began to come to Yeshua as Messiah and Lord because of this newly given tool. The Orthodox movement was shaken to the core. They were in an uproar. They wondered: *What is this book that is suddenly changing everything? And who is this rabbi's son who is exposing the previously hidden truth of Kaduri's Messiah note?*

Hell's Blast Furnace

That's when Yad L'Achim's[183] threats and other forms of persecution began.

We even began receiving death notes from unknown people. After six solid months of exposing the truth of the Kaduri note and using the *Rabbi* book to do so, I woke up one morning, after a long night of ministry, only to discover that someone had left us an unpleasant surprise. Apparently, someone had followed me home that night.

They knew exactly where I lived and which car was mine. When I went outside, I discovered that my car had been destroyed. Its wheels had been busted, the glass was broken, and the paint was heavily damaged. The perpetrators had painted across my windshield the words *Messianic Pig!* My insurance company, once I notified them, informed me, "We don't cover missionary activity."

To this very day, I have to park my car four or five blocks away from my home, and then I walk back and forth to it from my house. I take different routes home, and am very careful to make sure that I am not being followed. That's how a public convert from Orthodoxy to Yeshua often has to live in Israel.

But the problem is the Orthodox culture in Israel; it's not the government. The government protects freedom of religion. And it's only illegal to engage in missions and evangelism with someone under 18 years of age unless one has explicit permission from the youth's parents. It's also illegal to go into a private place and preach and evangelize—but it is not illegal to do so in a public place.

The government gives us quite a bit of leeway in sharing our faith, even faith in Yeshua. It's the nascent Sanhedrin and the other Orthodox rabbinic elite that are the problem—*the Orthodox Jews*—just like in the days of the New Testament persecution of the early Christians. By the way, almost all the earliest Christians were also Jews. Sadly, not much has changed in this regard in over two thousand years.

The Message That Won't Die

However, the Kaduri Revival is alive today in Israel and around the world. It will not be stopped. This is a prophetic movement of God. Jews in a returned Israel and around the world are coming to Jesus Christ as Lord because of Rabbi Kaduri's revelation.

After using my deep and reliable contacts in Israel, I, too, have become aware of the Kabbalistic curse placed upon the note as it was burned and thrown into the Dead Sea. I often ask the persecutors of the Kaduri story, "If the note was a fake, then why go to all this trouble to burn and destroy a note that's not even real in the first place? Why was it even on the website in the first place?"

I have never received an articulate answer to those questions. To me, the note's destruction *proves* its authenticity as well as the other rabbis' knowledge of this fact. Many Jews in Israel have now figured this out as well. Destroying the note was the worst thing those rabbis could have done. It was as though they screamed to the world, "We *must* burn this note, because it's real—and we can't let the world see it ever again!"

There are now many Jews in Israel who are believing in Yeshua. A number of those recent believers have come to faith in Him because of people secretly hearing the word about Kaduri's note and then seeking more information about it. I have become a part of that information flow.

As of now, at least thirteen of Kaduri's students are believers in Yeshua as Messiah and have given witnessed testimony to their salvation experience. Sadly, I must also tell you that their lives have become much more difficult because of their faith. They endure a lot of persecution. Some of them have had to move from their communities because of the incessant and intense persecution. One of these rabbinical students was in his sixties when he was born again.

Yet, all these students are still sharing their faith within their closer circles of family and friends. I also have been told by some of the same students that even more among Kaduri's original students are believers as well. They have since left the rabbinical yeshiva.

Now that you know my complete story, you can understand why so many people in Israel would come to me for answers about Yeshua—especially as this understanding relates to the Kaduri story. I understand that I am nothing. I am just a little person serving a big God, a big God who knew that many Jews in Israel would ultimately trust me to tell them the truth about this story. I have been on the same journey that many of them have trekked. I knew the major players of this story in a deeply personal way. This was the way God ordained it to be. And God is certainly not finished with this story yet.

Think of it: I have come from being an Orthodox Jewish boy growing up with Rabbi Kaduri and Ariel Sharon as personal friends of my family to experiencing my own Messiah journey and all the way to the collision of that journey with Kaduri's Messiah note, as well as personally connecting with some of the students of his own yeshiva who also believe. This was all in God's amazing master plan! That's why I call this story *The Kaduri Revival!*

I am a Jew from Israel. Carl Gallups is a Gentile from the United States. Together, along with many other Jewish and Gentile believers in Yeshua around the world, we are working in the fields of the prophesied end-time harvest as an example of the "one new man"!

> For he himself is our peace, who *has made us both one* and has broken down in his flesh the dividing wall of hostility by abolishing the law of commandments expressed in ordinances, *that he might create in himself one new man* in place of the two, so making peace, and might *reconcile us both to God in one body through the cross,* thereby killing the hostility. And he came and preached peace to you who were far off and peace to those who were near. For *through him we both have access in one Spirit to the Father.* (Ephesians 2:14–18, emphasis added)

Only the Lord of Glory could do such a marvelous thing.

34

A Great Cloud of Witnesses

Therefore, since we are surrounded by such a great cloud of witnesses…let us run with perseverance the race marked out for us, fixing our eyes on Jesus, the pioneer and perfecter of faith.

—Hebrews 12:1–2

The amazing account of Rabbi Zev Porat becoming a believer in *Yeshua Ha'Mashiach* is not terribly unusual. Neither is Rabbi Yitzhak Kaduri's story. The only reason Kaduri's story is so far-reaching is because of his unprecedented and renowned Orthodox status, both in Israel and abroad.

Zev Porat's conversion and subsequent ministry are viciously attacked because of his family's deep connections to Kaduri. Zev speaks with authority as a Jew—to the Jews. He is a formidable force for Yeshua, and the Jewish elite are well aware of him and his ministry outreach. They incessantly look for ways to shut him down and invalidate his message, especially the message of the Rabbi Kaduri Yeshua note.

However, history is replete with numerous instances of well-known rabbis and other renowned Jewish men and women who became believers in Yeshua as Messiah, Lord, and Savior. Kaduri and Porat are not the exceptions to the rule. Furthermore, the phenomenon continues in our time, despite the incessant efforts of the critics who would attempt to have the world think otherwise.

Believers

The number of Jewish people who now proclaim Yeshua/Jesus as Messiah is continuing to increase. As of December 2017, *The Jerusalem Post*[184] reported that an estimated 20,000 Messianic Jewish believers are living in Israel alone, and an estimated 350,000 are living worldwide.[185]

However, Messianic Rabbi Zev Porat says the true numbers representing the Jewish believers in Yeshua who live in Israel are much higher:

> I know for a fact there are many rabbis in Israel who believe Yeshua is the true Messiah. I know some of them personally, and they tell me of others who believe as they do. Some of them actually study the scriptures about Yeshua in secret study rooms that are located in different places throughout Israel. The officially reported number of total Jews in Israel who believe in Yeshua is much more than the twenty thousand you see reported in the newspapers and on the Internet.

Rabbi Porat's assertion is reflected by another person who claims to have personal contacts with various Orthodox rabbis. In an article posted at *Nazarene Judaism,* the following is found:

> Let me share a secret with you. Many of the Jewish Rabbis are well aware that Yeshua of Nazareth is the true Messiah of Judaism. I have spoken with many of them. These Rabbis know the truth but they fear that endorsing Yeshua as Messiah at this point would only serve to wrongly endorse the Paganism and antinomianism[186] of Christendom. The time is coming for those Rabbis and other Rabbinic Jews to start realizing they have a responsibility to get about the business of revealing Messiah to their people and the world.[187]

Rabbi Porat continued his staggering assessment concerning the correct number of Jews in Israel who are believers in Yeshua: "I believe, without exaggeration, that this number today is closer to 50,000—maybe even 60,000, and it is still growing."

Zev explained, "The state of Israel does not keep official numbers on Messianic Jews who live in Israel. But I deal with this community at the street level. This is where I was raised, and where I am still deeply engrained in Jewish and Messianic life. People would be shocked if they knew the real numbers."

He continued, "But many of the Messianic Jews in Israel are still hesitant to come forward. They know they will be heavily persecuted."

Even the *Jerusalem Post* appears to confirm what Rabbi Porat says about the potential inaccuracy of the reported numbers of Jewish believers:

> Very few Messianic Jews apply for aliya[188] from abroad, but the Jewish Agency does not have data on those who apply to immigrate while already residing in Israel. The Population and Immigration Bureau says it does not have statistics specifically for Messianic Jews.[189]

Rabbi Porat added, "Some who publicly say that they are Messianic Jews could even be deported. It's happened before. And some Messianic Jews who desire to come to live in Israel are sometimes denied entry."

Again, that December 2017 report in the *Jerusalem Post* confirms what Rabbi Porat asserted:

> Every now and again a story reaches the media about a self-identified Jew whose application for immigration to Israel, or aliya, has been denied on the basis that he or she is a Messianic Jew.
>
> Such was the case of Swedish psychologist Rebecca Floer, 64, who was deported from Israel last month. Though she does not define herself as a Messianic Jew, she does believe in Yeshua, the name used by Messianic believers for Jesus.
>
> After having lived part-time in northern Israel on a renewed tourist visa for the past three years, her passport has now been

> blacklisted, and her lawyer has warned her that she will find it difficult, if not impossible, to return to the country.
>
> Both in Israel and across the Jewish world, there is an almost blanket rejection of Messianic Jews, or Jews who believe in Jesus. They are ineligible to make aliya, because while they consider themselves to be Jews, it is not accepted that a Jew can believe in Jesus.
>
> Therefore, they are excluded from the Law of Return as people who have voluntarily converted out of Judaism.[190]

"I doubt if the Israeli mainstream press will ever tell the world how many actual Messianic Jews are here in Israel," Rabbi Porat says. "The fact is that the actual numbers would prove to be too devastating to the overall power structure in Israel, which is foundationally established upon the laws and teachings of Orthodox Judaism. Because of this, the rabbis, the Sanhedrin Council and the Sanhedrin courts have a lot of indirect sway over the government, business, and the culture in general."

As a striking example of the power wielded over the Jewish culture by the rabbinic courts in Israel, consider this *Haaretz* headline from August 2017: "Messianic Jews Cannot Be Married as Jews in Israel, Rabbinical Court Rules: Judges say couple are not Jews but converts to Christianity, and must either renounce their new religion or marry as Christians."[191]

That article reported that the judges in the case wrote that if the couple "declares before the court they have completely given up their Christian beliefs, including their belonging to a Messianic Jewish community and missionary activities, the court will discuss their matter anew."[192]

Such are the intense and very real difficulties a Messianic Jew living in Israel faces. To this day, the Israeli Jewish believers in Yeshua are still ordered by the religious ruling elite to "stop speaking in this name of Jesus!" Not much has changed in this regard since the days of the early Church (Acts 4:13–20). In the minds of the Orthodox, this is why the revelation of Kaduri's Messiah note is so devastating and why it must be stopped.

No Longer a Secret

In spite of the desire of the Orthodox elite to effectively suppress the truth about Orthodox Jews, and even some of their rabbis who are turning to Yeshua as Messiah, a number of credible ministry organizations are dedicated to exposing the truth. One such organization offers up the following insight:

> There have been many great rabbis among the Jews who came to faith in Jesus. But you have probably never heard of them, since the Jewish community casts them out and slanders them as soon as it comes to light that they believe in Jesus. When these rabbis were a part of the Jewish community, they were considered righteous and well-respected, but as soon as their faith in Jesus the Messiah became known, they were despised and considered traitors; sinners, fools and gentiles.[193]

From matters of immigration, deportation, marriage rights, potential disinheritance from family wills and businesses, a lifetime of shunning from family members and long-time friends, as well as out-and-out cultural persecution, the Jewish person living in Israel who professes a belief in Yeshua as Messiah has much to lose. The pressures to conform or to remain silent are immense.

35

So Much to Lose

Then Peter spoke up,
"We have left everything to follow you!"
—Mark 10:28

There is something else to be lost when a person living in Israel professes faith in Yeshua as Messiah.

When a prominent Jewish rabbi such as a man of Yitzhak Kaduri's stature professes Jesus Christ as the true Messiah, that statement turns the entire cultural perspective of Jewish Orthodoxy on its head—especially when it makes it to the headlines of Israeli news.

Consider the following words of a well-known, Israeli-based ministry that reaches out to Jewish people to lead them to Yeshua as Messiah. Like Zev Porat, the director of that ministry is a native-born Jewish-Israeli:

> If the Jewish people stopped following the rabbis, and instead followed the Messiah, the rabbis would lose their respect, their importance, and the source of their income. So unfortunately, those who are in a position to lose much prefer to do whatever they can to keep Jesus hidden from the Jewish people—quite possibly the best kept secret in Judaism.[194]

And there's the problem: Just like in the days of the first century, the rabbis of today cannot afford to proclaim Yeshua as Messiah. They fear the loss of their fame and fortune, as well as their power over the people. It appears that nothing much has changed in the last two thousand years.

Therefore, a celebrated national icon in Kaduri's position would have to handle his personal Yeshua revelation in the most judicious manner possible—not simply for his sake alone. Many lives, families, livelihoods, fortunes, government positions, and dynastic heritages would be at stake as well.

When one thinks of the step-by-step, calculated method whereby Rabbi Kaduri proceeded, resulting in the ultimate disclosure of the Yeshua note to the world, his plan turned out to be genius. Further considering that, all these years later, Kaduri's Messiah note saga continues to thrive, the distinct possibility that the *hand of God* is truly directing this story is not too far-fetched.

The Witnesses

In light of the ubiquitous documentation of similar rabbinic conversions, why should it surprise even the Orthodox Jew that Rabbi Kaduri, in more than one hundred years of poring over the Scriptures and searching for the truth concerning the identity of the genuine Messiah, might not have found that Messiah in the person of Yeshua? Now we know that not only was it possible, but apparently, this is exactly what happened. This is what history must truthfully record.[195]

For this reason, when the Kaduri story broke, the anti-missionary groups and Orthodox critics of Yeshua and Messianic Jews went berserk. They knew the most famous Kabbalistic Israeli rabbi would soon be attached to these kinds of documented lists. This was something they simply could not abide.

The Jewish elite in Israel obviously reasoned that it was because of this very phenomenon that the Kaduri note had to be destroyed and buried. Those insisting upon spreading the story must be silenced, and those persisting in spreading the news had to be marginalized and lampooned into irrelevance. That was their plan. But the plan has failed and continues to do so.

The Jewish ruling class in Israel never envisioned that a book about Kaduri's note would be written by a best-selling author. Nor could they have known that an Indiana produce farmer with deep and ingrained ties to a number of Israel's important people—even their own Sanhedrin Council—would read that book and personally deliver boxes of them into Israel.

How could they have further known that this American businessman and his wife would somehow contact an Israeli-born, Messianic rabbi living in Tel Aviv who had direct familial ties to Ariel Sharon, Israel's Sanhedrin, and countless important Israeli rabbis, as well as Rabbi Kaduri himself? And how could they have dreamed that the book about Kaduri's note would have been placed directly into the hands of that rabbi?

How in the world could those same Jewish elite—the anti-missionary organizations, Israeli media, and Orthodox rulers—have had even an inkling of an idea that all these factors would eventually collide, creating a massive and global explosion of knowledge concerning the very story they were desperately attempting to cover up? They had such a perfect plan. How could it fail? But Yahweh, the Lord of Heaven, had a different idea.

> For the Lord Almighty has purposed, and who can thwart him?
> His hand is stretched out, and who can turn it back? (Isaiah 14:27)

> Then Job answered the Lord and said, "I know that You can do all things, And that no purpose of Yours can be thwarted. Who is this that hides counsel without knowledge? Therefore I have declared that which I did not understand, Things too wonderful for me, which I did not know." (Job 42:1–3, NASB)

Seemingly, the Lord Himself would keep Kaduri's Messiah note and the prophetic connections to it in the headlines of the world's news cycle one way or the other until Yeshua comes again.

This was ordained by the Throne of God to be the *Yeshua revelation* that would stun the world.

Part Five

THE DIVINE AWAKENING

36

The Kaduri Revival in Israel

For this was not revealed to you
by flesh and blood,
but by my Father in heaven.
—Matthew 16:17

The revelation of Rabbi Kaduri's Yeshua note has become a global phenomenon, and it's still spreading. However, the international "Kaduri Revival"[196] began at home, in Israel, in some very powerful ways.

Messianic Rabbi Zev Porat has taken Kaduri's thoroughly documented revelation, along with the clear presentation of Yeshua, into the streets of Jerusalem. But he hasn't stopped there. He has also been to Bnei Brak, Ashdod, Tel Aviv, Haifa, the Old City of Jerusalem, several synagogues, and the Western Wall (Kotel),[197] among other locations.

Rabbi Porat was even allowed inside a prominent Israeli mosque, where he witnessed the message of Yeshua to the Imam. To be sure, the humble beginnings of the Kaduri Revival have had nothing short of supernatural and staggering results.[198]

Why Have We Not Heard?

In a striking video report of Kaduri's story, the viewer witnesses Rabbi Porat sitting on an outdoor bench in Tel Aviv. He is seated with an older

Jewish man. The man appears to be clinging to every word Zev is sharing with him. After the gentleman sees Rabbi Kaduri's note with his own eyes and learns of the decoded message the note contains, he exclaims, "Why have we not heard of this amazing revelation from our rabbis?"

"Because the media and the rabbis have colluded to cover up the story," Zev answers. "They are afraid of this revelation."

The man responds, "If this is true, and it appears to be so, then the media is keeping me from salvation!"

At this point, Zev places his hand on the man's shoulder, looks him in the eye, and says, "Only the Holy Spirit has revealed this to you."

The accounts of salvation encounters in Israel using the Kaduri Yeshua revelation are too numerous to recount in this book. But each one is profound, especially in light of just how difficult it is to help a Jewish person see that Yeshua is the genuine Messiah.

Western Wall Miracle

Zev related that on another witnessing occasion, he felt led by the Lord to go directly to the Western Wall (Kotel) at the Temple Mount in the Old City.

Upon entering the Kotel area, a group of Jewish men who had gathered for prayer saw Zev coming toward them, carrying the original book I had written. As always, he also was carrying his Hebrew-authorized Tanakh. When the group saw Rabbi Kaduri's picture on the cover of the book, they wanted to know what it was about. They all recognized the photo of Rabbi Yitzhak Kaduri and were fascinated by the book that bore his image. Zev began to share about the Kaduri note.

One man named Shem began to ply Rabbi Porat with sincere questions about the Kaduri story, especially the Yeshua note. Zev relates that his discussion with Shem went on for several hours as he answered question after question directly from the Tanakh.

Today, a photograph of Shem can be seen on Rabbi Porat's website wherein the young man is standing with his hands raised and placed up against the Western Wall. He is praying and asking Yeshua to save him.

"Think of it!" Zev says. "That may have been the first time in over two thousand years that an Orthodox Jew was saved right there at the Kotel!"

I am still deeply moved every time I look at that photograph because I have a direct attachment to that scene, an attachment about which Zev could not have known. In 1997, Hickory Hammock Baptist Church, in Milton, Florida,[199] sent my wife and me to Israel as a gift for our ten-year anniversary of ministry. On that excursion, of course, one of the main attractions for us was the Western Wall.

At the Kotel, I scribbled out a prayer on a piece of paper and wedged it into one of the many crevices of the wall. This is a custom for most people who visit that internationally known holy site.

When we returned home, I told our church family what I had written. One of the sections of my note read, "Lord, please give our church many increased opportunities to witness to the Gospel of Jesus Christ around the world—and especially to the Jewish people in Israel."

When Zev showed me the picture and told me the story of Shem's salvation experience, I couldn't help but wonder, "Could it actually be that Shem was saved somewhere near the exact location where my note was placed?" I may never know the answer to that question this side of glory. However, one thing is certain: my prayer *was* answered, and the salvation occurred in the locale where my prayer had been spoken and then deposited in the crevices of the original Temple Mount. Little did I know that seventeen years after placing the prayer note there, I would receive firsthand, photographic evidence of its answer.

The Kotel Synagogue

Zev related another witnessing encounter he experienced at the Kotel in early 2018. This time, the opportunity took place inside the Kotel Synagogue. Following is his account of that day:

> Our ministry team went back up to the Kotel to witness Yeshua to the Jews. Almost always we do this using the Kaduri revelation to

get the conversation started. While there, we were guided by the Holy Spirit to go inside the "cave" just to the left of the wall. That cave is actually a very large synagogue. The synagogue is open to the public, but it is also the place where all the important rabbis of Israel congregate when they are at the wall. They believe that it is a particularly holy place because of its location.

We knew when we entered the synagogue that this was going to be a place of intense spiritual warfare. We also knew that it could also be a very dangerous place to preach Yeshua as Messiah.

I remembered the promise of Luke 12:1. We are told that we should not worry about how we conduct ourselves at these kinds of moments; God would speak through us. I also think of Isaiah 49:10 in such moments: "Do not fear, for God is with you."

When our team entered the Kotel Synagogue, the rabbis were calling for people to pray aloud. So we joined them. And in our prayers we were audibly witnessing that Yeshua is the Messiah.

One of the main rabbis came up to us and said, "You need ten people with you, in order to pray." This is a rule that the rabbis will often invoke during the proceedings in that particular synagogue.[200]

"I don't need ten people to pray," I said to him. "Nowhere in the Tanakh does it say that in any kind of proper context. The God of Abraham, Isaac, and Jacob—which is *Yeshua Ha' Mashiach*—gives us the authority to pray to him directly. The number that are praying matters not; it's about our relationship with Him.

At that moment, in that synagogue cave, in the presence of all kinds of people from all over the world—the place went silent... utterly silent.

It was as though the rabbi had no idea how to respond. It was as if something supernatural had intervened. I suppose they were wondering to themselves: *How can this Israeli Jew be speaking about Yeshua as Messiah in this synagogue, of all places, and with such authority?*

I give all praise and glory to the Lord, of course. Before I went in, I had no idea what I was going to say, until I said it. But there it was—Yeshua's name was given as a witness inside the Kotel Synagogue on that day.

At this, one of the main rabbis, Eliezer Weitzman, approached me. He demanded, "Who sent you here? By what authority do you speak these things?"

I answered him saying that I came here by the authority of the God of Abraham, Isaac, and Jacob. The place was still silent, with all the attenders looking on in shock.

Rabbi Weitzman asked for the Bible I was holding, as if he desired to examine it for its authenticity. I had brought only the Tanakh with me on that day, as is usually my custom when witnessing to Jewish people, since they do not recognize the authority of the New Testament documents unless they are born again.

It just so happened that, on that day, I had taken with me the Tanakh that I had received while I was in the Israeli army. It is the officially accepted Tanakh of Israel. It is published by *Sinai Publishers* in Israel. Their own rabbis sign that version as the approved version of the scriptures. So he couldn't say a word against it. It was as if the Lord had specifically ordained for me to have that very edition with me. After he examined it and handed it back, I simply turned in the Tanakh and began to read aloud from Isaiah 53.

Something amazing happened. It was supernatural. The Jews in that Kotel Synagogue appeared to be absolutely fascinated by Isaiah 53. I've never seen anything like it. And then Rabbi Weitzman began to read the passage with me! Isaiah 53 is known among the Jews as the *forbidden chapter*[201]—yet here I was. I was reading it aloud, with the synagogue rabbi reading it with me, in front of all the congregants!

Then, Rabbi Weitzman tried to trip me up in front of the people. He asked me, "Who is this messiah?" The rabbi already knew what I was going to say, but now he was trying to confront me in front of the listening people.

The Lord gave me more supernatural strength. I told Rabbi Weitzman "*Yeshua is the Messiah.*" I told him that Yeshua is the only way of salvation and that no one comes to the Father but through Yeshua. I told him that only the blood of *Yeshua Ha' Mashiach* can redeem us.

The place remained hushed. The people appeared to be stunned. I continued to simply and lovingly relate more of the Gospel message, and then, before leaving, I urged the rabbis and the people gathered there to further search these things out for themselves.

I don't know for sure, but I am fairly certain this was the first time the clear Gospel of Jesus Christ had ever been preached inside the Kotel Synagogue. We were at the Kotel that day to share the Kaduri Messiah revelation—and wound up in the Kotel Synagogue proclaiming *Yeshua Ha' Mashiach* is Lord!

The Old City Cardo

Zev continued, describing another visit to the Kotel area:

> We were on our way out, and we took the route of the Cardo [the main East-West corridor].[202] The Cardo of the Old City begins at the Damascus Gate and crosses the city until it reaches the area of the Zion Gate. Near the Cardo's exit is a large, ornate menorah—a lampstand—created by the Temple Institute.[203]
>
> We stopped there, and began taking pictures. At that moment, a Jewish man walked up to us and asked why we were taking pictures. I explained that we believed the menorah was a perfect illustration of the true Messiah—the *Light of the World.* The young man asked, "Who is this messiah?"

I quickly opened the Tanakh and began to show him from the Hebrew Scriptures those passages that speak of Messiah. A crowd began to gather around us. Eventually I arrived at identifying the Messiah of the Tanakh as Yeshua. That man took our contact information so that he might speak further with us about Yeshua. A few others became angry and walked away, mumbling words of disdain. But some wanted to stay and talk.

At this point, I brought up Rabbi Kaduri's Yeshua revelation. Before I knew it, another crowd, almost twenty people in total, moved closer to hear this amazing news. Here we were, in the Old City, standing at the Cardo Menorah, sharing the Gospel of Yeshua—once again—using Rabbi Kaduri's proclamation as our foundation.

Then, just a few months later, we were back at the Cardo Menorah witnessing. This time we were able to venture into Isaiah 53 as we shared the Tanakh's revelation of Messiah. A Jewish man who was there that day, upon hearing and reading Isaiah 53 with us, began to exclaim "That's Yeshua! That's Yeshua!"

We spent a great deal of time, further teaching this young man in the truth of Yeshua. He has since professed his faith in Yeshua as Messiah and is now sharing his faith with his own family. We are currently in the process of intense discipling.

Once again, the documented account of Rabbi Yitzhak Kaduri and his Yeshua note are drawing the Jews out to hear the Gospel message. The Jews in Israel are simply fascinated by it.

No End in Sight

Several days each week, Messianic Rabbi Zev Porat and his team can be found somewhere in Israel sharing the good news of *Yeshua Ha' Mashiach*. In addition to continually implementing their creative, bold methods and seeking out specific locales to begin their witnessing encounters, Zev is also dedicated to conducting ongoing discipling sessions with those who are coming to Yeshua as Messiah. The Rabbi Kaduri Messiah revelation frequently makes its way into those witnessing and discipling encounters. The impact of Kaduri's written proclamation weighs profoundly upon the Jewish heart as a confirmation that even one of their greatest rabbis saw what they are now seeing regarding Yeshua.

The salvation stories are endless. Jews, Muslims, and Gentiles, in synagogues and mosques, and before rabbis, cantors, congregants, and Imams—the Rabbi Kaduri Messiah note is making its way through barriers that were once impenetrable. But the fire has now been lit and there's no putting out the flame of the light of truth.

Jewish Enough

The experiences recounted in this chapter are only a tiny sampling of what Messianic Rabbi Zev Porat can relate from his witnessing encounters using the Kaduri revelation. He uses that revelation as either a springboard for the initial gospel presentation, or sometimes, just as importantly, he uses it as the answer to the consistently heard protests of the Orthodox Jew: "That's not Jewish! That's the Gentile Messiah! That's not our Messiah!"

Zev responds to those protests with, "Really? Let me ask you this. Do you think Rabbi Yitzhak Kaduri was Jewish enough?" Without fail, the answer is, "Yes, of course!"

And then *out comes the Kaduri note.*

37

Kaduri and the Imam

And afterward, I will pour out my Spirit on all people. Your sons and daughters will prophesy, your old men will dream dreams, your young men will see visions.
—Joel 2:28

This next testimony is the most intriguing account of all the doors opened by the Kaduri note. The saga is told in Messianic Rabbi Zev Porat's own words.

The Mosque Visit

On another day of witnessing, our ministry team of fifteen people loaded up into four cars. We went to a specific city in Israel where we had predetermined to focus our outreach for that entire day.[204]

As our team dispersed to their assigned locations, the Lord spoke to my heart, "Go into a mosque." I couldn't believe what I heard.

The city had several mosques. So, believing I was being led by the Holy Spirit to do so, I went to the largest mosque in the city. In the car with me was my wife and one of our ministry partners.

When we arrived, the others in our party remained outside to pray. My wife and I approached the entrance alone. My heart was pounding.

I knew what I was doing could be extremely dangerous—at many levels. I am an obvious Israeli Jew, and I was going to knock on the door of a major mosque and dare to ask for a personal meeting with the imam! This was unheard of! To the Jewish mind, what I was doing was absolutely insane. But it had been directed by Yahweh, so I went to the door.

It is important to understand that once I went inside that mosque, for all practical and legal purposes, I would be "outside of Israel." If I were to go missing, there was a very slim chance that the Israeli police would enter that mosque to look for me. For Israeli police to go inside a mosque and search for a missing Jewish man would cause an absolute riot throughout the nation. As I knocked, I was well aware of these truths.

After a couple of sharp raps on the heavy mosque doors, a very large Arab man opened it. He was visibly upset. "What do you want?" he snapped. He recognized me as a Jewish man. Most of the Arabs in Israel speak both Arabic and Hebrew.

I answered in my native tongue, "I would like to speak to the imam."

"That will not be possible," he responded. Then he asked, "Who sent you here?"

I answered, "The God of Abraham, Isaac, and Jacob."

At that, the doorman curtly informed me that the imam would not see me, and he shut the door in my face.

I said, "Okay God, I did what you asked."

I don't mind telling you, I was a bit relieved as I turned to leave. However, the Lord spoke to my heart again and said, "Zev, do not go anywhere."

So, I stood outside the door, simply waiting. About two minutes later—it seemed like two hours—the door opened. The imam was standing there, right before me!

"I heard you were looking for me. Who sent you here?"

I gave him the same answer I had given his guards.

He said, "You are a Jew, right?"

I answered in the affirmative.

"Why do you wish to speak to me? Do you want to make trouble?"

I assured him that I wanted no trouble and that I had come in peace.

He stepped to the side and invited us into the mosque. Upon our entrance, he looked at his guards and gave them a stern order in Arabic. Immediately, the guards surrounded me and searched me for weapons. When they were satisfied that I was unarmed, the door closed. We were now "outside of Israel." We were in a major Israeli mosque with an imam and his guards. We were *alone*—yet, not really alone, for the Lord was with us.

I was told to remove my shoes. I remembered what Paul said, "To the Gentile I became a Gentile, so that I might reach them for Christ."

I slipped off my shoes. My wife, under the same conviction, put on a head covering in Arabic style. She removed her shoes as well. We wanted our hosts to know that our intentions were honorable. I was in the imam's "house." I was there as his guest, with his permission.

Please understand, I would never purposely compromise the truth of God's Word. But it is also important to be sensitive to the culture in which we are operating. Otherwise, we run the risk of shutting down our opportunity to share the Lord before we can even begin. This is hard work—it takes prayer and discernment—but it is a biblical principle.

The imam began by saying, "I also believe in the God of Abraham, Isaac, and Jacob." He then pulled out a Quran and began to read it aloud.

I did not turn to him and say, "Mohammad is a false prophet," or anything like that. I not only would have jeopardized my life at that point, but also, he would not listen to the gospel when that opportunity presented itself.

So, I respectfully listened as he read. If he had asked me if I thought Mohammad was a prophet, I would not have lied; I would have said "no." But, he did not ask. The Lord protected me. Yahweh was already moving in the prayers of our ministry team.

When the imam finished reading, I told him that Yeshua was central to my personal faith. He smiled slightly and said, "Yes, we Muslims also believe in Jesus. We believe he was a great prophet."

At that point, the Lord moved upon me to ask this imam a specific question. My question changed the subject completely, but, I had a plan.

I asked, "How long has man known that the world was round—like a globe?"

He answered, "I don't really know. I think about eight hundred to one thousand years at most."

"What if I showed you in the Bible that many thousands of years ago in Isaiah 40:22, God said the earth was *round*?" I had his attention.

"He sits enthroned above the **circle of the earth**, and its people are like grasshoppers. He stretches out the heavens like a canopy, and spreads them out like a tent to live in" (Isaiah 40:22, emphasis added).

I said, "This was written in the Bible by the prophet Isaiah, thousands of years before man discovered the actual shape of the earth. This proves that the Word of God is true. There is *no other book in the world* that proves something factual, like this, thousands of years before man discovers it."

The imam knew exactly what the word was. It was the Hebrew word *chugh.* It can mean a circle, but it also incorporates the idea of a round globe—a sphere, as is borne out by several translations and numerous commentaries.[205]

I had my Bible that is written in both Hebrew and Arabic. He read it with me, in both languages. As he read that word within that passage and context, he fell silent. He could not dispute the meaning of the word in either language.

In effect, I had just discredited the Quran without even mentioning it by name. After he saw that revelation and could not dispute it, he changed the subject, "Why do you come here to speak about this *Jesus*? Your own people don't even accept him."

This is exactly where I hoped he might take the conversation…

"But that is not correct," I said. "Many of our own people *do* accept Yeshua. In fact, have you ever heard of Rabbi Yitzhak Kaduri?"

"Yes, of course," he said. "He was one of your most famous rabbis."

"Yes he was. And even he believed that Jesus was the true Messiah," I answered.

"That's *impossible,*" the imam protested.

He put his Quran down and listened to me explain the Rabbi Kaduri story. He was fascinated.

Finally, I asked, "Would you like to see the note with your own eyes? I have a book about it in my car. You can see the note yourself and see that this is exactly what Rabbi Kaduri said regarding the real Messiah."

"Yes!" he replied. Interestingly, he never picked up his Quran again while I was there that day.

We walked outside together. When I got to the car, I grabbed up my backpack and showed his guards that there were only books in the bag. I had some Kaduri books, as well as twenty-five Bibles in that bag. We headed back inside the mosque. I couldn't believe what was happening! I was walking into a mosque with the imam, and I was carrying a bag full of Kaduri books and Bibles! The Lord was answering our prayers.

I opened the book and showed the imam the Kaduri revelation in the note—from the screen shot of Kaduri's own website in his own handwriting. The imam was amazed. He had no idea. I didn't press him any further, but I offered to leave the book with him as my personal gift to him.

In Middle Eastern culture, when Muslims are offered a gift, they must receive it. I knew that. So I said, "I have another gift for you." His eyes widened. "I'd like to leave all these Bibles for you as well." He graciously agreed.

The Garden

He put the Bibles on a table, then turned to me and said with a smile, "I'd like to show you my Garden."

I don't mind telling you that request unnerved me just a little bit. You are probably guessing why I might have been disturbed.

I had been talking with this imam about Jesus, Jews, Kaduri, the Bible, Isaiah, and a round earth; I had basically condemned his Scriptures as "not inspired"—and now I had given him a "gift" of Christian and Jewish literature and Scriptures! *Then* he asked me to "go outside and look at his garden with him."

Does he really want to show me his garden, or does he want to take me out back and do away with me? It sounds funny now to think about, but I still remember that day well. The thought did cross my mind.

But what did he do? The imam showed me his garden! It was gorgeous, and I told him so. We talked as though we were old friends. I could see what Yahweh was up to. Somehow, this man had connected with me. He actually liked me. *This,* I thought, *could be used to the glory of Yeshua…*

I looked at his garden and said, "Look at God's creation! This is gorgeous!"

"Yes! It's beautiful isn't it?" He was thrilled that I admired his handiwork. Here was a Jew—who was born again in Jesus—standing with a Muslim imam in a mosque on Islamic grounds in the middle of a city in the prophetically returned nation of Israel…and we were talking about the Creator of the universe *as if we were old friends*. Only Yahweh could arrange a day like this.

When we returned to the mosque, the imam's bodyguards were standing, lined up at the doorway to see me off. While I was shaking their hands, one by one, I noticed that every man had hatred in his eyes as he looked at me. The guards appeared to be livid that this visiting Jew, a believer in Jesus, was now a friend of their imam.

Even more incredible is that, just before stepping outside with the Imam, I gave him my contact information. My wife took photographs of the exchange. I didn't push him to contact me, nor did I ask for his contact information. I just wanted him to know that if he ever needed me, he could call me. When I left the mosque that day, I thought: *Well, I'll never hear from him again.*

I was mistaken.

Imam Calling

About six months later, I received an unexpected phone call. When I answered the unidentified number, the voice on the line said, "This is Saalik.[206] You were in my mosque." I immediately knew who he was.

"Yes, Saalik! Of course! How are you? It's great to hear from you," I replied.

What he said next astounded me.

"Zev, I need to tell you something. I have something to confess to you. Mohammad never spoke to me before. I have never heard from Mohammad in any personal way. But, I can tell you who *has* spoken to me!"

I could barely breathe. I had chill bumps on my arms as he continued.

"About three in the morning," Saalik continued, "some time back, I had a vision. I heard a voice telling me that He was *The God of Abraham, Isaac, and Jacob*. And then I saw Yeshua! I saw Him! He spoke to me! He is Messiah! Just like you said!"

Saalik went on to tell me that he had already left the mosque because of his Yeshua revelation. He has since had to go underground. But, he told me he is currently studying Yeshua and the Bible with other Muslims who are also believers. This is amazing!

This is what God is doing here in Israel. This is incredible end-time fulfillment, and with this imam, it started with the Kaduri Messiah revelation! He went from exclaiming "Impossible!" to now proclaiming, "I'm a believer!"

As you know, it is very dangerous for a Muslim to accept Jesus as Messiah. If his former cohorts find him, they will likely kill him. This is why he is in hiding to this day. Please pray for Saalik, who is now my brother in Yeshua.

Jesus Dreams?

Zev's mosque testimony certainly is stunning. But, believe it or not, what happened to the Muslim imam is not unheard of in these prophetic days. In fact, Muslims all over the world are reporting dreams and visions of Yeshua—and they are being saved.[207] Some are even going on to be pastors and preachers of *Yeshua Ha' Mashiach*.

Have a look at a few powerful examples of this phenomenon:

> Heidi Baker of Iris Ministries sees thousands of African Muslims receiving Jesus and getting baptized.
>
> "It's probably the only place in the world where they are coming so quickly," she said. "Many people are having dreams. They see Jesus appear to them. Probably half our pastors were leaders, Imams in Moslem mosques. They were leaders in these mosques, now they're pastors."
>
> "There is an end-time phenomenon that is happening through dreams and visions," said Christine Darg, author of *The Jesus Visions: Signs and Wonders in the Muslim World.*
>
> "[Yeshua] is going into the Muslim world and revealing, particularly, the last 24 hours of His life—how He died on the cross, which Islam does not teach - how He was raised from the dead, which Islam also does not teach—and how He is the Son of God, risen in power."
>
> "We receive lots of letters about people who have had dreams about the Lord, visions, even miracles," [said Nizar Shaheen, host of Light for the Nations, a Christian program seen throughout the Muslim world]. "When they watch the program, they say yes, we had a dream or a vision, and they accept Jesus as Lord." [208] (Brackets added)

Now, Messianic Rabbi Zev Porat can also testify firsthand to the phenomenon. Using the revelation given to 108-year-old Rabbi Kaduri, Zev was able to act as a divine conduit between a Muslim imam and Jesus Christ. No doubt we are living in amazingly prophetic times. And right in the midst of these prescient days, the Lord of Heaven is preparing the world for the return of the true Messiah—*Yeshua Ha' Mashiach.*

The way things are shaping up, the day of His coming may be sooner than we can imagine.

38

The China Connection

> Behold, these will come from afar; and lo,
> these will come from the north and from the
> west, and these from the land of Sinim.
> —Isaiah 49:12, NASB

Believe it or not, according to a number of renowned biblical scholars, China appears in the Old Testament in one specific verse.

That passage also connects China to an important end-time prophecy that now links directly to the Kaduri Messiah note event. This is certainly a fascinating twist in our Kaduri journey.

Let's first lay out the foundational material to place this truth in its proper context.

God's Servant and Witness to the Nations

The prophet Isaiah, in chapters 49–53 of the book by his name, unfolds a complex prophecy about the last-days return of a captive Israel to the Promised Land. Not only is the return of Israel emphasized in these passages, but, surprisingly to many, the prophecy indicates Israel's return would be brought about through Yahweh's use of the Gentile nations. Of course, this is exactly how it happened in 1948 and the decades leading up to that monumental event.

Through his vision, Isaiah identifies the faithful of the revenant nation of Israel as being God's true servants, eventually declaring that, as such, they are God's witnesses to the planet of His glory and salvation.

The prophecy is, at times, difficult to follow because it moves from the nation of Israel to an apparent personification of that nation—perhaps even in the person of Isaiah himself. Finally, the foretelling transitions into the ultimate revealing of God's servant, who came from Israel as the "Suffering Servant/Messiah" of Isaiah 53, the One who would be "pierced for our transgressions."

This multi-layered style of unfolding an end-time utterance is a common feature in the Hebrew Scriptures, familiar to classically trained biblical researchers as a *compound prophecy.*[209]

Following are a few scholarly commentaries concerning all that I have just laid forth.

Expositor's Bible Commentary:

> The passage is manifestly a piece of personification. The Servant is Israel—not now the nation as a whole, not the body and bulk of the Israelites, for they are to be the object of his first efforts, but the loyal, conscious, and effective Israel, realized in some of her members, and here personified by our prophet, who himself speaks for [Israel] out of his heart, in the first person.
>
> The Servant of Jehovah is a personification of the true, effective Israel as distinguished from the mass of the nation—a Personification, but not yet a Person. Something within Israel has wakened up to find itself conscious of being the Servant of Jehovah, and distinct from the mass of the nation—something that is not yet a Person.
>
> This brings us to the culminating passage—Isaiah 52:13–15 through Isaiah 53:1–12. Is the Servant still a Personification here, or at last and unmistakably a Person?[210]

MacLaren's Exposition of the Scriptures:

This grand prophecy is far too wide to be exhausted by the return of the exiles. There gleamed through it the wider redemption and the true return of the real captives. The previous promises all find their fulfilment in the experiences of the soul on its journey back to God.[211]

Keil and Delitzsch Biblical Commentary on the Old Testament:

Not only is the restoration of the remnant of Israel the work of the servant of Jehovah; but Jehovah has appointed him for something higher than this. He has given or set him for the light of the heathen ("a light to lighten the Gentiles," Luke 2:32), to become His salvation to the end of the earth.[212]

Gentile Nations Will Be Used to Restore Israel

Note the following commentary entries that speak to the fact that Yahweh would use the "Gentile nations" to restore Israel to the land. Also notice that each was written a century or more before Israel did return in 1948—with the help of the Gentiles, just as the prophecy had declared.

Pulpit Commentary:

It is usual to expound this and parallel passages (Isaiah 60:4; 66:20) of the return of the Jews to their own land by favor of the Gentiles.[213] (Published in 1880)

Jamieson-Fausset-Brown Bible Commentary:

The Gentiles shall aid in restoring Israel to its own land (Isa 60:4; 66:20).[214] (Published in 1871)

Matthew Henry's Concise Commentary:

> God can raise up friends for returning Israelites, even among Gentiles.[215] (Published in 1706)

Ellicott's Commentary for English Readers:

> The Gentiles…the people…both words are used of the heathen. They are summoned by the uplifted signal of Jehovah to do their work as nursing fathers, carrying the children in their bosom (Numbers 11:12). [The words "carrying the children in their bosom" are found in Numbers 11:12, as noted by the commentator. That passage is a direct reference to the Hebrews settling in Israel under God's direction].[216] (Published in 1877) (Bracketed words added)

So much for the modern argument that "the State of Israel that now exists in the Middle East can't be the *real Israel*…because it was "brought back" by Gentiles—the United Nations, United States, Great Britain, and the Balfour Declaration, etc."

Now we know, straight from God's own mouth, that the current nation of Israel is a direct fulfillment of a very specific prophecy: Israel was brought back by the decrees and assistance of the Gentile nations! And we are the first generation to witness the fulfillment of that prophecy.

Sinim/China

Let's now look at that unique Bible verse that mentions China. It is found in Isaiah 49:12:

> Behold, these will come from afar; and lo, these will come from the north and from the west, and these from *the land of Sinim.* (NASB, emphasis added)

The word "Sinim" is the clue. The Modern Hebrew word for China is *Sin* (pronounced *seen*).[217] The Hebrew suffix *-im* (in *Sinim*) denotes that the word is plural, effectively translating as "peoples from the land of Sin."

Even though in Isaiah's day there was no nation of China, various Asian nation-states existed that would eventually make up what we know today as China. However, we must also keep in mind that Isaiah's prophecy in chapter 49 was not primarily about his time. It was about a time in the distant future, 2,700 years, when Israel would return to the land and when there would, indeed, be a nation called China ...in *our time.*

Again, we will appeal to well-known, scholarly sources for the identification of Sinim with the people of what is now known as China.

The International Standard Bible Encyclopedia:

> The name occurs in Isaiah's prophecy of the return of the people from distant lands. [The] Septuagint points to an eastern country. Many scholars have favored identification with China...from very early times trade relations were established with the Far East by way of Arabia and the Persian Gulf.[218]

Ellicott's Commentary for English Readers:

> Modern scholars are almost unanimous in making [Isaiah 49:12] refer to the Chinese.... All recent discoveries tend to the conclusion that the commerce of the great ancient monarchies was wider than scholars imagined. The actual immigration of Jews into China is believed to have taken place about B.C. 200.[219]

Jamieson-Fausset-Brown Bible Commentary:

> Sinim—The Arabians and other Asiatics called China *Sin,* or *Tchin*; the Chinese had no special name for themselves, but either adopted that of the reigning dynasty or some high-sounding titles. This view of "Sinim" suits the context which requires a people to

be meant "from far," and distinct from those "from the north and from the west."[220]

Pulpit Commentary:

They shall also come from the land of Sinim by which most recent interpreters understand China.[221]

Barnes' Notes on the Bible:

This very ancient and celebrated people…was known to the Arabians and Syrians by the name Sin, Tein, Tshini; and a Hebrew writer might well have heard of them, especially if sojourning in Babylon, the metropolis as it were of all Asia.… The Chinese have been known from time immemorial by the name Tschin. Tschin means a Chinaman.[222]

Strong's Exhaustive Concordance:

Plural of an otherwise unknown name; Sinim, a distant Oriental region—Sinim.[223]

Brown-Driver-Briggs:

Adjective, of a people plural = substantive; Isaiah 49:12, identification with Chinese.[224]

Now that our contextual foundation for Isaiah 49–53, and especially 49:12, has been established, we can move to the Rabbi Kaduri connection.

39

Kaduri Goes to China

> But you will receive power when the Holy Spirit comes on you; and you will be my witnesses in Jerusalem, and in all Judea and Samaria, and to the ends of the earth.
>
> —Acts 1:8

As mentioned earlier, Messianic Rabbi Zev Porat's wife is Chinese. She speaks Mandarin Chinese, the official language of China and Taiwan. She also speaks Hebrew and English. Her family still lives in China. Over the years, they have been involved in a sizable amount of missionary work in China, both in government-approved churches as well as underground churches.[225]

China is currently on track to comprise the world's largest population of Christians by 2030. In recent years, even the Council on Foreign Relations has addressed the phenomenon:

> The number of Christians in the early 1980s was estimated at about six million.... In 2010 the Pew Research Center calculated a total of sixty-seven million...Christians in China, approximately five percent of the country's population. Other independent estimates suggest somewhere between 100 and 130 million. Purdue's [Fenggang] Yang projects that if "modest" growth rates

are sustained, China could have as many as 160 million Christians by 2025 and 247 million by 2032.[226]

Just as Isaiah predicted, not only did Jews living in China return to the newly resurrected Israel after 1948, but there had long been Jews in China before that date who were continually trickling back to the land of their origins. Isaiah appears to acknowledge this ancient fact in his prophecy, long before it happened.[227]

Whedon's Commentary on the Bible:

"Sinim," is China; at least its westernmost borders, or a name given to the eastern-most parts of the world known to Semitic people in Isaiah's times, perhaps as far back as 800 B.C.[228]

Barnes' Notes on the Bible:

And so [Isaiah] here mentions the several quarters of the world, where the generality of the Jews were dispersed.[229]

A Light to the Gentiles

The prophecy in Isaiah 49:12 also appears to speak to the fact that during the years *after* Israel's return to the land, there would be an outpouring of the Spirit of God, eventually producing untold numbers of believers from among the many Gentile nations, even from the remotely located land of Sinim. To many scholars, then, Isaiah's prophecy is distinctly twofold.

Keil and Delitzsch Biblical Commentary on the Old Testament:

Not only is the restoration of the remnant of Israel the work of the servant of Jehovah; but Jehovah has appointed him for something higher than this. He has given or set him for the light of the heathen ("a light to lighten the Gentiles," Luke 2:32), to become His salvation to the end of the earth.[230]

Barnes' Notes on the Bible:

The passage furnishes an interesting prediction respecting the future conversion of the largest kingdom of the world.... There may be some plausibility in the supposition that while so many other nations, far inferior in numbers and importance, are mentioned by name, one so vast as this would not wholly be omitted by the Spirit of Inspiration.[231]

Matthew Poole's Commentary:

[Isaiah] speaks here, and in many other places, of the conversion of the Gentiles, with allusion to that work of gathering and bringing back the Jews from all parts where they were dispersed into their own land.[232]

Gill's Exposition of the Entire Bible:

This is a prophecy of the conversion of the Jews, or of the Gentiles, or of both, in the latter day, in the several parts of the world; who shall come to Christ.[233]

The Ingathering

This predicted modern-day revival among the Chinese is not happening without cost. The Chinese government has been a relentless antagonist of the biblical faith and sees Christianity particularly as a direct threat to its communist intentions.[234] Nevertheless, the last-days ingathering of the Chinese people continues, *for it has been declared* by the Word of God.

There can be no doubt that in the midst of the apparent falling away in America and Europe, there is simultaneously a great ingathering in other parts of the world. In Asia, Africa, and Latin America, the numbers of those coming to Jesus Christ continue to soar, with more coming to faith in the last twenty-five years than at any time in world history.[235]

After the Rabbi Kaduri story broke, and once that account, in book format, was in the hands of Messianic Rabbi Porat, the stunning message of the Messiah revelation went straight to China. When it arrived, it spread like wildfire—and continues to do so.

Zev gives us the information in his own words.

Kaduri Goes Underground

By the grace of our Lord, we have now been able to get the story of Rabbi Kaduri's last-days revelation into at least 150 churches throughout China, perhaps in as many as 170 churches. These numbers include churches that are government-sanctioned, as well as underground.

There are still a few government churches that preach the truth of the gospel of Jesus Christ, but it is very dangerous to do so. It is also dangerous to preach that Israel's existence is a prophetic fulfillment of end-time prophecy. The Chinese government is very much opposed to these kinds of messages. If a government-approved church is caught teaching and preaching such things, it can be shut down immediately. The penalties are even worse for the underground churches.

In 2008–2009, official government restrictions on China's underground church were lifted until revival started throughout the nation. China's largely communist government has recently responded with a repressive crackdown on the church as a whole, but particularly on the underground churches.

But now, thanks to the story of Rabbi Kaduri and his earth-shattering Yeshua revelation going out to the nations, the message of last-days visions and revelations—even to a returned Israel's most revered Orthodox rabbi—is blazing throughout the land of Sinim!

The Kaduri message has gone all over China, Hong Kong, and Taiwan, as well as inner and outer Mongolia. In our missionary excursions into those places, we often preach to three congregations a day. Thus, in a ten-day period, we might reach at least thirty churches with the Kaduri revelation—sometimes even more.

The main message of the first Kaduri book, written by Carl Gallups, has been translated into the Chinese language on Chinese web platforms. There are now between ten and fifteen million Chinese who have already read or heard of Kaduri's revelation. They have seen the note for themselves. They have seen its decoded translation that Yehoshua is the real Messiah! This message has sparked a major revival in China. As a result, many are coming to salvation in Yeshua.

Entire churches have been awakened to the prophetic times in which we are living, and especially the truth of the returned nation of Israel and its place as God's last-days witness to the nations. The Chinese Christians are thrilled to see that their nation is specifically mentioned in Isaiah 49:12. They are elated to understand that they were ordained by Heaven's Throne to have a place in the end-times awakening that is sweeping the planet.

I can testify firsthand that many Chinese pastors are now preaching the biblical truth of the "one new man" as found in Ephesians 2:15. Now they understand that even the Christians in China are also a part of the last-days *spiritual Israel* (Ephesians 2:11–13; Romans 11:25–26) so wonderfully foretold by the prophet Isaiah.

Muslims living in China are also coming to faith in Yeshua! They are fascinated by the true and documented story of a Jewish Rabbi of Kaduri's stature believing in Jesus as Messiah. From that fascination, they are then led straight into the contextual Word of God to salvation in Jesus Christ. It's absolutely astounding what God is doing in China!

God is even using the Chinese people to bring the gospel of Jesus back into Israel. Chinese Christians love to come to Israel. Now, many of them are actually witnessing to Israeli Jews—and they are using the Kaduri revelation to do so! We are watching Kaduri's revelation of Yeshua as Messiah link up directly with the prophecy of Isaiah 49:12. To know that we are having a small part in the fulfillment of that specific Bible prophecy is humbling and thrilling.

No doubt, the fire of the "Kaduri Revival" still burns brightly.

40

The Forbidden Chapter

He was despised and rejected by men, a man of sorrows and acquainted with grief; and as one from whom men hide their faces he was despised, and we esteemed him not.
—Isaiah 53:3

How does opening a new Chinese restaurant in Israel help lead a Jewish person to Yeshua as Messiah?

I know, the question sounds ridiculous. But the answer illustrates a powerful testimony to the "living" nature of the Word of God.

Messianic Rabbi Zev Porat has often shared the account of how he and his Chinese wife have employed a creative but surprisingly effective way to get a Jewish person thinking and talking about one of the most stunning passages concerning the Messiah in all of the Old Testament. I first heard the story when Zev appeared on one of my radio broadcasts and shared it with our listening audience.

Following is his explanation of the process he used.

The Chinese Restaurant

The Israeli people generally love Chinese food. Because of that, they are keenly interested when a new Chinese restaurant opens in Israel, and they are usually anxious to try it out as soon as possible.

So, here's what we did. We took the Old Testament passage of Isaiah 53 and printed it on a flyer in Modern Hebrew. The little handout did not reveal the fact that it was a passage from the prophet Isaiah's book. Instead, it was written in simple paragraph form, without any verse descriptions. We never claimed this was an advertising flyer for a restaurant. But, because my wife is obviously Chinese and we had a group from China helping us, many who took the pamphlet assumed we were advertising for a new Chinese restaurant.

When we took these leaflets to the streets of Tel Aviv, an amazing thing happened. As we started handing them to the people who were walking on the sidewalk or sitting on public benches, some of them came back to us and asked us, "What is this? Are you Christians?" Remember, there was nothing on the paper to indicate the writing was from the Bible. Neither was the name of Jesus mentioned anywhere.

I would answer, "Yes, we are—but why would you ask this?"

Their response was something like, "Because this writing declares what you Christians say about Jesus. This is the story of Jesus."

I would just look at them, smile, and say, "Really? Would it surprise you to find out this writing is actually the 53rd chapter of Isaiah? These words are not from the New Testament at all, and they are not from a Christian sermon or lesson; they are taken directly from the Jewish Tanakh. Yet, you are telling me that the words sound exactly like the New Testament Yeshua? How can this be?"

At this point they are usually quite stunned. They can't believe what they are reading on our flyer is in their Scriptures. So, I open the Tanakh to Isaiah 53 and have them read it aloud.

When they are finished reading, they ask, "How is it that I've never seen this, or heard this?"

I tell them, "It is because your rabbis don't want you to know about it. They know it sounds just like Yeshua of the New Testament, and they are afraid that you might become believers. After all, without any pressure or preaching on my part, you saw it for yourself simply by reading the words—straight from the Tanakh. If the rabbis are not afraid of it, why have you never heard them read it aloud? Why have they never encouraged you to read it or ask questions about it?' "

We are now personally ministering to several of those who returned to ask us about our flyer. This technique has been a powerful way to start a conversation about the Tanakh and its revelation of Yeshua.

As Zev's account illustrates, Isaiah 53 is probably the most powerful passage in the entire Old Testament for reaching a Jewish person for Yeshua as Messiah. To be sure, other passages are also mightily used of Yahweh for this purpose, but even the rabbis know that Isaiah 53 is particularly potent. This is why they try so hard to explain that this passage does not mean Yeshua—or, most often, they simply ignore the chapter completely.

Remember also, Isaiah 53 is the passage Rabbi Yitzhak Kaduri alluded to in his 2005 Yom Kippur preaching service just three months before his death. It was in that same service when Rabbi Kaduri revealed he had met the real Messiah and would be leaving the Messiah's name in a note.

Objections and Counter-Objections

Of course, the majority of today's Orthodox Jewish leaders strongly dispute the Messianic claims regarding Isaiah 53.

In the interest of academic fairness, we will once again appeal to the argument of Rabbi Tovia Singer. Not only does he have a widespread and highly influential Orthodox voice in Israel, but, as you will remember, he was also the one who resoundingly dismissed the Messiah note of Rabbi Yitzhak Kaduri as being "not about Jesus of the New Testament." Singer's assessment of Isaiah 53 is fairly typical of the Orthodox elite's view of the passage.

Rabbi Singer posted an article on his website titled, "Who Is God's Suffering Servant? The Rabbinic Interpretation of Isaiah 53." The piece begins with this paragraph:

> Despite strong objections from conservative Christian apologists, the prevailing rabbinic interpretation of Isaiah 53 ascribes the

> "servant" to the nation of Israel who silently endured unimaginable suffering at the hands of its gentile oppressors. The speakers, in this most-debated chapter, are the stunned kings of nations who will bear witness to the messianic age and the final vindication of the Jewish people following their long and bitter exile. "Who would have believed our report?" the astonished and contrite world leaders wonder aloud in dazed bewilderment (53:1).[236]

Many others whose roots are deeply embedded in the Jewish faith disagree with Rabbi Singer's assessment. Rabbi Rachmiel Frydland was a Holocaust survivor coming from a deeply Orthodox family, and was a former rabbinical student in Warsaw, Poland. He also became a Messianic Jewish teacher—a believer in Yeshua.[237]

Rabbi Frydland has also written about Isaiah 53. Frydland's article is titled, "The Rabbis' Dilemma: A Look at Isaiah 53." Following are a couple of pertinent excerpts:

> The subject was never discussed in my pre-war-Poland Hebrew school. In the rabbinical training I had received, the fifty-third chapter of the book of Isaiah had been continually avoided in favor of other, weightier" matters to be learned. Yet, when I first read this passage, my mind was filled with questions.... Who is this chapter speaking about? The words are clear—the passage tells of an outstanding Servant of the Lord whose visage is marred and is afflicted and stricken....
>
> Rashi (Rabbi Shlomo Itzchaki, 1040–1105) and some of the later rabbis, though, interpreted the passage as referring to Israel. **They knew that the older interpretations referred it to Messiah.**
>
> However, Rashi lived at a time when a degenerate medieval distortion of Christianity was practiced. He wanted to preserve the Jewish people from accepting such a faith and, although his intentions were sincere, other prominent Jewish rabbis and leaders realized the inconsistencies of Rashi's interpretation. They pre-

> sented a threefold objection to his innovation. **First, they showed the consensus of ancient opinion. Secondly, they pointed out that the text is in the singular. Thirdly, they noted verse eight.**
>
> This verse presented an insurmountable difficulty to those who interpreted this passage as referring to Israel.[238] (Emphasis added)

In an excellent ministry article titled "The Forbidden Chapter," the outline of the entire history of Isaiah 53's Jewish interpretation is laid out. The summation of that article is succinctly stated:

> It's important to understand we're not just talking about a Christian interpretation here—**the Jewish Sages of ancient times also always interpreted Isaiah 53 to be about the Messiah.** In fact, the well-known term "Messiah ben Yosef" is actually from this very text.[239] (Emphasis added)

Messianic Rabbi Zev Porat also attests, from the standpoint of his own deeply Orthodox background, that this passage has indeed long been avoided, hidden, and sometimes outright forbidden by the rabbis from being read and studied among the Orthodox Jews. When it is *studied*, Zev affirms, it is adjusted so that the interpretation is about Israel rather than the Messiah.

Zev says that often the naysayers deny this truth, but his answer is, "Ask those Jews who have been saved because of the passage. Or the ones who have dared to ask their rabbis the tough questions about this passage. They will tell you."

Turn the page for examples of those amazing testimonies.

41

Portrait of Our Redeemer

Kings take their stands. Rulers make plans together against the LORD and against his Messiah.
—Psalm 2:2, GOD'S WORD® Translation

Indeed, there are myriad testimonies on the Internet and in printed materials concerning the power of Isaiah 53, especially regarding its effectiveness in reaching the Jewish heart.

The following is an example of that type of testimony. It was penned by a Jewish woman named Geri Ungurean. Ms. Ungurean has been a Jewish believer in Yeshua since 1983.

> To say that I was shocked [when I first read Isaiah 53] would be a gross understatement. I remember reading the words over and over. I wondered **why I had never heard this in my synagogue.** It was a clear picture of our Redeemer—Yeshua—and why He went to that cross to suffer and die.
>
> The 17th century Jewish historian, Raphael Levi, admitted that long ago the rabbis used to read Isaiah 53 in synagogues, but after the chapter caused "arguments and great confusion" the rabbis decided that the simplest thing would be to just take that prophecy out of the *Haftarah*[240] readings in synagogues. That's

> why today when we read Isaiah 52, we stop in the middle of the chapter and the week after we jump straight to Isaiah 54.[241] [Bracketed words and emphasis added]

Ms. Ungurean's claim concerning how the ancient rabbis used to read Isaiah 53 in the synagogues is historically accurate. Many of the earliest Jewish commentators and rabbis claimed this passage referred to the Messiah, not to Isaiah, and not to the nation of Israel, as is often insisted upon by the more modern rabbis and Jewish expositors.[242]

Plainly Stated

Read the chapter for yourself. Written in paragraph form, it's easy to understand why Orthodox rabbis would rather their congregants not be intimately familiar with this passage about Messiah.

The following version of Isaiah 53 is from the *English Translation of The Holy Scriptures, Revised in Accordance with Jewish Tradition and Modern Biblical Scholarship*:

> Who would have believed our report? And to whom is the arm of the Lord revealed? For he grew up before him as a tender plant, and as a root out of a dry ground: he had no form nor comeliness; and when we see him, there is no beauty that we should desire him. He was despised and rejected of men; a man of sorrows, and acquainted with grief: and as one from whom men hide their face he was despised, and we esteemed him not.
>
> Surely he hath borne griefs inflicted by us, and suffered sorrows we have caused: yet we did esteem him stricken, smitten of God, and afflicted. But he was wounded through our transgressions, bruised through our iniquities: the chastisement of our peace was upon him, and with his wounds we were healed. All we like sheep have gone astray; we have turned everyone to his own way; and the Lord hath caused the iniquity of us all to fall upon him.

He was oppressed, and he was afflicted, yet he opened not his mouth: as a lamb which is brought to the slaughter, and as a sheep before her shearers is dumb, so he opened not his mouth. He was taken away from rule and from judgment; and his life who shall recount? For he was cut off out of the land of the living; through the transgressions of my people was he stricken. And one made his grave among the wicked, and his tomb among the rich; although he had done no violence, neither was any deceit in his mouth.

But it pleased the Lord to bruise him; he hath put him to grief; if his soul shall consider it a recompense for guilt, he shall see his seed, he shall prolong his days, and the pleasure of the Lord shall prosper in his hand. He shall see of the travail of his soul, and shall be satisfied: by his knowledge shall my servant justify the righteous before many, and he shall bear their iniquities. Therefore will I divide him a portion with the great, and he shall divide the spoil with the strong because he hath laid open his soul unto death, and was numbered with transgressors; and he took off the sin of many, and made intercession for the transgressors.[243]

Messianic Rabbi Jonathan Sacks

Rabbi Jonathan Sacks comes from a family that includes nineteen generations of rabbis. Raised in a kosher (satisfying the requirements of Jewish law) home, Jonathan became convinced that Yeshua is the promised Messiah of Israel through his study of Messianic prophecies in the Tanakh. He says that particularly compelling to him were the vivid prophecies of Isaiah 53. Today, he is the leader of a Messianic congregation in Bowling Green, Kentucky. Rabbi Sacks says of Isaiah 53:[244]

The **overwhelmingly dominant Jewish view throughout history** has been that this extended passage **speaks of Messiah**.

For over a thousand years after the death of Yeshua, this

> remained essentially **the only Jewish view** concerning Isaiah 53. In the late 11th century, **a new view** that the passage spoke of Israel, was introduced, but was **vehemently rejected by the vast majority of rabbis for the next 700 years.**
>
> Rabbi Moshe El-Sheikh...writing in the latter half of the 16th century stated: "Our Rabbis of blessed memory with one voice accept and affirm the opinion that the prophet is speaking of the King Messiah, and we shall ourselves also adhere to the same view."[245] (Emphasis added)

On his webpage titled, "What Rabbis Have Said about Isaiah 53," Messianic Rabbi Sacks quotes twenty-four renowned rabbis who examined Isaiah 53 from the first century AD through the twentieth century AD. Each of them solidly represents the traditional Jewish view of Isaiah 53 as speaking of the suffering and redeeming Messiah—not the nation of Israel.[246]

The truth is apparent. There is a reason Isaiah 53 is known among many of the Jews as the "Forbidden Chapter."

42

The Heart of the Tanakh

And the Lord has laid on him
the iniquity of us all.
—Isaiah 53:6

The following is a portion of the testimony of a dear friend of mine. He is Messianic Rabbi Eric Walker and the executive director of the Igniting a Nation ministries and television program headquartered in Birmingham, Alabama.

Rabbi Eric Walker says:

I grew up in the Jewish Community within Pittsburgh, Pennsylvania. I was born in 1952 to a father whose family immigrated from Hungary and a mother whose father came from Galicia (Southern Poland/Western Ukraine). My father's family changed their name from Wolowitz to Walker in 1934 to avoid religious persecution. They did this at the insistence of my Hungarian Grandfather, Bernat, who spoke seven languages and was the *maître-d'* at the German American Club in NYC during WWII. As a child, I remember many conversations about one cousin of my grandfather who was the only survivor in her family in the Holocaust. She was a seamstress who worked in a labor camp where she was assigned to sew and repair German officers' uniforms.

Being Jewish was not a "title," it was our way of life—the only life we knew. We lived in the Jewish community, our friends were Jewish, and our entire family belonged to the Jewish country club. At that time, we belonged to a Reformed Synagogue, but they did not perform Bar Mitzvah, so I began to attend my grandparents' synagogue in preparation for this important rite of passage.

My grandfather loved Israel and told of his service in the US Navy in World War I and his desire to enlist to fight those who persecuted us in the *shtetls* (small Jewish communities) of Eastern Europe. He was a Zionist, but did not want to move to Israel or even encourage any of us to do so. His position was clearly that if all American Jews moved to Israel, then no one would be left to raise money in support of the new Jewish State. His contribution to Israel was commemorated when he was named "Israel Bonds Man of the Year" in 1959.

This great honor brought him personal introductions to Israel's first prime minister, David ben Gurion, and Israel's ambassador to the United Nations, Abba Eban. A picture of my grandfather with Ben Gurion hangs in my office to this very day. My grandmother, Lillian Amper, was the president of Hadassah, the Women's Zionist Organization of America, Inc. Together they labored side by side to lead fundraising drives in support of Israel and the return of Soviet Jews to Israel.

I maintained my Jewish identity throughout college, but not much different than my youth, my college friends were many from high school who grew up in the same Jewish community that I did. There were varying degrees of observance, but we still attended synagogue with our families during the High Holy Days of Rosh Hashanah and Yom Kippur.

A Spiritual Journey

After graduation, I ultimately wound up in Atlanta, Georgia, in 1975. I joined an Orthodox synagogue and took a profound dive into my Jewish identity. It was there that I was intensely exposed to the Talmudic teachings and rabbinic traditions of Judaism.

At no point in time had anyone ever shared the gospel of Yeshua with me, nor had they even attempted to open a dialogue. Again, I was surrounded by Jews and lived within the confines of the Jewish community. It wasn't until I was 40 that I began to question many things about my Jewish faith and the Jewish teachings. At age 40, I began a new life and launched a personal spiritual journey looking for a deeper meaning to life and my ultimate identity. I tried out everything that came my way, even the New Age movement.

However, on December 21, 1996, at the invitation of a new friend, I wound up in a Messianic Jewish Synagogue. I was still stumbling along upon my spiritual journey. However, after that first Messianic synagogue experience, I began to fervently devote myself to the in-depth study of the Bible, comparing my Jewish foundation to the contextual connections in the Tanakh.

The Heart of God's Word

The more I studied, the more on fire I became—and it wasn't long before I realized that the heart of the Jewish Bible, Isaiah 53, had been omitted from my entire traditional Jewish life. If it was there in the Bible I used as a young man in synagogue, it was certainly never read as a part of the Haftorah readings of the Prophets under any of the rabbinical systems.

As I look back on this reality, I saw a picture of myself as a little boy in elementary school learning how to make a valentine heart. You would take a piece of red paper and fold it in half and cut a curve in the fold. Out would pop a heart-shaped cutout. When you opened the sheet of red paper, you also saw where the heart had been cut out. This is what has been done to my people for thousands of years.

Now, twenty-two years later, I see two different aspects of the prophecies of Isaiah in complete context of the life and times of Isaiah. I see the prophetic content of Isaiah 53, and now an even more profound question—and answer—in reference to this most important chapter. *Almost everyone, Jew or Gentile, who reads this chapter comes away with a vision of Yeshua on the cross.* It truly is the heart of God's Word.

I also see Isaiah 53 as the divine prayer that brings about the salvation of Israel. When reading the words of God through the prophet Isaiah, it paints an unmistakable picture of the rejected, despised, and beaten Messiah. When read in a prayerful manner, Isaiah 53 contains all the elements needed to bring about salvation. In God's own words through this prophet, I believe He has given us the very words that will usher in Messiah's return.

Isaiah 53 is written like a gospel tract for today's Jewish person. The passage begins with a confession that we have rejected God's Messiah. It then moves to the acknowledgment that Messiah is the one who takes away our sin—through His sacrifice alone. The passage further emphasizes that God's true Messiah would indeed come back from the dead and rule and reign forever. It reads like something that would be printed by a modern-day evangelistic outreach ministry. It really is quite remarkable—and very powerful. Of course, this is the very reason that most rabbis avoid discussing or acknowledging this particular passage altogether.

Rabbi Kaduri's Students

Messianic Rabbi Zev Porat says:

I was also told by several of Rabbi Kaduri's believing yeshiva students that not only did Rabbi Kaduri teach the Messianic prophecies of the Tanakh, but he specifically taught the significance of Isaiah 53 in helping the Jewish mind to make the biblical connection to Yeshua. So you see, not all of today's Orthodox Jewish rabbis see Isaiah 53 as being about Israel. There was none more Orthodox than the famed Rabbi Yitzhak Kaduri!

When we consider that this was apparently a key passage Rabbi Kaduri was teaching in his yeshiva, as well as in his October 2005 Yom Kippur synagogue message, its power becomes even more pronounced.

Rabbi Kaduri discovered this power. He knew this power.

He also knew the Messiah of Isaiah 53: He is *Yeshua Ha' Mashiach.*

43

Witnessing to Jewish People

As was his custom, Paul went into the synagogue, and on three Sabbath days he reasoned with them from the Scriptures, explaining and proving that the Messiah had to suffer and rise from the dead. "This Jesus I am proclaiming to you is the Messiah," he said.
—Acts 17:2–3

How might one go about witnessing the truth of Messiah to a Jew, especially when desiring to use the "Forbidden Chapter"—Isaiah 53—as the foundational starting point?

Zev Porat says:

We can't put God in a box when it comes to exactly how to approach a Jewish person with the gospel of Yeshua. In general, we witness to them from the Old Testament. We have had a few situations where we can start in the New Testament, especially when a Jewish person asks us to do so, sometimes they even bring up the New Testament before we do. However, the vast majority of the time, we have to begin with the Tanakh, because most Jews are taught from their childhood that the New Testament Scriptures are perverted and corrupt and that Jesus is a fake and the Gentile Messiah.

Even when witnessing to the Jew from the Old Testament, we still have a mountain of bias and misinformation to surmount before we can begin to make meaningful headway.

However, once we can get them to see that Yeshua is found throughout the Old Testament, and that the passages that have been purposely hidden from them are the most powerful representations of Yeshua as Messiah, we can begin to finally break the ice.

All of this is a spiritual matter. The Holy Spirit of Yahweh has to reveal these things to the one you are witnessing to. We are certainly not always successful, but when a Jews does come to Yeshua, when their eyes are truly opened to the truth, they usually become very seriously committed witnesses. After all, they often are persecuted, and even rejected by their families for their newfound faith in Yeshua.

Our ministry uses a variety of Old Testament passages and witnessing techniques when we are talking about Messiah with the Jewish people, but I agree—Isaiah 53 is probably the most powerful one of all. Apparently, Rabbi Kaduri realized this truth as well. If you are a Jew, seeing this passage for the very first time, it is a hard passage to ignore.

The Yeshua Project

The Yeshua Project was formed out of three organizations partnering together to share the gospel with Israelis: Kehilat haCarmel, Heart of G-d Ministries, and Tree of Life Ministries.[247]

Using the Internet and social media, and by producing a video in Hebrew and English called "'The Forbidden Chapter' in the Hebrew Bible—Isaiah 53," the Yeshua Project has reached many millions of people around the globe, demonstrating the evangelizing power of Isaiah 53 as it is supernaturally revealed by the Holy Spirit.[248]

Isaiah in the Streets

This potent, documentary-styled video is a little less than ten minutes in length. It portrays a young man speaking, in Hebrew, in a "man-on-the-street" witnessing approach. All the listeners are speaking Hebrew as well.

The first statement the witness presents to the individual men and women in the video is: "There is a chapter in the Tanakh that used to be read in synagogues in the past. But later the rabbis decided to take it out of the *Haftarah* readings. Today it is called the 'forbidden chapter.' Have you ever heard of it before?"

The listeners are then treated to an overview of Isaiah 53. They are told that it is a passage about the prophecy of who the Messiah would be. They are also made historically aware that for almost 1,700 years after the prophecy was written by Isaiah, virtually all the rabbis believed and taught that this passage was indeed about Messiah.

From this point in the video, we see a montage of several listeners who are reading aloud various verses of the passage in Hebrew. After reading the ominous and Spirit-filled words of Isaiah 53, they voluntarily respond with affirmation: "This is about Messiah. That's really powerful! It's about the Messiah who will be despised and rejected by society."

One woman says, "Our people were convinced that he was a bad person." Another man sadly admits, "I don't know why." Yet another man says, "They didn't accept him. They rejected him."

One by one, the listeners are taken through the entire chapter as they repeat back the meaning of what they see in every verse. They voluntarily express their understanding of the rejection, suffering, abuse, and death of the Messiah of whom Isaiah 53 speaks.

Then comes the clincher. The listeners are asked if they have ever before heard of this passage and these specific details about the real Messiah. Each responds, "No." This truly is the hidden or "forbidden" chapter.

The witnessing man then presents the heart of God's message of salvation to fallen humanity—straight from the Tanakh. He shows them the truth that because of our sin nature, we deserve death (Ezekiel 18:4) and ultimately our sin will separate us from God forever (Daniel 12:2). Of course, Isaiah 53, which they have already seen, clearly outlines God's provision for the penalty of our sin through Messiah's sacrifice. The witness reminds them of this fact as well.

The presenter continues by explaining the importance of recognizing that God's Messiah, as presented in Isaiah 53, would be a specific man who would willingly become that ultimate sacrifice for our sin. The listeners appear to understand these truths. It all makes perfect sense to them, now that they have read the words of the prophecy with their own eyes.

He Has Already Come

It is explained to the listeners that, according to Daniel chapter 9, the Messiah had to come before the destruction of the Second Temple. It is then explained that, of course, the destruction of the Second Temple happened in AD 70. The listeners are very familiar with this fact as well. Consequently, Messiah must have already come, sometime *before* AD 70.

They are reminded that Micah 5 says Messiah would be born in Bethlehem. Next, the presenter reminds them that Messiah would lay down His life, but would be rejected by His own people. Then they are reminded that Isaiah 53 says that after His death, He would live again—and many Gentiles would come to Him as Messiah as well. Those same Gentiles would come to know the God of Israel because of Him (Isaiah 49).

Then comes the "closer."

Who Has Believed Our Message?

The listeners are finally asked, "Based upon those descriptions of Messiah, from Isaiah, is there anyone in history, that you are aware of, who has fulfilled these things?" Four of the listeners answer, "No, I don't know anyone who has fulfilled these things." The fifth one answers, "Um... *Yeshua*!" The sixth says, "Listen, I need to mention again that I don't believe in Him at all. But, based upon the stories and everything I've heard, yes, it fits Yeshua."

Shockingly, one of those who previously said he had no idea who fit these prophecies of Isaiah finally admits, "Look, I believe that Yeshua, who came before the destruction of the Second Temple, fulfilled these things precisely." The man appears as if he is about to cry.

Another man, after being presented with the complete message of

Messiah from the Tanakh, says, "I think I haven't heard these things because when the conversation turns to Yeshua, there's already some kind of 'barrier' where people don't even want to talk about him, don't want to open their minds or think about it a bit. People look at him like…just like that verse said…they rejected him."

Then the video—clearly aimed at nonbelieving Jews—ends with these words over the next three frames:

"Could we have missed our own Messiah?"

"Over five hundred thousand Jews have found our Messiah."

"He's dramatically changed our lives."

True to what Messianic Rabbi Zev Porat has said about the constant persecution of such witnessing material—information that is designed to get the truth of God's Word to the Jewish people—the video has the following words posted under the YouTube version of this documentary edition:

> The older version with many views had to be re-edited for security reasons. Apparently, some people don't want this message to spread.[249]

As we have already documented, we clearly understand exactly who those "some people" might be.

44

Desperately Seeking Messiah

"Do you believe in the Son of Man?" "Who is he, sir?" the man asked. "Tell me so that I may believe in him." Jesus said, "You have now seen him; in fact, he is the one speaking with you."
—John 9:35–37

Another powerful video testimonial focuses on a Jewish man named Mordechai Mottel Baleston.[250]

The video begins with Mr. Baleston affirming his Orthodox Jewish upbringing, especially as it relates to the anti-Christian, anti-New Testament, and anti-Jesus teachings he continually received. He was told that the New Testament was written by Gentiles to teach them how to more effectively persecute the Jews.

Laughingly, Mr. Baleston then admits that the forbidding Jewish atmosphere surrounding the New Testament was the very reason he went to the library one day to secretly begin reading the New Testament for himself, so that he could see this "horrible, Jew-hating" book with his own eyes.

He goes on to acknowledge that from the very opening words of the book of Matthew, he was shocked. It was not a book about how to persecute Jews. It was nothing like what he had been told. It was about a thoroughly Jewish Messiah, and it was written by Jews, to the Jews, from the land of Israel. The New Testament, he said, turned out to be a message of love, not hate.

Mr. Baleston said he discovered the message of the New Testament was that the Jewish Messiah had indeed come—in the person of Yeshua—fulfilling all the prophecies of the Tanakh. He admitted to being overwhelmed as he read the New Testament and the truth about Yeshua.

"It was as beautiful as anything I had ever read in any other part of the Bible," he said of the New Testament. "As I came to faith that Yeshua—that Jesus—was the Messiah, it was clear that was the most Jewish thing I could do!... This is the One who was promised in our Bible!"

Isaiah 53 Speaks Again

The last half of the video begins with Mr. Baleston proclaiming, "The fifty-third chapter of Isaiah—*it is astonishing*! If you would just read that chapter without the [rest of the] Bible around it, you would say 'Uh!' this is some Christian Bible—this is Jesus!"

Mr. Baleston then relates that it was several months after placing his faith in Yeshua as Messiah before he finally told his deeply Orthodox father what he had done. When he did tell his father, his dad was very skeptical about the whole affair. But then, on his own, his dad started to study about Yeshua for himself.

Mr. Baleston next tells the story about how he and his dad attended a lecture in New York City around a year and a half after his dad had started reading about Yeshua as the Messiah. The speaker that night was the author of a book about Yeshua—a book his dad had been reading. The speaker asked, "Would everyone here who is a Jew, but a believer in Yeshua, please raise your hand?"

"Naturally, I raised my hand," Baleston said.

Mr. Baleston said that his dad also raised his hand. He turned to his dad and said, "Pop, the speaker said will all the Jews *who are believers in Yeshua* raise their hands. He didn't say would *all the Jews* raise their hands."

His dad looked at him and said, "I heard what he said."

Mordechai Baleston and his dad had become professing believers in Yeshua as Savior and Messiah!

The Rabbi Kaduri Fire

Messiah of Israel Ministries has also launched multiple CD-placement campaigns. Zev Porat's ministry teams have deposited hundreds of thousands of evangelistic CDs into Israeli mailboxes all over the nation.[251]

In those CDs are a multitude of instructions about the Messianic passages in the Tanakh as well as the powerful information of Rabbi Yitzhak Kaduri's Yeshua revelation. Email addresses and phone numbers are provided in the CDs as well so that interested persons can contact Messiah of Israel Ministries.[252]

"These campaigns have been highly effective," Zev says, "—so effective, in fact, that Yad L'Achim actually went to the radio airwaves and was warning the people of Israel of our outreach efforts. The Jewish people were told to immediately discard the CD and to not look at it. Of course, many of them did look at its material, simply because Yad L'Achim sparked their curiosity with this outrage! What they meant for evil, Yahweh turned it to good."

Zev claims the response has been overwhelming. "We have had calls and emails pour into our office, with Jews from all over Israel wanting to know more about Yeshua and Rabbi Yitzhak Kaduri's revelation," he said. "We continue witnessing to unbelievers and discipling many who have responded to this unique method of outreach. The power of Rabbi Kaduri's faithful revelation continues to sweep Israel like a fire!"

Yad L'Achim Goes to "War"

The Orthodox anti-missionary (anti-Christian) organization Yad L'Achim responded to Rabbi Porat's CD campaign with an acerbic warning to its followers. In part, they titled their article to be a "preemptive war" response. Following is an excerpt from that article:

> Caution! Mission to the Brothers announces: Hundreds of thousands of CDs were distributed today in mailboxes throughout the country by a missionary sect [Rabbi Zev Porat's Messiah of Israel Ministries] with the aim of converting Jews to Christianity. As soon as you accept it, take care of yourself and your children!
>
> At the same time, Yad L'Achim gave a series of interviews on the subject in many media outlets.
>
> "We will not rest until the final halt of the missionary campaign," Yad L'Achim promised this week.[253] (Bracketed words added)

"Think of what we must overcome in order to reach a single Jewish person in Israel with the truth of Yeshua," Zev opines.

"There is the basic vitriolic Jewish rejection of the New Testament and the name of Yeshua that we must contend with," he said. "Then we have to overcome the idea of centuries of persecution of the Jews—in the name of Jesus. On top of that, we have to deal with the clouding of the gospel and the truth of Yeshua by the rabbis, and by synagogue traditions that are thousands of years old and deeply ingrained in our culture."

Zev continued:

> Then there is the influence of Kabbalah, as well as the influential rabbinical power and persuasion over almost every aspect of Orthodox life, as well as the legalistic system of Judaism, forbidden Tanakh chapters, misinformation about translations, constant Yad L'Achim persecution, the orthodox *Two-Messiah* hurdle, and finally—Judaism's powerful connections to the Israeli media and government. Then, when you add the factor of familial pressure—even the absolute shunning from family members—the walls are insurmountable in the human sense.
>
> However, with Yahweh, all things are possible. We are only small people, but we are serving a big God! And with Rabbi

Yitzhak Kaduri's Yeshua note—many of these walls are broken down immediately!

This is what the Orthodox elite know and fear. This is why there is so much resistance to the Kaduri story getting out. It isn't because the story and the note are not true. They know it's true. That's why they destroyed the note!

The fact is that when a Jew hears this truth—their traditional defenses are immediately penetrated, and they are now open to the good news about Messiah Yeshua. *After all,* they say, *their greatest rabbi in all of Israel was also a believer in Yeshua and wrote it down for the whole world to see!* God is doing a great work in these amazingly prophetic days!

The Kaduri Genius

When all things are considered, it appears that the way in which Kaduri chose to reveal his note, leave student witnesses as well as synagogue witnesses, and arrange for the note to be in coded form and then finally posted on his Internet website for the world to see, was absolute genius. It's almost as though the whole affair might have been orchestrated from the *Throne of God.*

Imagine that.

Part Six

THE DIVINELY PROPHETIC

45

Prophetic Days

And so I will show my greatness and my holiness, and I will make myself known in the sight of many nations. Then they will know that I am the Lord.

—Ezekiel 38:23

We are living in the most profoundly prophetic days since the first coming of *Yeshua Ha' Mashiach*. There's really no way around that biblical and historical truth.

For starters, we are now on the other side of the miraculous return of Israel—the biblically prophesied event that would serve as a definitive marker of the last days.[254]

The revenant nation of Israel also serves as God's end-time sign to the nations testifying that He alone is *God of gods* (Ezekiel 38:23, 39:7, 21–29). Dozens of generations that came before us longed to see this prophecy fulfilled. But only in our historical lifetime did it come to pass. We are now more than seventy years on the other side of God's "sign to the nations" (1948–2018).

We are also the first generation to see Jerusalem restored as Israel's legal and rightful capital (May 14, 2018). It really doesn't get much more prophetic than these two occurrences alone. But these amazing prophetic fulfillments are not the only part of the last-days convergences closing in upon our generation.

We are also the first generation to witness:

- Every end-time technology listed in the Bible either fulfilled or in the immediate process of being fulfilled (i.e., the whole world seeing something at once, the whole world taking a "mark," the whole world worshiping a man and/or global governance system, images made to "live and breathe," "fire" being called down from "heaven," etc.; Revelation 13).
- The gospel being preached to all the nations (Matthew 24:14).
- The ever-present spirit of an outburst of World War III (Matthew 24:7; Ezekiel 38–39; Revelation 9:13–19).
- The invention of the Internet. Some see this as the modern-day Tower of Babel—instantaneously connecting the entire globe to all manner of debauchery, terror, demonic oppression, apostasy, and filth.
- The pervasive "corruption of all flesh"—animal and human—through various methods of genetic editing. Some believe this is a requirement necessary to fulfill Jesus' prophecy of the last-days characterization of the "Days of Noah" (Luke 17:26–30).
- The pervasive corruption of gender identity, sexuality, marriage, and family—also believed to be necessary to fulfill Jesus' prophecy of the last-days characterization of the "Days of Lot" (Luke 17:28–37).
- The universal, end-time demonic outpouring, corruption of truth, apostasy, and spirit of global deception, complete with the technological innovations to carry out the scourge every second of every single day (Revelation 12:1; Timothy 4:1; Revelation 6:14, 20:8).
- The global spirit of "terror and dread" (Luke 21:26; 2 Timothy 3:1; Matthew 24:21).
- The burgeoning sense that we are right on the verge of the nations of Ezekiel 38 formally shaping the prophesied coalition that will eventually come against the returned nation of Israel (Ezekiel 37–39).

- The nation of Turkey currently collapsing into an emergent resurrected Ottoman Empire—the potential chief Islamic caliphate headquarters of the Middle East and world.[255]

These are just a few of the most important biblical signs. But also, think of this: Every one of the foregoing, convergent signs has only come about since Israel's relatively recent return.

Of course, I have not even ventured to discuss: CRISPR Cas9 (the recently employed method of using existing biological mechanisms for the "cutting and pasting" of genetic information within a genome[256]), the explosion of invasive and potentially dangerous artificial intelligence (AI), sex robots, robotic militias, or the ever-present Orwellian spy technology used against practically every citizen on the planet. Along with that comes invasive and deadly drone technology; space warfare; and the burgeoning, universal fascination with potential UFO visitation—not to mention the existing technologies for the implementation of a global marking and identification agenda.

Neither have we delved into the various scourges of abject human depravity, runaway drug-abuse epidemics, and the plague of pervasive pornography and its resulting horrors of pedophilia, abuse of women, sex trafficking, and so forth. The prophetic signs are almost too numerous to discuss in these few remaining pages. However, these well-recognized facts intensely bolster the opening sentence of this chapter: *We are indeed living in unprecedentedly prophetic times.*[257]

Kaduri, the Rabbis, and the End Times

All this brings us back to Rabbi Yitzhak Kaduri and his understanding of the prophetic nature of our days, as well as the understanding of the current influential Orthodox rabbis in Israel.

Let's begin with today's Israeli rabbis. Very often, one can find on the Internet a story or two about how some highly recognized rabbi has uttered yet another last-days observation. The writings are often about the imminent expectation of Messiah's appearance, the soon beginning of a Third Temple, the world on the brink of a global war, and Israel's impending "national repentance" necessary for Messiah to finally appear. We also hear these rabbis speaking about the Ezekiel 38–39 prophecy being fulfilled in our days; new, end-time revelations discovered in the "Bible codes" phenomenon[258] (very popular among certain Orthodox rabbis); and several other observations of equal significance.

Those are not the only "prophetic" topics the Orthodox rabbis around the planet are discussing. On December 3, 2015, the Center for Jewish-Christian Understanding & Cooperation (CJCUC) published an official declaration that rocked the Judeo/Christian world. The statement was titled, "Orthodox Rabbinic Statement on Christianity. To Do the Will of Our Father in Heaven: Toward a Partnership between Jews and Christians."[259]

The proclamation was signed by several dozen Orthodox rabbis from more than twelve nations, including many from the United States and Israel.

Among other shocking admissions within the document is the following: "As did Maimonides and Yehudah Halevi,[260] we acknowledge that the emergence of Christianity in human history is neither an accident nor an error, but the willed divine outcome and gift to the nations."[261]

The opening statement of that CJCUC decree states:

> After nearly two millennia of mutual hostility and alienation, we Orthodox Rabbis who lead communities, institutions and seminaries in Israel, the United States and Europe recognize the historic opportunity now before us. We seek to do the will of our Father in Heaven by accepting the hand offered to us by **our Christian brothers and sisters. Jews and Christians must work together** as partners to address the moral challenges of our era.[262]

Sharon's Death

Of course, Rabbi Yitzhak Kaduri was quite vocal about the fact that he also believed the "spirit of the last days" was upon us. Naturally, his vision of Messiah Yeshua was the most significant prophetic revelation. And don't forget, attached to that disclosure was also the generational "proximity marker" of the death of Ariel Sharon on January 11, 2014.

Even though the mainstream media didn't flat out identify Ariel Sharon as some sort of literal Messiah (i.e., Messiah ben Joseph), they still frequently applied Messianic epitaphs to him, especially at his passing. Consider the following headlines:

- "Ariel Sharon, Lion of Israel" (*New York Daily News*)[263]
- "Ariel Sharon: The 'Lion of God' Departs" (*Times UK*)[264]
- "The Lion of Israel—Ariel Sharon" (*Jewish News*)[265]
- "Sharon: The Life of a Lion—'He was on the threshold of the Promised Land, he already took the step, he was about to place his foot on the Promised Land, and then he fell'" (*Jerusalem Post*)[266]
- "'My name is Ariel Sharon': His name means 'Lion of God'" (*Guardian UK*)[267]
- "The Left Is Waiting for a Messiah 'Sharon radiated magnetic power'" (*Haaretz*)[268]
- "The Architecture of Ariel Sharon 'Trumpeted…as the "saviour of Israel" (sometimes even as its "king")'" (*Aljazeera*)[269]

Rabbi Kaduri himself was no stranger to making public prophetic proclamations either. Consider the following statement he made in September 2005, just three months before his death. Especially note the words in bold type:

In a class between the Mincha (afternoon) and Maariv (evening) prayers at his Jerusalem yeshiva seminary, Rabbi Kaduri issued the following call:

> This declaration I find fitting to issue for **all of the Jews of the world** to hear. It is incumbent upon them to **return to the Land of Israel** due to **terrible natural disasters** which threaten the world.
>
> In the future, the Holy One, Blessed be He, will bring about great disasters in the countries of the world to sweeten the judgements of the Land of Israel.
>
> I am ordering the publication of this declaration as a warning, so that Jews in the countries of the world will be aware of the impending danger and **will come to the Land of Israel for the building of the Temple and revelation of our righteous Mashiach (Messiah).**[270]

Notice Kaduri's main prophetic emphases: the necessity for the Jews to hasten their return to Israel, the onslaught of impending natural disasters, the building of the Third Temple, and the final revealing of the Messiah.

The Jewish return to the land and the looming natural disasters of the very last days are thoroughly biblical revelations. The building of a new Temple is primarily an Orthodox Jewish desire, although many evangelical Christians also see this as a potential prophetic marker of end-time events.

As for Kaduri's prediction concerning the revealing of Messiah, that would be accomplished, at least as a preliminary revelation, through his Yeshua note—a "revelation" that would cause a global spiritual earthquake.

But what was this talk from Rabbi Kaduri concerning the "building of the Temple" in Israel? When Kaduri spoke those words, one huge obstacle to the building of a new one remained: Jerusalem was not the officially recognized capital of Israel. If Jerusalem was not the sovereign capital of Israel, building a Jewish Temple there, especially anywhere near the Temple Mount, would be all but impossible. What did Rabbi Kaduri know that the rest of the world did not know at that time?

46

The Third Temple

Jesus left the temple and was walking away when his disciples came up to him to call his attention to its buildings. "Do you see all these things?" he asked. "Truly I tell you, not one stone here will be left on another; every one will be thrown down."

—Matthew 24:1–2

In speaking of the Third Temple, one is usually referring to an edifice similar to the First and Second Jewish Temples that were built upon the Temple Mount in the epicenter of Jerusalem. Of course, the Muslim Dome of the Rock is currently located there and has been in that locale since AD 688.

The First Temple, built by King Solomon around 800 BC, was destroyed by the Babylonians in 586 BC. The Second Temple was relatively completed in 516 BC, then refurbished and overhauled by King Herod during Jesus' day. That structure was eventually razed by the Romans in AD 70. There has never been another Jewish Temple since that time. The Jews have longed for another one to finally sit upon the Temple Mount. They also believe this specific Third Temple must be built in order for their Messiah to finally come to Israel. "After all," they would say, "this truth is found in some of the last words of Messianic promise found in the very last book of the Tanakh."

> "I will send my messenger, who will prepare the way before me. **Then suddenly the Lord you are seeking will come to his temple**; the messenger of the covenant, **whom you desire**, will come," says the Lord Almighty.
>
> But who can endure the day of his coming? Who can stand when he appears? For he will be like a refiner's fire or a launderer's soap. He will sit as a refiner and purifier of silver; he will purify the Levites and refine them like gold and silver.
>
> Then the Lord will have men who will bring offerings in righteousness, and the offerings of Judah and Jerusalem will be acceptable to the Lord, as in days gone by, as in former years. (Malachi 3:1–4, emphasis added)

The Jews have, of course, rejected Jesus Christ as Messiah. So they fail to realize the literal fulfillment of Messiah actually "coming to His temple" throughout His ministry, specifically during the final week of His earthly life.

Varying Interpretations

There are several schools of thought within evangelical Christian circles regarding whether the Bible contextually requires that a literal Third Temple structure must be completed before the return of Yeshua. Some believe this is indeed a strict biblical requirement and the appearance of a third structure will happen sometime before the Rapture of the Church.

Others believe a Third Temple will be built upon the Temple Mount, but only sometime *after* the Rapture. Most of those who hold to one of these two persuasions believe the Third Temple ultimately will be commandeered by the coming Antichrist (Matthew 24:15; 2 Thessalonians 2:1–4).

Yet another school of eschatology believes the Third and ultimate Temple will finally appear on the Temple Mount only *after* the literal return of Jesus Christ, and that the true Third Temple of our current time is the body of Christ itself. They argue that the only New Testament statement concerning a "new temple" in the very last days concerns the "temple" that is the Church.[271]

> Consequently, you are no longer foreigners and strangers, but fellow citizens with God's people and also members of his household, built on the foundation of the apostles and prophets, **with Christ Jesus himself as the chief cornerstone. In him the whole building is joined together and rises to become a holy temple in the Lord.** And in him you too are being built together to become a dwelling in which God lives by his Spirit. (Ephesians 2:19–22, emphasis added)

> Don't you know that **you yourselves are God's temple** and that God's Spirit dwells in your midst? (1 Corinthians 3:16)

Accordingly, some Christians insist the Third Temple is meant to be understood in the "spiritual" sense. Others argue that it is literal and physical reality. Still others say that it is probably *both.*[272] They insist the Jews will likely rebuild a literal Temple (that will not be blessed by Yahweh; see Isaiah 66) in which the Antichrist will ultimately seat himself as "God." At the same time, they argue, the Church is becoming the true "spiritual" temple, under the blood of Jesus and through the Holy Spirit—the "one new man" (Ephesians 2:14–16).

The Jewish View

In addition to these various evangelical interpretations, there is also the strictly Orthodox Jewish view of a literal new Temple—to be constructed *as a Messianic necessity,* because without the structure's physical presence, many Jews believe they will not see their long-awaited Messiah.[273]

This belief is concurrent with several important factors that have, only in our historical lifetime, begun to converge: a massive return of Jews to the land of Israel; an increased participation in the "keeping of the Law of God;" an expectation for Messiah's imminent return; and, for a number of Jews, the rebuilding of the Temple on the Temple Mount.

More Jews in Israel

In July 2018, a prominent Israeli news organization proclaimed, "Government Announces 'Majority of Jews in Israel' Sanhedrin Responds 'Time for Jubilee':"

> **The Israeli government recently announced that the largest community of Jews in the world is in Israel.** This demographic fact has far-reaching Messianic ramifications in Jewish Law, requiring the Jews to reinstate Biblical commandments that have not been seen in two millennia and bringing redemption [coming of the Messiah] one, rather significant step closer.[274] (Emphasis added)
>
> Rabbi Hillel Weiss, spokesman for the nascent Sanhedrin, explained:
>
> "Having a majority of Jews in Israel creates a different halachic (Torah law) reality, requiring Jews to perform certain mitzvoth (Torah commandments) they have not had to perform in 2,000 years." Rabbi Weiss explained that this condition of a majority of Jews in Israel was anticipated in prophecy as the final return of the Jews to Israel. It is referred to as the third inheritance of the land, the first being by Joshua, the second after the Babylonian exile.
>
> The third inheritance refers to Jews' prophesied return from the exile that followed the destruction of the Second Temple by the Romans in 70 CE. Jewish tradition holds that **this return will usher in the building of the Third Temple, the return of the Davidic Dynasty, and the messianic era.**[275] (Emphasis added)

Today, there are several Jewish-led Temple reconstruction movements. A 2012 *Haaretz* article describes one such interdenominational assembly:

> Temple? Sacrifices? In the 21st century… [At] the joint directorate's monthly meeting…around the table were a few men and women who did not look especially off-the-wall—though they may have thought this was my perception of them. The participants represented the range of Temple movements.[276]

As a matter of fact, one sect of Orthodox Jews argues that only an altar, rather than an entire structure, is needed in order to once again resume the prescribed "sacrifices" upon the Temple Mount.

> The institute [Rabbi Yisrael Ariel] founded is busy reconstructing and recreating all the material elements necessary for a Third Temple to be ready to function. He is particularly involved in the crafting of **a mobile altar, which can be installed quickly when sacrifices are again performed.**[277] (Emphasis added)

Although I am familiar with the intricacies and eschatological schematics of each of the foregoing Third Temple scenarios, the purpose of this book is not to debate the various theological arguments. Rather, we will primarily consider the Jewish view of the matter, because this relates directly to the story we are examining now.

From the nascent Sanhedrin Council in Israel to the mainstream Israeli media, Prime Minister Benjamin Netanyahu, members of the Israeli parliament, and the declarations of several very significant Israeli rabbis—including Rabbi Yitzhak Kaduri—the issue of a Third Temple in Jerusalem is front and center in today's news.

Bible prophecy continues to unfold before us.

47

The Temple Zeitgeist

The time has come to rebuild the
Temple on Mount Moriah in Jerusalem.
—The Sanhedrin Court, May 2018[278]

Once again, review the words of Rabbi Kaduri, written just three months before his death:

> I am ordering the publication of this declaration as a warning, so that Jews in the countries of the world will be aware of the impending danger and **will come to the Land of Israel for the building of the Temple and revelation of our righteous Mashiach (Messiah).**[279]

Since we can be assured that Kaduri knew Yeshua/Jesus was the true Messiah, most likely he also thought, because of his 108 years of traditional Hebrew upbringing, that when Yeshua returned, He would ultimately return to a rebuilt Temple on the Temple Mount.

The point is that Rabbi Kaduri obviously believed the rebuilding would somehow connect to the ultimate revealing of the true Messiah. He may or may not have been correct in his theory, but one thing is certain: We know he was not mistaken in his revelation of the name of the true Messiah.

What do other prominent Jews or Jewish bodies of influence say about the matter of a Third Temple?

The Sanhedrin Court

In a stunning turn of events, the Sanhedrin Court of Israel, just days before the official move of the US Embassy to Jerusalem, issued a letter to the Arab world. The letter was written in Hebrew, English, and Arabic.

That May 2018 dispatch read:

> Dear brothers, the distinguished Sons of Ishmael, The great Arab nation,
>
> With the gracious help of the protector and Savior of Israel, Creator of the world by covenant, we declare that the footsteps of Messiah are evidently heard and that the time has come to rebuild the Temple on Mount Moriah in Jerusalem in its ancient place.
>
> We, the Jews who advocate building of the Temple, are applying to your Honorable ones, who were nominated by their peoples to give oath, raise vows and gifts to the Temple as prophesied by prophet Isaiah concerning your essential role and honorable position in keeping the Temple and **supporting it with lamb sacrifices** and incense in order to receive God's Blessings.[280] (Emphasis added)

Note especially the Orthodox Jewish view regarding the rebuilding of the Temple. The nascent Sanhedrin acknowledges their belief that this feat must be accomplished for Messiah to appear, and that there must be lamb sacrifices.

Sadly, they have completely missed the true Lamb of God—*Yeshua Ha' Mashiac*h.

The Rabbis, Evangelicals, and Donald Trump

In an earlier chapter, we examined the 2016–2018 Trump Messiah furor in Israel. Much of that zeal centered around President Trump's signing of the Jerusalem Embassy Act, then officially moving the US Embassy to Jerusalem on May 14, 2018—the exact day of the seventieth anniversary of the return of Israel.

Attached to Trump's extreme popularity in Israel at that time were the prevalent Messianic expectations and the accompanying hope of a soon-to-be rebuilt Temple on the Temple Mount.

A key online, Israeli-based news source reported:

> Rabbi Yosef Berger, the rabbi in charge of King David's Tomb on Mount Zion, revealed to Breaking Israel News a 600-year-old Jewish source stating that the Third Temple will be prepared by descendants of Edom as a "reparation" for destroying the Second Temple. Additional hints from esoteric sources indicate that US President Donald Trump has already begun this process.[281]

On March 29, 2018, the headlines of *Israel Today* screamed, "Top Israeli Rabbi Believes Trump Will Build Third Temple in Jerusalem."[282]

In that article, Rabbi Yosef Berger was also quoted as saying:

> No leader in history has recognized Jerusalem as the capital of the Jews and Israel. [President Donald Trump] has already created a great *tikkun* (reparation) for the Christians through his unprecedented relationship with Jerusalem. Trump is the representative of Edom that will perform that final historic reparation for his entire nation by building the Temple.

At the close of 2017, just months away from enacting President Donald Trump's signing of the Jerusalem Embassy Act, Israel's mainstream Orthodox publication, *Haaretz,* proclaimed:

> Christians and Jews Now Compare Trump to Persian King Cyrus—Will He Build the Third Temple?—Like Cyrus 2,500 years ago, Trump is seen as an instrument of God. And the plan [is] to build the Third Temple on the Temple Mount—where the Al-Aqsa Mosque currently stands.[283]

Even *Newsweek* got in on the zeitgeist of the Third Temple fever with this December 2017 headline: "Will Trump Hasten the Arrival of the Messiah? Jews and Evangelicals think so."[284]

That article opened with these words:

> In the wake of President Donald Trump's controversial decision to recognize Jerusalem as the capital of Israel, some Jewish activists argued that the U.S. president was being guided by God to restore Jewish control over sacred sites.
>
> Activists lobbying for the construction of a Jewish Temple in Jerusalem said Trump was playing a similar role to the Persian emperor Cyrus the Great, who allowed the Jews to return to Israel from exile.

The Trump/Cyrus/Temple Coin

In March 2018, an Israeli media source proclaimed: "Global Support for Third Temple Coin." The article's first two paragraphs claim:

> A newly minted coin featuring President Trump, King Cyrus,[285] and the Third Temple has been featured in media around the world, graphically illustrating that support for the Jewish Temple on the Temple Mount is now a global phenomenon that is transcending political and religious boundaries.
>
> Three weeks ago, the nascent Sanhedrin and the Mikdash (Temple) Educational Center, a non-profit organization for education about the Temple, partnered in a risky venture to mint a

commemorative medallion with an image of President Donald Trump and the Persian King Cyrus. The flip side features a stylized image of the Third Temple.[286]

Rabbi Hillel Weiss, spokesman for the Sanhedrin, said of the Trump Coin:

> This is enormously popular among America's friends and very unpopular among the people who hate America," Rabbi Weiss told *Breaking Israel News*.
>
> Obama hated Israel and Jerusalem, and as a result, America's enemies became stronger while he was president, many acquiring or developing nuclear weapons. It is important to realize that the most powerful and enduring hope America has is to side with Hashem. The only hope for this is to support Jews taking their place as a Nation of Priests and a Light Unto the Nations.[287]

The online site *Hamikdash.org,* which is prominently promoting and selling the Trump/Cyrus coin, pulls no punches in describing its main goal and prayer regarding the global distribution of the coin:

> With the advent of the 70th anniversary of the State of Israel—and Donald Trump's Jerusalem Declaration… [It is our prayer that] the unique coin, will find its way into homes and institutions the world over, [as] a portent to usher—God willing, **the period which the new Temple will be restored.**[288] (Emphasis added)

Rabbi Chaim Kanievsky

Rabbi Kanievsky, touted as "one of the world's leading Jewish scholars" of our time, lives in Bnei Brak, Israel. In a July 2018 edition of *The Star* (UK), Rabbi Kanievsky made several startling claims regarding the soon coming of Messiah and the building of the Third Temple in Jerusalem:

> The signs of redemption are slowly appearing. But the Messiah himself has yet to show himself to the world.... We are seeing all of the conditions described in the Talmud appear before us.... It is for this reason that we anticipate the appearance of the Messiah at any moment, God-willing.[289]

Kanievsky claims to believe the Messiah was born on Saturday, July 21, 2018. He bases this date upon his reading of ancient mystical texts and that date's connection to *Tisha B'Av*, an annual day of fasting and sorrow that memorializes certain monumental disasters in the history of the Jewish people. That day specifically marks the destruction of the two previous Temples in Jerusalem. *The Star* article then says, "with the construction of a third being key to the prophecy of the Jewish Messiah."

Rabbi Kanievsky is also quoted as saying, "It seems to me that the sages intended to teach us that even when the Temple is destroyed, in any case the Redemption exists."

Needless to say, the air in Israel is thick with Messianic anticipation, complete with a rebuilt Third Temple.

48

The World Holds Its Breath

> People will faint from terror, apprehensive of what is coming on the world, for the heavenly bodies will be shaken.
> —Luke 21:26

As of this writing, Israeli Prime Minister Benjamin Netanyahu has not made a definitive statement regarding the literal rebuilding of a new Temple on the Temple Mount. However, a number of prophecy watchers believe that Netanyahu did indeed telegraph several strong hints in that regard.

For example, during his US Jerusalem Embassy dedication speech on March 14, 2018, which was carried live around the world, Netanyahu emphasized the Jewish Temple's presence on the Temple Mount three different times. The context of his remarks concerned the recitation of the history of Israel's first two Temples in that location. Some believed Netanyahu was covertly signaling his support for an agenda to rebuild the structure. That feeling was further reinforced when, near the end of his speech, he proclaimed, "The Temple Mount is in our hands!" At those specific words, the crowd erupted into riotous applause.[290]

But, back in late 2015, Netanyahu was insisting that Israel was only committed to the *status quo* regarding the Temple Mount, and that claims to the contrary were merely a part of "a campaign of incitement."[291]

However, to counter that claim, a corresponding *Haaretz* investigation uncovered:

> Netanyahu's deputy defense minister, as well as one of his key donors in the United States, have financially supported those who wish to impose Israeli sovereignty over the Temple Mount.[292]

The *Haaretz* investigation was reported to have revealed that Deputy Defense Minister Eli Ben-Dahan donated fifty thousand shekels ($12,000) to the Temple Institute, which exists solely to promote the construction of the Third Temple.[293]

But, there is also this: Just a couple of weeks after President Trump signed the Jerusalem Embassy Act, it appeared to many prophecy watchers that Benjamin Netanyahu expressed his innate desire to see the Third Temple constructed in Israel's recognized capital.

The *Times of Israel* reported Prime Minister Netanyahu as saying:

> I want to tell you that the Jewish people have a long memory, so we remember the proclamation of the great king, Cyrus the Great, the Persian king 2,500 years ago. He proclaimed that the Jewish exiles in Babylon could **come back and rebuild our Temple in Jerusalem.** We remember a hundred years ago, Lord Balfour, who issued **the Balfour Proclamation that recognized the rights of the Jewish people in our ancestral homeland.** We remember 70 years ago, President Harry S. Truman was **the first leader to recognize the Jewish state.** And we remember how a few weeks ago, President **Donald J. Trump recognized Jerusalem as Israel's capital.** Mr. President, this will be remembered by our people through the ages.[294]

To many around the world who heard those words, Netanyahu's speech appeared to directly connect Israel's right to exist and Jerusalem being the lawful capital of Israel with Israel's inherent right to rebuild the Temple in Jerusalem.

Fuel to the Fire

Then, on July 19, 2018, another monumental piece of the puzzle appeared to have fallen into place. Israel's parliament passed a "law in stone" declaring "Jerusalem, complete and united, is the capital of Israel."[295]

That declaration of Israel's sovereignty over the land, particularly the city of Jerusalem, appeared to signal a continued march toward the potential of the soon-coming construction of a new Temple.

After Israel's lawmakers passed the legislation, Prime Minister Netanyahu employed the use of particularly strong nationalistic language. "[This is a] historic moment in the history of Zionism and the history of the state of Israel. Israel is the nation state of the Jewish people, which honors the individual rights of all its citizens," he said. "I repeat this is our state. The Jewish state."

> "Lately, there are people who are trying to destabilize this and therefore destabilize the foundations of our existence and our rights," he added. "So today we have made a law in stone. This is our country. This is our language. This is our anthem and this is our flag. Long live the state of Israel."[296]

Destroy the Mosque and Rebuild the Temple?

Added to the zeal of Israel's Orthodox who wish to see the reconstruction of the Temple was another shocking statement delivered in 2016 by an Israeli Knesset member. Likud lawmaker and Deputy Speaker of the Knesset Oren Hazan spoke the following words at a town-hall-style meeting in Petach Tikvah, an Israeli city twenty kilometers east of Tel Aviv:

> "If the day comes and I have the opportunity to lead the country, not to mention become the prime minister, **I will build the temple on the Temple Mount.**"
>
> After the panel discussion organized by the group Students For The Temple Mount, **we asked Hazan how he would demolish Al-Aqsa mosque and Dome of the Rock in order to make way for a temple,** he replied, "It would not be responsible at this point in time to tell you how we would do it, but **I will say it clear and loud: When I have the opportunity to do it, I will.**"[297]

By the time Netanyahu made his Jerusalem Embassy speech on March 14, 2018, as well as his pointed declarations of July 19, 2018, concerning Israel's sovereignty over Jerusalem, one can see why so many thought the prime minister was potentially sending Third Temple smoke signals—especially to the Orthodox of Israel.

Prominent Israeli Rabbis

Additionally, many renowned Israeli Orthodox rabbis have gone on record concerning their view that the US Embassy move to Jerusalem was a prophetic precursor to the rebuilding of the Third Temple. Following are four examples of those stunning rabbinic interpretations.[298]

Rabbi Jeremy Gimpel, the founder of the Land of Israel Network:

> Now, we are seeing just the beginning of this prophecy [Isaiah 62:6–7] as nations begin moving their embassies from Tel-Aviv to Jerusalem. This is a step in the prophetic *process of redemption.* [The Jewish understanding of the coming of their Messiah. In the minds of many Orthodox, this process requires the building of a Temple.]. (Emphasis and bracketed words added)

Rabbi Hillel Weiss, spokesman for the nascent Sanhedrin:

> The opening of the US Embassy in Jerusalem is not the end; it is a means. It is one step in the Geula process [redemption process] that is moving towards the Temple, which must, by necessity, involve all the nations and even the Temple is merely a means for sanctifying all of creation.

Rabbi Shimon Apisdorf, renowned Torah teacher and author:

> The Kol Hatur laid out 156 steps in the process of Moshiach, One of the steps is called Koresh Meshichi based on King Cyrus allowing and even enabling the Jews to come back to Israel and build the Temple. This step is the role non-Jews and their leaders play in the Moshiach. It is specifically for non-Jews and as such, is not a mitzvah that Jews are commanded to perform.

Rabbi Yosef Berger, Rabbi of King David's Tomb on Mount Zion:

> No one forced the US president to do this. This is clearly a case of the non-Jews coming to Jerusalem to praise God, as they did in the First and Second Temples, and as the Prophets said they would again.

While the Orthodox Jewish world was obviously thrilled with President Trump's American Embassy move, those in the Islamic world were much less than thrilled. They were livid.

Harbingers of a Looming War?

President Donald Trump signed the Jerusalem Embassy Act on December 6, 2017. But, by December 12, 2017, the prominent and highly controversial Turkish media source *Yeni Safak* published an article titled, "What if a Muslim Army Was Established against Israel?" The second line of that article's title explained, "If the member states of the OIC unite militarily, they will form the world's largest and most comprehensive army."[299]

Yeni Safak[300] reported:

> The Organization of Islamic Cooperation (OIC), which was established in 1969 following the criminal arson of al-Aqsa Mosque in occupied Jerusalem, will meet in Istanbul on Wednesday for an extraordinary summit to discuss Jerusalem following U.S. President Donald Trump's decision last week to recognize the holy city as Israel's capital and relocate the U.S. embassy to the city. It is expected that clear messages and steps against Israel will emerge as a result of the summit….
>
> The establishment of a possible Muslim army would ensure that Israel is militarily surrounded.[301]

Echoing the basic theme and sentiments of the *Yeni Safak* article, and just four days after the May 14, 2018, dedication of the United States Embassy in Jerusalem, President Erdogan of Turkey called yet another OIC assembly. On Friday, May 18, 2018, *Al Jazeera*[302] reported on that meeting and the accompanying rally in an article titled, "Erdogan Calls on Muslim Countries to Unite and Confront Israel":

> Turkish President Recep Tayyip Erdogan has called on Muslim leaders to unite and confront Israel, days after scores of Palestinians were killed by Israeli snipers as they marked 70 years of Israeli occupation.
>
> Speaking at an extraordinary summit of the Organization of Islamic Cooperation (OIC) on Friday, Erdogan said Israel should be held accountable over the killings which drew widespread international condemnation and triggered a wave of protests from Asia, through the Middle East, to North Africa….
>
> Erdogan told a raucous crowd of more than 10,000 people in Istanbul's Yenikapi fairground that the Muslim world had to unite and "pull themselves back together"….

"Since 1947, Israel has been free to do what it likes in this region. They do whatever they feel like. But this reality can be undone…if we unite."[303]

FrontPage Magazine[304] also ran a detailed report of that reactionary OIC conclave. Portions of the first two paragraphs of that piece read:

> Turkey's Dictator Recep Tayyip Erdogan, assembled with great urgency Sunni-Muslim leaders from the Middle East, Asia, and Africa, as well as Iran's Shiite President Hassan Rouhani. The assembled representatives of the 57 member-states of the Organization of Islamic Cooperation (OIC) held this "emergency meeting" in Istanbul, Turkey, by virtue of Turkey's holding the presidency of the OIC. The ostensible reason for the meeting was…the U.S. embassy relocation to Jerusalem.
>
> According to Al-Jazeera, the Qatari based network also funded by the Qatari regime, Erdogan called on Muslim leaders to "unite and confront Israel." He mentioned "70 years of Israeli occupation."[305]

Obviously, this matter of a new Temple on the Temple Mount in a restored Israeli capital of Jerusalem is truly monumental to Jews and Muslims alike.

We are the only generation to live in the midst of these converging prophetic phenomena. A growing number of prophecy watchers believe the previously unthinkable possibility of rebuilding another Temple on the Temple Mount, in a Jerusalem that had been declared the lawful capital of Israel, might actually have its beginnings in our day.

Perhaps the renowned Rabbi Yitzhak Kaduri was on to something.

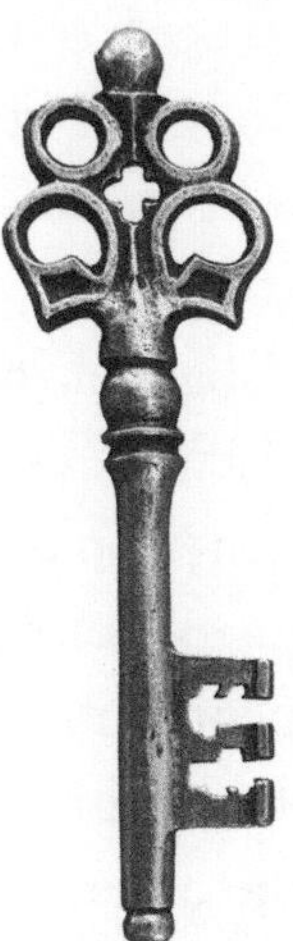

49

It's a Jewish Thing

To God's elect, exiles scattered throughout the provinces of Pontus, Galatia, Cappadocia, Asia and Bithynia.

—1 Peter 1:1

For our Jewish friends reading this book, please do not continue to accept as *truth* the blatant falsehood that believing in Yeshua as Messiah is not Jewish. When the matter is understood in its proper historical and biblical context, nothing could be *more* Jewish! This is exactly why hundreds of thousands of Jewish people and former Orthodox rabbis the world over are now followers of Messiah Yeshua.

Here are the Jewish facts. The vast majority of the New Testament account occurred squarely in the midst of the ancient land of Israel—the Promised Land of the Jews.

Most important, when God put on human flesh, He put on *Jewish* flesh. In the person of Yeshua/Jesus, Yahweh revealed Himself as the promised Messiah of Israel (Isaiah 53; Zechariah 12:10; Psalm 22; Colossians 1:15–18; Hebrews 1:1–3; John 1:1–14, etc.).

And don't forget this important tidbit: All of Yeshua's original followers were Jews! Furthermore, every one of the New Testament writers was Jewish. One book, Hebrews, was written specifically to help the Orthodox Jewish believers in Christ see how He completely fulfilled the Old Testament Messianic prophecies of the promised Great High Priest.

The book of Hebrews alone contains at least thirty-five direct quotations from and fifty-three distinct references to the Old Testament. The books of the Tanakh referenced in Hebrews are Genesis, Psalms, Deuteronomy, Jeremiah, Isaiah, Numbers, Haggai, Exodus, 1 Chronicles, Proverbs, Habakkuk, and 2 Samuel.[306]

In fact, the entire New Testament contains quotes from all of the Old Testament books except five: Ezra, Nehemiah, Esther, Ecclesiastes, and the Song of Solomon. Yeshua Himself, throughout the pages of the New Testament, quoted from twenty-four Old Testament books.[307] It is highly possible that in the unrecorded portions of His ministry, He also quoted from the others. Yeshua and Paul were often invited into the synagogues of their day, where they stood before congregations and read the Scriptures of the Tanakh—and from them they preached the Kingdom of God.

The original twelve disciples were all Jews as well, as were the 120 in the Upper Room on the day the Church was birthed. According to Acts 4:4, the three thousand who came to faith on that Jewish holiday of Pentecost eventually grew to about five thousand—all of whom were Jews or Gentile converts to Judaism.

History bears out that many thousands of Jewish believers in Yeshua were living and witnessing in Israel from the very beginning. Even a number of rabbis and priests of the first century believed in Yeshua as Lord and Messiah (Acts 6:7). Furthermore, it was these first Jewish believers in *Yeshua Ha' Mashiach* who took the gospel "unto the whole world" (Matthew 28:19–20).

In fact, for years, the first Jewish believers in Yeshua worshiped in their synagogues and at the Temple! There were no church buildings with stained glass windows. These believers were all Jews. Some years later, most of the Jewish believers either left the synagogues or were expelled from them. However, this was not their first choice. They left because of the pressure and threats leveled upon them by the nonbelieving Jews. Gentiles were eventually, after several decades, included in this faith—but faith in Yeshua certainly is not only a Gentile thing. It is first and foremost a thoroughly Jewish thing.

If it were not for the Jewish prophecies of a coming Messiah, a Jewish Messiah, Jewish disciples, Jewish followers, the birth of a Jewish body of believers in Yeshua, a body of Jewish testimonial writings called the New Testament, and Jewish missionaries to the Gentiles, there would be no faith system called Christianity.

In reality, to be a believer in *Yeshua Ha' Mashiach* is about as Jewish as a person can get.

The most powerful witness of this truth in our lifetime is Kaduri's Yeshua note. It is still circulating before the eyes of the world, and apparently there's no stopping its supernatural reach.

This truly is the story that will not end—until the return of *Yeshua Ha' Mashiach* Himself.

50

He Knew

See, I am doing a new thing! Now it springs up; do you not perceive it? I am making a way in the wilderness and streams in the wasteland.
—Isaiah 43:19

An amazing story like that of Rabbi Kaduri's might be a little difficult to wrap one's mind around at first. However, after examining the pertinent facts, you probably agree by now that the entire affair certainly has the distinctively recognizable fingerprints of Yahweh all over it.

Apparently, Rabbi Yitzhak Kaduri was divinely entrusted with the humanly impossible task of opening up the hearts, eyes, and ears of the entire Jewish world to the understanding that Yeshua is the Messiah. It makes sense that the Lord might choose him for that mission; after all, Rabbi Kaduri was one of the most renowned and globally recognized Orthodox leaders in Israel's history. Most of today's Orthodox Jews would never consider a message about Yeshua unless it had, indeed, originated from the handwriting of a celebrated Orthodox rabbi of the caliber and standing of Yitzhak Kaduri. And that's exactly what happened.

Heaven's Choice

Messianic Rabbi Zev Porat explains:

> What many Christians do not yet understand is just how important the word of a powerful rabbi really is within the Orthodox Jewish life. A Jew will not believe anything out of the ordinary—until he first hears it verified from a trusted rabbi. When confronted with a difficult scriptural situation, the Orthodox Jew will often say, "I must first find out what my rabbi says about this."
>
> So, for a rabbi of Yitzhak Kaduri's universally recognized and exalted stature to leave a note in his own handwriting verifying that Yeshua is the real Messiah is beyond description in its importance and impact.
>
> Rabbi Kaduri's sphere of influence was huge! He accomplished something that few rabbis *ever* accomplish—he was revered, and sought out for counsel, by both the Sephardic and the Ashkenazi Jews.[308] This often-overlooked factor cannot be ignored, especially in the case of the Messiah note.
>
> Because of this fact, it is Kaduri's Yeshua note alone that often opens the door to modern Jewish hearts, enabling them to explore the Scriptures to discover the real truth about Messiah Yeshua. I can't even begin to describe the importance of this Kaduri story in the quest to lead Jews to Yeshua as Messiah. Please understand—witnessing to a Jew would not be *impossible* without Kaduri's note, but there is no doubt whatsoever that this note has opened up an entirely new universe of witnessing opportunities and salvations in Yeshua!
>
> This is the main reason the Orthodox elite are so upset about the note. The potential of its impact across the global Jewish population is enormous.

Prescient

Regardless of the fact that Rabbi Kaduri appeared to know very little about the complete gospel message of Yeshua, he obviously understood the signs of his times. He particularly understood his role in what Yahweh was doing at the very last of his days. He knew there was a great Messianic fervor in Israel, perhaps more than at any other time in that nation's modern history.

He also sensed that the world was nearing a time of the potential construction of a Third Temple in Jerusalem. This was the predominant reason Kaduri passionately called Jews from all over the world to "immediately return to the Land of Israel." But, Rabbi Kaduri would also *had to have known* that, in order for this amazing thing to happen, Jerusalem would eventually become the lawful and recognized capital of Israel again.

Even though he didn't live to see that occur, the human impossibility of the matter finally did come to pass. It happened in our lifetime, only twelve years after Kaduri's death. Had the Lord somehow made Rabbi Kaduri aware of the marvelously impossible chain of events that would soon come to fruition?

Rabbi Kaduri's Messiah revelation might have been more prophetically connected to monumental biblical events than anyone could have ever imagined. I expect our generation to see further prophetic stunners burst into existence—perhaps right around the corner.

Part Seven

THE DIVINE NAME

51

The Name

They will deliver you to synagogues and prisons, and you will be brought before kings and governors, and all on account of my name.
—Luke 21:12–13

The Rabbi Kaduri story boils down to one supremely important factor. It's all about *the Name.*

The name Rabbi Kaduri revealed as the true Messiah—*Yeshua*—has been a global dividing point since Jesus first began His ministry along the shores of Galilee. Since then, practically every person who has ever called upon the name of Yeshua has discovered, to one degree or another, just how deep that divide can become.

We also know that, as the Day of the Lord approaches, the division over *the Name* will only grow deeper. This is exactly the way Yeshua told us it would be. He said that His name would become a reproach among the nations, especially among the unbelieving Jews. Even the hallmark of the coming Antichrist will be that he shamelessly slanders *the Name* and everything it represents:

> **Why do the nations conspire and the peoples plot in vain**? The kings of the earth rise up and the rulers band together **against the** LORD and **against his *anointed*.**[309] (Psalm 2:1–2, emphasis added)

> [Jesus said] They will **treat you this way because of my name,** for **they do not know the One** who sent me. (John 15:21–22, emphasis added)

> But the Lord said to Ananias, "Go! This man [Saul/Paul] is my chosen instrument to carry **my name** before the Gentiles and their kings and before the people of Israel. I will show him **how much he must suffer for my name.**" (Acts 9:15–16, emphasis added)

> You have persevered and have **endured hardships for my name,** and have not grown weary. (Revelation 2:3, emphasis added)

> Yet you have kept my word and **have not denied my name.** I will make those who are of the synagogue of Satan, **who claim to be Jews though they are not**, but are liars—I will make them come and fall down at your feet and acknowledge that I have loved you. (Revelation 3:8–9, emphasis added)

> The beast was given a mouth to utter proud words **and blasphemies** and to exercise his authority for forty-two months. **He opened his mouth to blaspheme God**, and **to slander his name** and his dwelling place and those who live in heaven. (Revelation 13:5–6, emphasis added)

The Name of God

The most important of all the names by which God is known is the four-letter one represented by the Hebrew letters *Yud-Heh-Vav-Heh* (יהוה), reading from the right to left as Hebrew is properly written.

That designation is used in the Tanakh almost seven thousand times for the name of God. This arrangement of Hebrew letters is sometimes called the Tetragrammaton.[310]

In English, יהוה is transliterated as YHVH or JHVH and articulated as "Yahweh" (*Yah'- way*) or "Jehovah."[311]

The name YHVH is directly related to the Hebrew root verb *Heh-Yud-Heh* ("to be") and reflects the fact that God's existence is eternal. This is why, when God first speaks His name to a human being (Moses), He reveals himself as "I Am" or "I will be what I will be" (Exodus 3:14).

Too Holy

Among the Orthodox Jews, the Tetragrammaton is often referred to as the "Ineffable Name." It is frequently taught that, from time immemorial, the Jews refused to pronounce YHWH because "it is too holy" to utter that name aloud, lest it might be "taken in vain" unintentionally. As a result, many Orthodox Jews, and even some Messianic congregations, vocalize YHWH as *Ha Shem*—"the Name." Often, they will even write the name of God as G-d. See the books of 2 Samuel 6:2, 1 Kings 3:2, and Isaiah 18:7 for examples of where this idea might have taken root.

However, the practice of not pronouncing *the Name* did not occur—at least in an all-inclusive manner—until the destruction of the Temple in AD 70 and in the years beyond.

Throughout the Bible, Yahweh specifically instructs His people to "proclaim His name" (Isaiah 12:4; Psalms 105:1). He even tells them to sing His name and "chant praises to His Name" (Psalms 68:4 and 148:13). There is not a single verse of Scripture wherein God Himself forbids speaking His name. This practice was devised, at first, only by limited sects of Orthodox Judaism, in what is sometimes described as a purely superstitious application.

Consider the following, as iterated in several prominent sources of Jewish history:

> Nothing in the Torah prohibits a person from pronouncing the Name of God. Indeed, it is evident from scripture that God's

Name was pronounced routinely. Many common Hebrew names contain "Yah" or "Yahu," part of God's four-letter Name. The Name was pronounced as part of daily services in the Temple.

The Mishnah confirms that there was no prohibition against pronouncing The Name in ancient times. In fact, the Mishnah recommends using God's Name as a routine greeting to a fellow Jew. Berakhot 9:5.

However, **by the time of the Talmud,** [compiled between the second and fifth centuries AD] **it was the custom to use substitute Names for God**. Some rabbis asserted that a person who pronounces YHVH according to its letters (instead of using a substitute) has no place in the World to Come, and should be put to death. Instead of pronouncing the four-letter Name, we usually substitute the Name "Adonai," or simply say "Ha-Shem" (lit. The Name).

With the Temple destroyed and the prohibition on pronouncing The Name outside of the Temple, pronunciation of the Name fell into disuse.[312] (Emphasis added)

In another example of scholarly research, we find the following:

Some very old fragments of the Septuagint Version of the Old Testament that actually existed in the Messiah's day have survived down to our times; and it should be noted that the personal Name of God appears in them. In 1944, W. G. Waddell discovered the remains of an Egyptian papyrus scroll (Papyrus Fued 266) dating to the first or second century B.C. which included part of the Septuagint. In no instance, however, was YHVH translated into any other form. Instead the Tetragrammaton itself—in square Aramaic letters—was written into the Greek text. This parallels the Qumran sect's use of the paleo-Hebrew script for the Divine Name in a document which was otherwise written in square Aramaic script.

> There are three separate pre-Christian copies of the Greek Septuagint Bible extant today; **and not a single instant** of the Tetragrammaton translated into a Greek form—or, for that matter, translated at all—can be found. As a result, **we can now say, with certainty, that it was a Jewish practice—before, during, and after the New Testament period—to write the Divine Name in the paleo-Hebrew or square, Aramaic script—or in transliteration right into the Greek text of Scripture.**[313] (Emphasis added)

The New International Dictionary of New Testament Theology states:

> Recent textual discoveries cast doubt on the idea that the compilers of the LXX [Septuagint] translated the Tetragrammaton YHVH by [the Greek] *kyrios*. **The oldest LXX MSS (fragments) now available to us have the Tetragrammaton written in Hebrew characters in the Greek text.** This custom was retained by later Jewish translators of the Old Testament in the first centuries A.D.[314] (Emphasis added)

The *Anchor Bible Dictionary* further affirms:

> There is some evidence that the Tetragrammaton, the Divine Name, Yahweh, appeared in some or all of the OT quotations in the NT when the NT documents were first penned.[315]

The Connection

As Rabbi Zev Porat explained in an earlier chapter, the ancient practice of applying Hebrew pictograms to each letter, along with its corresponding meaning, was also discontinued at about the same time the Temple was destroyed and during the dispersion of the earliest New Testament documents. During this same period, the widespread practice of not pronouncing the Tetragrammaton was beginning to bloom.

Why was this period so important? As we have discovered, the most probable reason is directly related to the fact that the pictographic name of Yeshua is represented by the *aleph* and the *tav*—"the one" (*aleph*) "upon the cross" (*tav*). This representation was apparently more than the Orthodox elite could bear.

More than likely, the discontinuation of pronouncing YHWH among the Jews was also the result of a similar problem. We'll discover that particularly challenging snag in the following chapter.

52

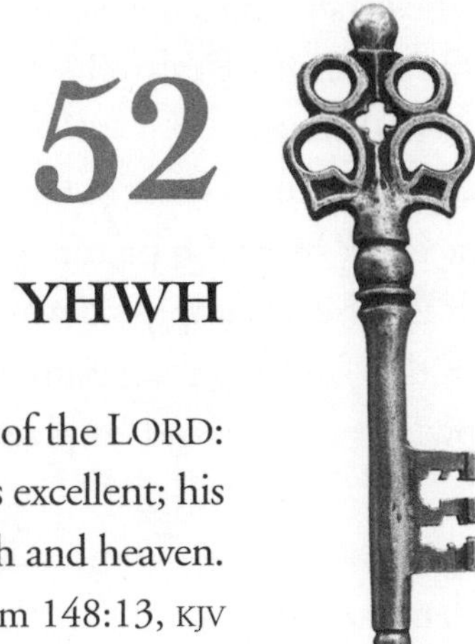

YHWH

Let them praise the name of the LORD:
for his name alone is excellent; his
glory is above the earth and heaven.
—Psalm 148:13, KJV

As we saw in the preceding chapter, the Hebrew letters representing the Name of God are יהוה. Quite shockingly, the pictographic representations of those four letters also link directly to the person of Yeshua.[316]

- The letter *yud* (or *yod*) is represented as *a hand.* It means "a mighty work."
- The letter *waw* (or *vav*), is represented as a *nail* or *spike*, or *tent peg*. It means "to secure—or to save."
- The letter *heh* is represented as a stick-figure man, with his arms raised in amazement. It means "Behold!" or "to look upon" and it occurs twice in the Tetragrammaton.

Taken together, in the most ancient representations known to the Hebrew people, the name YHWH declares: "Behold the hand! Behold the nail!"

On the other hand, if we simply use the ideographic renderings of the letters, the message of Yahweh's name reveals: "Behold! The mighty work that saves and secures."

Really? The Holy Name of God is represented in the Hebrew language as portraying a stunning picture of Yeshua's sacrificial work on the cross? Indeed it is. There's simply no way around it.

Does this startling revelation remind you of anything else? Consider the following passages and emphasized words:

> Then saith [Jesus] to Thomas, Reach hither thy finger, and **behold my hands;** and reach hither thy hand, and thrust it into my side: and be not faithless, but believing. (John 20:27, KJV, emphasis added)

> **They pierce my hands and my feet.** All my bones are on display; people stare and gloat over me. They divide my clothes among them and cast lots for my garment. (Psalm 22:16–18)

> **But he was pierced** for our transgressions, he was crushed for our iniquities; the punishment that brought us peace was on him, and **by his wounds we are healed.** (Isaiah 53:5)

> And I will pour out on the house of David and the inhabitants of Jerusalem a spirit of grace and supplication. **They will look on me, the one they have pierced,** and they will mourn for him as one mourns for an only child, and grieve bitterly for him as one grieves for a firstborn son. (Zechariah 12:10)

> These things happened so that the scripture would be fulfilled: "Not one of his bones will be broken," and, as another scripture says, "**They will look on the one they have pierced.**" (John 19:36–37)

> Look, he is coming with the clouds, and every eye will see him, **even those who pierced him**; and all the peoples of the earth will mourn because of him. (Revelation 1:7)

While this revelation is stunning, it is by no means the only one like it.

Elohim

Elohim (אלוהים) is the first name of God to which we are introduced through the Scriptures. Genesis 1:1 states, "In the beginning, God [*Elohim*] created the heaven and the earth." We are also told that Elohim created the world by separating "the waters" from the midst of the "void" or "chaos" (Genesis 1:1–7).

The word "elohim" is found thousands of times in the Old Testament, second only to the name "Yahweh." Most of the time, the word means "God." However, it is sometimes used to describe the angels of Heaven's court, as well as the fallen realm of Satan (disobedient angels). In those cases, the English translations render the word as "angels," "divine beings," "sons of God" (*bene elohim)*, or simply as "gods." Sometimes the word is used to describe faithful human beings who belong to God through Jesus Christ (Matthew 5:9; John 1:12; Romans 8:14, 19; and Galatians 3:26).

The use of the word, therefore, depends upon the context and the grammatical qualifiers that surround it. By calling the angels "elohim," God is giving something of "His Name" to the angelic realm. He is identifying with the beings of His first creation—a concept that is reinforced, even in the New Testament.[317]

> For this reason I kneel before the Father, **from whom** every family in heaven and on earth **derives its name**. (Ephesians 3:14–15, emphasis added)

> But as many as received him, **to them gave He power to become the sons of God** [*bene elohim*], even to them that believe on his name. (John 1:14, emphasis added)

> Blessed are the peacemakers, for they **will be called sons of God** [*bene elohim*]. (Matthew 5:9, emphasis added)

> Because those who are led by the Spirit of God are **called sons of God** [*bene elohim*]. (Romans 8:14, emphasis added)

Stunningly, the word "elohim," in its ancient pictographic representation, also points directly to *Yeshua Ha' Mashiach*—especially in tying together the biblical truth that Yeshua is none other than "God with us."

Have a look at the Hebrew letters that make up the word "elohim" and what those letters represent when they speak of our Creator:

Aleph – God Himself, the most powerful One

Lamed – The shepherd, represented by the symbol of a shepherd's staff

Heh – Behold, look at

Yod/yud – The mighty work, "the hand"

Mem – Waters, "chaos"

Consequently, the letters that make up the name "Elohim" as it applies to our Creator would easily express something like this: "God, the most powerful Creator, is also our loving Shepherd. Behold! It is He who calmed the waters and brought order out of chaos!"

> So God made the vault and separated the water under the vault from the water above it. And it was so. (Genesis 1:7)

> The [disciples] were amazed and asked, "What kind of man is this? Even the winds and the waves obey him!" (Matthew 8:27)

> The LORD is my shepherd, I shall not want. (Psalm 23, KJV)

[Jesus said to them:] "I am the good shepherd. The good shepherd lays down his life for the sheep." (John 10:11)

Yeshua

Now let's examine the name Yeshua in the same pictographic manner. In Hebrew, Yeshua is spelled with the letters (reading from right to left) *yud–shin–waw–ayin* (עושי).

Following the same Hebrew pictographic charts, we arrive at yet another striking conclusion.

- *Yud:* "A mighty work"; this is represented by the symbol of a hand.
- *Shin:* Since the most ancient of days, this letter has represented Yahweh Himself.[318] It is the single Hebrew letter that stands alone as the "signature stamp" of God's name. It is His "divine mark." It is also the symbol emblazoned on practically every mezuzah that is posted on the doorposts of Orthodox homes and businesses around the world.[319]
- *Waw* (or *vav):* This means "to save, or secure" and is represented by the symbol of a nail or spike.
- *Ayin:* This is represented by the symbol of an eye. Its meaning is "to make known, to see, to understand, or to experience."

By connecting the meanings of all four of those letters, the name Yeshua easily translates to this ideographic meaning: "The mighty work of God's hand of salvation was accomplished by Yahweh Himself. Through this work you are now able to see and know Yahweh, and to experience Him in a personal way; Yeshua is God with us."

Understanding this amazing disclosure, certain New Testament passages now burst forth with new life and fresh contextual perspective:

Jesus answered: "Don't you know me, Philip, even after I have been among you such a long time? Anyone who has seen me has seen the Father. How can you say, 'Show us the Father'?" (John 14:9)

For now we see only a reflection as in a mirror; then we shall see face to face. Now I know in part; then I shall know fully, even as I am fully known. (1 Corinthians 13:12)

Jesus answered, "I am the way and the truth and the life. No one comes to the Father except through me. If you really know me, you will know my Father as well. From now on, you do know him and have seen him." (John 14:6–7)

[Yeshua] is the image of the invisible God, the firstborn over all creation. (Colossians 1:15)

[Yeshua] is the radiance of God's glory and the exact representation of his being. (Hebrews 1:3)

They **will look on me**, the one they have pierced, and they **will mourn for him** as one mourns for an only child. (Zechariah 12:10, emphasis added)

A Potent Witness

Messianic Rabbi Zev Porat says:

What we have been doing in our ministry with a greater urgency than ever is to take these revelations directly to the Jewish people—so they can see these things with their own eyes. When they see them for the very first time, they are absolutely stunned. They simply can't believe it. Some of them even get angry that the rabbis have hidden this information. They actually feel betrayed.

I believe that by revealing these irrefutable connections, the attempt of the rabbis to hide the truth will ultimately backfire on them. The Jewish people love the history of their ancestors. They love learning about the origins of our ancient language. When they discover that an important part of that history has been effectively eliminated or purposely concealed, they become very upset. They are ready to listen. They know that there must be a reason for the concealment.

With today's technological advancements in spreading information to the entire planet within minutes, there's no way that the truth of these discoveries can be contained any longer. The more this evidence gets out, the more the Jewish people will understand that Rabbi Kaduri's Yeshua note was not far-fetched at all. They will understand that it was not some sort of trick. Rabbi Kaduri's note actually revealed the eternal truth; *Yeshua is Messiah!* And that truth has been there since the beginning—hidden in the names of YWHW, Elohim, and Yeshua!

The Word Became Flesh

Is there any wonder, then, that the disappearance of the teaching of the Hebrew pictograms happened to correspond with the destruction of the Temple and the first several decades just after the ministry, crucifixion, and resurrection of Yeshua/Jesus?

The elimination of that important linguistic teaching also parallels the arrival of the first New Testament documents, which were being profusely circulated among the first-century Church—a body consisting primarily of Jewish believers in Yeshua. Mere coincidence? Probably not.

The pictograms God originally put in the minds of the very earliest Hebrew people, as they were hammering out those symbols on stone, would later testify to the most complete meaning of God's Holy Name. Surely, the primeval Hebrews would have had no clue as to how those symbols would one day in the distant future declare the truth of the gospel message. It was as if the ancient words had actually turned into a physical reality—*in the flesh.*

This is why an ancient Jewish man by the name of John, an original follower of *Yeshua Ha' Mashiach*, penned the following divinely inspired words:

> In the beginning was the Word, and the Word was with God, and the Word was God. He was with God in the beginning. Through him all things were made; without him nothing was made that has been made....
>
> The Word became flesh and made his dwelling among us. We have seen his glory, the glory of the one and only Son, who came from the Father, full of grace and truth. (John 1:1–3, 14)

The Word "that became flesh" is none other than the Holy Name that pictographically translates to "behold the hand, behold the nail." That Living Word became flesh in the person of Yeshua, through Whom the world can now *see* Yahweh and His mighty act of salvation. He is the same One who parts the waters of chaos.

This is exactly what many Jews today are coming to understand. Yeshua/Jesus is indeed Messiah. He is "God with us." He is the heavenly "sign" upon whom they have long been waiting.

> Therefore the Lord Himself shall give you a sign: behold, the young woman shall conceive, and bear a son, and shall call his name Immanuel [God with us]. (Isaiah 7:1, JPS Tanakh 1917)

Of course, it helps tremendously that the Jews' most beloved Orthodox rabbi, Yitzhak Kaduri, confirmed this through his Yeshua note back in 2007.

By now you can clearly understand why the Orthodox elite in Israel eventually did away with "speaking" God's Name, as well as with the pictographic meanings of the most ancient form of the Hebrew language. They all point to Yeshua as Messiah and LORD.

It appears the "deep state" and the "fake news" have been alive and well...all the way back to the Garden of Eden.[320] This is why the Apostle Paul warned that our battle is not really against flesh and blood.

> Finally, be strong in the Lord and in his mighty power. Put on the full armor of God, so that you can take your stand against the devil's schemes. For our struggle is not against flesh and blood, but against the rulers, against the authorities, against the powers of this dark world and against the spiritual forces of evil in the heavenly realms. (Ephesians 6:10–12)

53

Yeshua Shemi

And they shall call his name Emmanuel,
which being interpreted is, God with us.
—Matthew 1:23

Ecclesiastes 1:9 declares, "What has been will be again, what has been done will be done again; there is nothing new under the sun."

In so many ways, the world is swinging right back to the days of Jesus' earthly ministry. The Sanhedrin Council is once again seated in the heart of Israel. The Jewish-elite power structure is strong and often exerts tremendous pressure upon government and media figures as well as the general populace. The abject rejection, even hatred, of the very Name of Jesus is as strong as ever—perhaps stronger. The vitriolic reaction to His Name has now had over two thousand years in which to stew and ferment.

In addition to those prophetic elements, the direct persecution of Christians the world over is now at an all-time high.[321] Most of that persecution—and not by mere happenstance—takes place in the Land of the Bible (the Middle East, North Africa, and parts of Asia).[322] Here is the place where humanity and its fallen civilizations commenced, and this is the place where God's Word and final plan will culminate. Here is where the prophesied "war of the ages" is heating up right before our eyes. This area of the planet truly is the spiritual *Ground Zero*...and it always has been.[323]

Of Whom Does the Prophet Speak?

Since we have spent quite a bit of time focusing upon the prophecy of Isaiah 53—the last known special preaching focus of Rabbi Yitzhak Kaduri in his synagogue just before his passing—let's take one final moment to reconsider a passage from the New Testament regarding that same message.

The book of Acts contains striking commentary on what the first-century Jews believed about Isaiah 53, especially that passage's predictions concerning the Messiah:

> 30 Then Philip[324] ran up to the chariot and heard the man reading Isaiah the prophet. "**Do you understand what you are reading?**" Philip asked.
> 31 "How can I," he said, "unless someone explains it to me?" So he invited Philip to come up and sit with him.
> 32 This is the passage of Scripture the eunuch was reading: "He was led like a sheep to the slaughter, and as a lamb before its shearer is silent, so he did not open his mouth.
> 33 In his humiliation he was deprived of justice. Who can speak of his descendants? For his life was taken from the earth."
> 34 The eunuch asked Philip, "Tell me, please, **who is the prophet talking about, himself or someone else?**"
> 35 Then Philip began with that very passage of Scripture and told him the good news about Jesus. (Acts 8:30–35, emphasis added)

Yes indeed. In the end of it all, Rabbi Yitzhak Kaduri got it right—just like the man in the chariot. Kaduri saw it! Apparently, along with a huge number of other Jewish people around the world, he recognized the revelation of *Yeshua Ha' Mashiach* within the words of the prophet Isaiah.

And, according to his own testimony, like the Apostle Paul, Rabbi Kaduri actually met Yeshua in a vision.

At the time of his death, almost a hundred years after Rabbi Chaim's prophecy had originally been spoken over him in the land of Iraq, Yitzhak Kaduri had become the most venerated rabbi in Israel's modern history. After he had gathered up a following of millions around the world, and in the waning years of his extensive life, the Lord of Glory revealed to him the truth upon which he had been patiently waiting …

Yeshua Shemi!… "Jesus is my name."

54

The Note That Shook the World

Once Rabbi Yitzhak Kaduri picked up his pen and arranged that now-legendary collection of six specific, coded Hebrew words on a piece of paper, he set in motion a divine course that would spark a spiritual firestorm, ultimately leading a multitude of Jewish people to Christ. In so doing, he laid upon *the altar of sacrifice* his amazingly renowned Orthodox Jewish legacy, while at the same time leaving numerous disciples to carry on that eternally significant message.

No, this story is not a lie, a fraud, or a trick. Neither is it a case of "mistaken interpretation." What it became was nothing short of earth-shattering. That mysterious Yeshua note was the very revelation the Jewish world needed, and it came from just the one through whom it needed to be heard—and at just the right time. From Heaven's Throne to Rabbi Yitzhak Kaduri's heart.

The rage of Satan's domain still rails against Rabbi Kaduri's global revelation and against those who continue to proliferate the stunning message it reveals. Regardless, the Kingdom of Jesus Christ continues to rush forward in victory—smack in the middle of the most prophetic days in the history of humanity's existence.

You are living in the midst of those days right now.
This story is not yet over—*not even close.*
In fact, I believe it has only just begun.

For I tell you, you will not see me again until you say, "Blessed is he who comes in the name of the Lord." (Matthew 23:39)

His intent was that now, through the church, the manifold wisdom of God should be made known to the rulers and authorities in the heavenly realms. (Ephesians 3:10)

ABOUT THE AUTHORS

Carl Gallups

Carl Gallups has been the senior pastor of Hickory Hammock Baptist Church in Milton, Florida, since 1987. He is a graduate of the Florida Law Enforcement Academy, Florida State University (BSc., Criminology) and New Orleans Baptist Theological Seminary (MDiv), and serves on the Board of Regents at the University of Mobile in Mobile, Alabama.

Carl is a former decorated Florida law enforcement officer, having served under three sheriffs with two different sheriff's offices. He was also appointed as a special deputy, in January 2016, under former Sheriff Joe Arpaio, Maricopa County, Arizona.

Pastor Gallups is a critically acclaimed, Amazon Top 60 bestselling author of multiple books, a talk-radio host since 2002, and a regular guest pundit on numerous television and radio programs as well as various print media sources. He is also a frequent guest preacher at national prophecy and Bible conferences. He has preached the Gospel of Jesus Christ on three continents, in four nations, and all over the United States and Canada—including Hawaii and Alaska.

Carl was featured on *Fox News Business Report* in 2016 as an "influential evangelical leader," publicly endorsing candidate Donald Trump for the office of president. Carl was asked by the Trump campaign to open the internationally broadcast Trump for President Rally in Pensacola, Florida, in January 2016. More than twelve thousand people attended that rally.

Pastor Gallups and Messianic Rabbi Zev Porat have been in close ministry affiliation since 2014. They often travel and speak together in television and radio media appearances, as well as at prophecy conferences and church settings.

Carl lives in Milton, Florida, with his wife, Pam. You can find more information about him at www.carlgallups.com.

Zev Porat

Messianic Rabbi Zev Porat was born and raised in Israel. As a child, because of his father's Orthodox rabbinic work, he spent a great deal of time on both the East and West Coasts of the United States. Hebrew is Zev's first language, but he also speaks, reads, and writes fluent English.

Zev served several years in the Israel Defense Forces and its reserves. He was raised in an Orthodox rabbinical family. His father, grandfather, and great-grandfather were all very influential rabbis in Israel. He and his family are still deeply connected to important Israeli government officials as well as the Orthodox rabbinical community.

He is the founder and director of the world-reaching Messiah of Israel Ministries centered in Tel Aviv, Israel. Zev is frequently featured in numerous international media venues, mainly in Europe and the United States, in addition to being a sought-after conference speaker and guest preacher. Zev has ministered in hundreds of underground church congregations in China as well.

Messianic Rabbi Zev Porat lives in Tel Aviv, Israel.

You can find more information about Messianic Rabbi Zev Porat at www.messiahofisraelministries.org.

ACKNOWLEDGMENTS

I want to give a special thanks to my ministry partner Carl Gallups—also, to his wife Pam, his son Brandon Gallups, and to PNN Executive Editor Mike Shoesmith. You are all a huge part of this amazing Kaduri journey.

I wish to thank Tom Horn and the remarkable team at Defender Publishing, as well as the entire SkyWatch TV team—particularly Joe Horn, Derek Gilbert, and Sharon Gilbert.

I especially would like to extend a word of gratitude to my ministry team at Messiah of Israel Ministries in Tel Aviv and the believers around the world for faithfully standing with us in the middle of these crucially prophetic times.

—Zev Porat

To Pam. Long before we were married, I became keenly aware that my life would be forever and profoundly impacted by yours. Thank you for walking this journey with me, faithfully by my side. You are an amazing blessing from the Lord.

To Tom Horn and all the crew at Defender Publishing and SkyWatch TV, and especially my amazing and patient editor—Angie Peters. You guys are the greatest! What a blessing you are to my family and me.

As the reader has already discovered, this book would not have been possible without the ministry partnership and deep friendship that I share with Zev Porat. I praise Yeshua for him and his amazing ministry team.

—Carl Gallups

NOTES

1. Gallups, Carl. "The Rabbi Who Found Messiah: The Story of Yitzhak Kaduri and His Prophecies of the Endtimes." WND Books, Washington D.C., November 2013.
2. Dictionary, "Divine," Merriam-Webster, Accessed April 22, 2018, https://www.merriam-webster.com/dictionary/divine.
3. WND.com. "Messiah Mystery Follows Death of Mystical Rabbi," WND.com, 5-18-07, http://www.wnd.com/2007/05/41669.
4. Yom Kippur is the holiest day of the year for the Orthodox Jew. *Yom Kippur* means "Day of Atonement." As Leviticus 16:30 states, "For on this day He will forgive you, to purify you, that you be cleansed from all your sins before God." See also Leviticus 23:26–32 for the Day of Atonement as one of the seven Holy Feasts of the Lord.
   Also See:
   a.) Rabbi Steinberg, Paul. "Erev (Night Of) Yom Kippur," My Jewish Learning, Accessed June 23, 2018, https://www.myjewishlearning.com/article/erev-yom-kippur.
   b.) Rabbi Posner, Menachem. "What You Need to Know About Yom Kippur Synagogue Services," Chabad.org, Accessed June 12, 2018, https://www.chabad.org/library/article_cdo/aid/1965282/jewish/What-You-Need-to-Know-About-Yom-Kippur-Synagogue-Services.htm.
5. The Jews referred to the "teacher's seat" in the same way we might speak of a professor's "chair" in a university (*Clarke's Commentary*, vol. 5, p. 217). "By 'the seat of Moses' (Matthew 23:2) we are to understand 'authority to teach the law.' It had long been the custom of the Jewish teachers to sit as they taught from the Law and the Prophets, but to stand as they read from these works [see: Luke 4:16, 20–21]."
6. *The Sh'ma Prayer* serves as a focal point of the morning and evening Orthodox Jewish prayer services. *Shema Yisrael* translates to: "Hear O' Israel." These are the opening words of Deuteronomy 6:4. Often, the one reciting that prayer will do so with eyes covered, one hand resting gently over the brow.
   See: Dr. Tigay, Jeffery. "Deuteronomy 6:4—The Shema," *My Jewish Learning*, https://www.myjewishlearning.com/article/deuteronomy-64-the-shema.
7. Dr. Tigay, Jeffery. "Deuteronomy 6:4—The Shema," *My Jewish Learning*, https://www.myjewishlearning.com/article/deuteronomy-64-the-shema. At this link is an article outlining in detail the extremely ritualistic and codified services of a typical Orthodox Yom Kippur. There is no mention of anyone

actually "preaching" or bringing an extemporaneous message of any kind. That is simply not done in a Yom Kippur service.

8. Rabbi Yitzhak Kaduri's actual age is unknown. He is widely reported to have been between 104 and 108 years old at the time of his death. The date of his birth is apparently uncertain. See: https://ffoz.org/discover/yahrzeit/the-man-to-whom-messiah-revealed-his-name.html.
9. Joffe, Lawrence. "Rabbi Yitzhak Kaduri: Mercurial Jewish Mystic Who Threw His Weight behind Rightwing Israeli Politicians," *The Guardian*, 1-30-2006, https://www.theguardian.com/news/2006/jan/31/guardianobituaries.israel.
10. France-Presse, Agence. "Tens of Thousands Attend Funeral of Kabbalist Rabbi," *The New York Times*, January 30, 2006, https://www.nytimes.com/2006/01/30/world/middleeast/tens-of-thousands-attend-funeral-of-kabbalist-rabbi.html.
11. Hillel, Fendel. "Over 300,000 at Funeral of World's Senior Kabbalist Rabbi," *Israel National News*, 1-29-06, https://www.israelnationalnews.com/News/News.aspx/97471.
12. Rabbi Ovadia Yosef's funeral, in 2013, would have some eight hundred thousand people present. Rabbi Yosef and Rabbi Kaduri were contemporaries and were both Sephardic rabbis. See: Fiske, Gavriel. "Rabbi Ovadia Yosef Buried in Largest Funeral in Israeli History," *Times of Israel*, October 7, 2013, https://www.timesofisrael.com/jerusalem-closes-down-for-rabbi-ovadia-yosefs-funeral. Also see: Wagner, Matthew. "Kaduri Obituary," *Jerusalem Post*, 1-25-06, https://www.jpost.com/Jewish-World/Jewish-News/Kaduri-obituary.
13. Later in this book you will read the exact words, spoken by an extremely credible witness and prominent US Jewish media figure who claimed to be connected to the sources of the note's destruction. His stunning disclosure was given live over a nationally broadcast radio program on which I was the guest interviewee.
14. As of this writing, that interview can be seen at: "Carl Gallups/Pat Boone (TBN) The Rabbi Who Found Messiah," https://www.youtube.com/watch?v=hFih3XFDels.
15. **Jew**…The English term "Jew" originates in the Biblical Hebrew word *Yehudi*, meaning "from the Kingdom of Judah." The term "Jews" first appears in 2 Kings 16:6. See: Gilad, Elan. "Why Are Jews Called Jews?" *Haaretz*, 2-15-17, https://www.haaretz.com/archaeology/why-are-jews-called-jews-1.5410757.
16. The word "Hebrew" occurs for the first time in Scripture in Genesis 14:13. It is a title used of the Israelites. The word probably means "descendant of Eber." Eber was an ancestor of the Israelites and the Ishmaelites. See the Table of Nations in Genesis 10–11 and 1 Chronicles 1.

    Eber was a great-grandson of Noah's son Shem. Some scholars believe the term "Hebrew" means "from the other side"—particularly of the Euphrates River—

where Abraham originated, the land of Ur of the Chaldees. Those who trace their lineage to Abraham are the Hebrew people.

17. **The Use of the Title "Rabbi"**: A Messianic rabbi is a teacher/preacher who, usually coming from an Orthodox Jewish background, becomes a believer in Yeshua/Jesus as Messiah and Savior. Usually that rabbi leads a congregation or study group of other Jews who believe in Yeshua as well. Many Gentile believers in Jesus Christ also belong to these Messianic Jewish congregations and study groups. Generally, the desire of most Gentiles who choose to belong to such congregations is that they might learn more about the Hebrew foundations of Scripture and biblical interpretation since, sadly, the vast majority of typical evangelical congregations do not delve deeply into these matters.
18. Zev Porat (www.messiahofisraelministries.org); Messiah of Israel Ministries now possesses a huge gospel ministry footprint around the world, particularly in the Jewish world within Israel.
    Every word attributed to Zev Porat in this book was provided either in writing or digital recording provided exclusively for this work. The content has been read and approved by him and attested to as an accurate representation of his words and testimony.
19. *Yahweh*. The God of the Israelites and of the Bible, whose name was revealed to Moses as four Hebrew consonants (YHWH) called the Tetragrammaton. See: https://www.britannica.com/topic/Yahweh.
20. A Yeshiva is a Jewish rabbinical training school or "seminary." As of June 2018, two of these videos featuring Kaduri's yeshiva students can be seen at the following addresses:
    a.) Rabbi Kaduri Student Saved, https://www.youtube.com/watch?v=zIldXZcs8pg.
    b.) The Kaduri Revival Continues in Israel, https://www.youtube.com/watch?v=BtuhmEuDpQs&t=27s.
21. "Organization of the Nascent Sanhedrin," Accessed June 12, 2018, http://www.thesanhedrin.org/en/index.php/Organization_of_the_Nascent_Sanhedrin.
22. Gallups, Carl. *The Rabbi Who Found Messiah: The Story of Yitzhak Kaduri and His Prophecies of the Endtimes*. WND Books, Washington D.C., November 2013.
23. Arutz Sheva. "Audio: 20th VJRI Noahide Conference with Larry Borntrager," *Israel National News*, 6-14-10, https://www.israelnationalnews.com/Radio/News.aspx/2292#.WzOTD9JKhdg.
24. Kress, Michael. "The Modern Noahide Movement," *My Jewish Learning*, Accessed June 22, 2018, https://www.myjewishlearning.com/article/the-modern-noahide-movement.

25. The following explanations of the "Noahide" are found at: Korn, Eugene. Boston College Center for Jewish Christian Learning. "Noahide Covenant: Theology and Jewish Law," Accessed June 12, 2018, https://www.bc.edu/content/dam/files/research_sites/cjl/texts/cjrelations/resources/sourcebook/Noahide_covenant.htm.
The descendants of Noah were commanded with seven precepts: to establish laws, (and the prohibitions of) blasphemy, idolatry, adultery, bloodshed, theft, and eating the blood of a living animal.—Babylonian Talmud, Sanhedrin 56a. As such, classical Judaism subscribed to a double covenant theory: Jews have the Torah covenant of 613 commandments and all gentiles have a covenant of seven Noahide mitzvot, each covenant being valid for its respective adherents. Conventionally, only those accepting the covenant are termed 'b'nai Noah' (sons of Noah, or Noahides). Noahides are not expected to convert to Judaism, for they have an independently authentic covenant that governs a valid way of life.
Noahides are accorded positive status in this worldview, to the extent that gentiles who faithfully keep the Noahide commandments are regarded as more beloved by God [i.e., more valued] than Jews who violate the fundamentals of their covenant of 613 commandments. This is clearly evidenced by the Talmudic and medieval rabbinic claim that "righteous gentiles have a share in the world to come" [i.e., salvation earned by their exemplary lives on earth], whereas Jews who commit grievous sins do not earn that status.
26. Fendel, Hillel. "Noahide Archaeologist Vendyl Jones Passes Away," *Israel National News*, 12-37-10, https://www.israelnationalnews.com/News/News.aspx/141371.
27. *Yeshua Ha' Mashiach* is a Hebrew phrase meaning "Jesus the Christ" or "Jesus the Messiah."
28. The rabbis teach that *Messiah ben (son of) Joseph* (a strictly human figure—a military or political leader) will be anointed by God to battle the enemies of Israel and then lead Israel and the Jews to a place of strength and righteousness so that the ultimate Messiah, the true Savior of Israel, can finally appear. The second Messiah figure is known as *Messiah ben David*, and is the one who will finally establish the longed-for Messianic Kingdom on earth. He is the "ultimate" Messiah upon whom the Orthodox Jews are desperately waiting. This understanding is the Jewish "Two Messiah" teaching.
29. Chuck Mohler's testimony was sent to me in a personal email. His testimony has been reviewed by him and approved in writing for printing in this book.
30. Staff. "The Bible Society in Israel Brings the Scriptures to the Holy Land," *Kehila News*, 4-14-17, https://kehilanews.com/2017/04/14/the-bible-society-in-israel-brings-the-scriptures-to-the-holy-land. **The Bible Society's** website is the only all-Hebrew online source for the free study of Scriptures. This website

is seeing traffic from Israel and around the world. See: http://www.haktuvim.co.il.

31. France-Presse, Agence. "Tens of Thousands Attend Funeral of Kabbalist Rabbi," *New York Times*, January 30, 2006, https://www.nytimes.com/2006/01/30/world/middleeast/tens-of-thousands-attend-funeral-of-kabbalist-rabbi.html.
32. Sephardic Jews. "After their Expulsion from Spain in 1492, Sephardic Jews Mostly Settled in Amsterdam, North Africa and the Middle East." Shephardic Jews are of Mediterranean and Middle Eastern descent and the Ashkenazi Jews are of European descent. These are the two main "divisions" or "denominations" among the Orthodox Jews. See: "Who Are Sephardic Jews?" https://www.myjewishlearning.com/article/who-are-sephardic-jews/.
33. Shas Party. "Shas (Hebrew acronym for *Shomrei Sfarad*, literally meaning "ephardi Guards") is an ultra-Orthodox political party in Israel founded by Rav Ovadiah Yosef in 1984." See: "Israel Political Parties: Shas," http://www.jewishvirtuallibrary.org/shas-political-party.
34. The Likud Party is a right-wing political party in Israel founded by revolutionary leader Menachem Begin and was the first right-leaning party to lead the Israeli government. It is currently headed by Prime Minister Benjamin Netanyahu. See: Jewish Virtual Library, "Likud Party: History & Overview," Accessed July 23, 2018, https://www.jewishvirtuallibrary.org/history-and-overview-of-the-likud-party.
35. Joffe, Lawrence. "Rabbi Yitzhak Kaduri: Mercurial Jewish Mystic Who Threw His Weight behind Rightwing Israeli Politicians," *The Guardian*, 1-30-2006, https://www.theguardian.com/news/2006/jan/31/guardianobituaries.israel.
36. *The Christian Science Monitor*. "Why Is Israel Pulling Out Settlers from Gaza, West Bank?" August 15, 2005, https://www.csmonitor.com/2005/0815/p10s01-wome.html.
37. **Kabbalah and *Pulsa Denura*** – Definitions:
Pulsa Denura – Hebrew for "lashings of fire," or "bullets of fire."
Quoted from *ReformJudiasm.org:*
"**Kabbalah** (also spelled Kabalah, Cabala, Qabala)—sometimes translated as "mysticism" or "occult knowledge."
"The Zohar, a collection of written, mystical commentaries on the Torah, is considered to be the underpinning of Kabbalah. Written in medieval Aramaic and medieval Hebrew, the Zohar is intended to guide Kabbalists in their spiritual journey, helping them attain the greater levels of connectedness with God that they desire.
The practical dimension of Kabbalah involves rituals for gaining and exercising power to affect change in our world and in the celestial worlds beyond.
This power is generated by performing commandments, summoning and

controlling angelic and demonic forces, and otherwise tapping into the supernatural energies present in Creation. The practical aspect of Kabbalah furthers God's intention in the world, advancing good, subduing evil, healing, and mending. The true master of this art fulfills the human potential to be a co-creator with God."
Reference: Rabbi Dennis, Geoffrey W. "What Is Kabbalah?" *ReformJudiasm.org*, accessed 4-25-18, https://reformjudaism.org/what-kabbalah.
Quoted from *Haaretz*:
"***Pulsa Denura*** is commonly considered the most severe of kabbalistic curses. According to descriptions found in books and the media, ten righteous kabbalists gather at midnight in a synagogue, by the light of black candles, blow shofars and recite the curse. If the curse has been uttered by worthy and righteous men and against an appropriate target, the target is supposed to die within the year." Reference: Ilan, Shahar. "The Original Pulsa Denura," *Haaretz*, 05-04-05, https://www.haaretz.com/1.4853346.

38. Barkat, Amiram. "Extremists Put Pulsa Denura Death Curse on PM Ariel Sharon," *Haaretz*, 07-27-05, https://www.haaretz.com/1.4925355.SEE ALSO: Weiss, Efrat. "Extremists Curse Olmert with Pulsa Denura," *Ynet News*, 06-26-06, https://www.ynetnews.com/articles/0,7340,L-3268259,00.html.
39. The collective body of Jewish religious laws derived from the written and oral Torah.
40. Barkat, Amiram. "Extremists Put Pulsa Denura Death Curse on PM Ariel Sharon," *Haaretz*, 07-27-05, https://www.haaretz.com/1.4925355.
41. Joffe, Lawrence. "Rabbi Yitzhak Kaduri: Mercurial Jewish Mystic Who Threw His Weight behind Rightwing Israeli Politicians," *Guardian*, 01-30-2006, https://www.theguardian.com/news/2006/jan/31/guardianobituaries.israel.
42. Marciano, Ilan. "Rabbi Kaduri in Serious Condition," Ynet News, 01-16-06, https://www.ynetnews.com/articles/0,7340,L-3200573,00.html.
43. WND.com. "Messiah Mystery Follows Death of Mystical Rabbi," 05-18-07, http://www.wnd.com/2007/05/41669.
44. That original article is no longer available on *Israel Today's* website. However, it was reproduced, word-for-word, by several other website owners before it was reprinted with the mysterious disappearance of the section titled, "The Rabbi's Followers React." You can see those reproductions at the following websites as of 05-04-18.
    a.) Unleavened Bread Ministries, "Rabbi Reveals Name of Messiah," (reprint from Israel Today's 4-30-07 article), accessed 05-04-18, http://www.ubm1.org/?page=rabbireveals.
    b.) Rav. Reuven ben Gershom, "Prominent Israeli Rabbi Reveals the Name of the Messiah," Teshuva International, 10-14-08, http://www.rmi-ministries.com/rabbi-reveals-the-messiah.htm.

c.) World Historia, "Rabbi Reveals Name of the Messiah," 10-30-2007, https://archive.fo/OYIbV. (This copy/paste of the original article was posted within months of the original's posting—once again proving that the original has since been significantly altered.)

d.) The original Web-posted article (at an archived URL): Schneider, Aviel, "Rabbi Reveals Name of the Messiah," 04-30-07, https://web.archive.org/web/20070702085646/http://www.israeltoday.co.il:80/default.aspx?tabid=128&view=item&idx=1347.

45. Fraser, Giles. "Christians Must Understand That for Jews the Cross Is a Symbol of Oppression," *Guardian*, 04-25-14, https://www.theguardian.com/commentisfree/2014/apr/25/jews-cross-symbol-of-oppression-christians.
46. Ryan Jones, e-mail message to author on April 2013 and May 29–30, 2013.
47. I am in possession of the lengthy email exchange between the *Israel Today* representative and me. He has asked to remain anonymous. Since he had been so cooperative with me in getting to the bottom of the discrepancies, I was more than glad to oblige. I can assure the reader that this *Israel Today* representative is legitimate and trustworthy, as I have been in correspondence with him several times since writing my first book. Everything he has told me in the past has proven accurate. I have no reason to doubt his explanation as represented in this chapter.
48. Gallups, Carl. "Hebrew Alphabet/Pictograms Chart," Carlgallups.com, accessed July 12, 2018, http://www.carlgallups.com/hebrewpictograms.gif.
49. Studylight.org. "Ancient Hebrew Alphabet," (Al-Aleph), Accessed June 23, 2018, https://www.studylight.org/lexicons/hebrew/ahl_alphabet.html.
50. In ancient Judaism, the ox was a significant offering. The Bible lists it as the animal to be used for the peace offering. It was the most valuable of all the animal sacrifices in ancient Jewish life, representing the wealth, livelihood, and continued prosperity of the owner. See: "The Spiritual Significance of the Ox in Scripture - Part One," Accessed July 12, 2018, http://www.iswasandwillbe.com/The_Spiritual_Significance_Of_The_Ox_In_Scripture_Part_One.php. "The ox is…associated with service and production, and increase of wealth. In early ancient Israel, the ox was the single most valuable animal one could own. To steal a man's ox was just like stealing his livelihood. It was his most valuable possession."
51. See Psalm 22:16–18; Zechariah 12:10; and Isaiah 53:5–6.
52. In several of the last chapters of this book, I explore the pictographic meanings of the Hebrew words *Yahweh, Elohim*, and *Yeshua*. Combining the information about the *aleph* and *tav* that you just read, with the amazing revelations yet to come, will open up an entirely new world of understanding, especially if you have never before seen these connections.
53. Handelzalts, Michael. "In the Beginning: The Origins of the Hebrew

Alphabet," *Haaretz*, 08-04-13, https://www.haaretz.com/jewish/.premium-why-hebrew-should-be-called-jewish-1.5316745.

54. Various screen captures, an archived original article, and copy/paste repostings of that original *Israel Today* Internet article, complete with the material about the "angel" and the "cross signs," are still available on the Internet as of this writing. Apparently, however, they are no longer a part of *Israel Today's* official reporting of the Kaduri note.
    a.) The original Web-posted article (at an archived URL): Schneider, Aviel, "Rabbi Reveals Name of the Messiah," 04-30-07, https://web.archive.org/web/20070702085646/http://www.israeltoday.co.il:80/default.aspx?tabid=128&view=item&idx=1347.
    b.) The reposted article: Schneider, Aviel. "The Rabbi, the Note and the Messiah," *Israel Today*, Thursday, May 30, 2007, http://www.israeltoday.co.il/NewsItem/tabid/178/nid/23877/Default.aspx.
55. *WND,* "Messiah Mystery Follows Death of Mystical Rabbi," WND.com, 05-18-07, http://www.wnd.com/2007/05/41669/.
56. The original Web-posted article (at an archived URL): Schneider, Aviel, "Rabbi Reveals Name of the Messiah," 04-30-07, https://web.archive.org/web/20070702085646/http://www.israeltoday.co.il:80/default.aspx?tabid=128&view=item&idx=1347.
57. *Month of Mercy*. "What Is Elul? A Month of Mercy," Jewishcontent.org, accessed April 24, 2018, http://www.jewishcontent.org/cgi-bin/calendar?holiday=tishrei201.
58. For further reference concerning Hebrew acrostics, see J. A. Motyer, "Acrostic," in *The New International Dictionary of the Bible* (Grand Rapids: Zondervan, 1987), p. 12.
59. *Yehoshua* and *Yeshua* are, in effect, the same name, derived from the same Hebrew root of the word "salvation." (Some researchers claim that inserting the divine abbreviation *ho* into the name *Yeshua* points to the God-Man nature of the true Messiah, who would be both God and man at the same time.) The name *Yeshua* corresponds to the Romanized, Greek spelling, *Iesous*, from which comes the English spelling "Jesus." Dr. Price, James. "The Names Yeshua and Yehoshua," Essene.com, accessed April 12, 2018, http://www.essene.com/Yeshua/yehoshua.htm. "Thus, it can be concluded that in post-exilic times of the Biblical era, the names Yeshua and Yehoshua were regarded as equivalent.... As far as the Talmud is concerned, it is evident that the old uncensored editions of the Talmud associated Jesus [Yeshua] of Nazareth with the name Joshua [Yehosua]. This is demonstrated by the following passage: Sotah 47a."
60. *HELPS Greek Word-Studies* – NT 2424 Iēsoús – Jesus, the transliteration of the Hebrew term, OT 3091 ("Yehoshua"/Jehoshua, contracted to "Joshua")

which means "Yahweh saves" (or "Yahweh is salvation"). See: http://biblehub.com/greek/2424.htm.

61. Meyer, Stan. "Why Do Most Jews Not Believe in Jesus?" Jews for Jesus, 03-28-18, https://jewsforjesus.org/answers/why-do-most-jews-not-believe-in-jesus.
62. Foote, George W.; Wheeler, J.M., eds. (1885). *The Jewish Life of Christ: Being the Sepher Toldoth Jeshu* (London: Progressive Publishing Company). Accessed April 21, 2018, http://www.ftarchives.net/foote/toldoth/tjtitle.htm.
63. Howard, George (1995). "Shem-Tob and the Tol'doth Yeshu." Hebrew Gospel of Matthew. Macon, Georgia: Mercer University Press. pp. 206–211. Also see: Edman, L. (1857). Sefer Toledot Yeshu: sive Liber de ortu et origine Jesu ex editione wagenseiliana transcriptus et explicatus [Sefer Toledot Yeshu: or *The Book of the Rising and Origin of Jesus from the Wagenseiliana edition: Transcription and Explanation*]. (Nabu Press, May 25, 2010), C. A. Leffler. p. 8.
   Michael H. Cohen, *A Friend of All Faiths*, page 42, 2004: "In Hebrew school, one of my teachers had explained that Yeshu (Hebrew for Jesus), rather than meaning "Saviour," in fact was an acronym that stood for *yimach shemo ve-zichrono*: "may his name and memory be erased."
   Proceedings: Volume 4 Akademyah ha-le'umit ha-Yiśre'elit le-mada'im – 1969: "Perhaps the most significant of these is the passage where instead of the printed 'that certain man' we find 'Jesus the Nazarene—may his name be obliterated' (thus also in a Genizah MS, British Museum, Or. 91842)."
64. Maltz, Steve. "Bad Names for Jesus," January 2013, accessed April 19, 2018, https://www.premier.org.uk/Blogs/Yeshua-Explored/Bad-Names-for-Jesus.
65. The Talmud is an immense body of Jewish civil and ceremonial law and legend comprising the Mishnah (collection of oral traditions) and the Gemara (a rabbinical commentary on the Mishnah). There are two versions of the Talmud: the Babylonian Talmud (which dates from the fifth century AD but includes earlier material) and the earlier Palestinian or Jerusalem Talmud.
66. There are no undisputed examples of any Aramaic or Hebrew text wherein Yeshu refers to anyone other than Jesus. See: *Jesus Outside the New Testament*, p. 124, Robert E. Van Voorst—2000: "This is likely an inference from the Talmud and other Jewish usage, where Jesus is called Yeshu, and other Jews with the same name are called by the fuller name Yehoshua, 'Joshua' (e.g., b Sanh. 107b)." However, a popular Jewish tradition states that the shortening to Yeshu relates to the *Y-SH-U* of the *yimach shemo,* "may his name be obliterated." See: Michael H. Cohen, *A Friend of All Faiths,* Page 42, 2004: "In Hebrew school, one of my teachers had explained that Yeshu (Hebrew for Jesus), rather than meaning 'Saviour,' in fact was an acronym that stood for *yimach shemo ve-zichrono*: "may his name and memory be erased." Also see: *Proceedings: Volume 4, Akademyah ha-le'umit ha-Yiśre'elit le-mada'im* – 1969: "Perhaps the most significant of these is the passage where instead of

the printed 'that certain man' we find "Jesus the Nazarene—may his name be obliterated' (thus also in a Genizah MS, British Museum, Or. 91842)."

67. Wikipedia, "Yeshu," Accessed June 3, 2018, https://en.wikipedia.org/wiki/Yeshua#cite_note-33. This statement in the Wikipedia article on Yeshu references the following sources of the assertion: J. Maier Jesus von Nazareth 1978. G. Theissen, *Historical Jesus*, 1998. R. Voorst, Jesus Outside the New Testament 2000.
68. *The Book of the Generations/History/Life of Jesus*, often abbreviated as Toledot Yeshu, is an early Jewish text taken to be an alternative biography of Jesus. It exists in a number of different versions, none of which is considered either canonical or normative within rabbinic literature. See: Dan, Joseph (2006). "Toledot Yeshu." In Michael Berenbaum and Fred Skolnik. *Encyclopaedia Judaica*. 20 (2nd ed.). Detroit: Gale Virtual Reference Library. pp. 28–29.
69. Dr. Kjaer-Hansen, Kai. "An Introduction to the Names Yehoshua/Joshua, Yeshua, Jesus and Yeshu," *Jews for Jesus*, 03-23-92, https://jewsforjesus.org/answers/an-introduction-to-the-names-yehoshua-joshua-yeshua-jesus-and-yeshu. Dr. Kjaer-Hansen begins his paper by stating: "This paper was originally presented at the Ninth North American Coordinating Committee Meeting of the LCJE, Los Angeles, California, 23–25 March 1992."
70. Messianic Rabbi Rosenberg, Matt. "Yeshua means salvation. Yeshu does not. Yahshua means nothing," 12-06-12, http://ravmatt.blogspot.com/2012/12/yeshua-means-salvation-yeshu-does-not.html.
71. The Messianic Jewish site "One for Israel," further confirms this. See https://www.oneforisrael.org/bible-based-teaching-from-israel/jesus-vs-yeshua.
72. Ibid. Maltz, Steve. "Bad Names for Jesus."
    Also see:
    a.) Collins, Andrew. "Jesus—Son of the Panther and the Cult of Bacchus-Dionysus," Accessed May 25, 2018, http://andrewcollins.com/page/articles/Jesus.htm.
    b.) Dalman, Gustaf. "Jesus Christ in the Talmud, Midrash, Zohar, and the Liturgy of the Synagogue," CreateSpace Independent Publishing Platform (October 24, 2013): 22–23, https://books.google.com/books?id=p0nuAgAAQBAJ&pg=RA1-PA23&lpg=RA1-PA23&dq=Jesus+the+son+of+panther&source=bl&ots=Zw8rlhm71S&sig=We1xeQEZFFFe96MH7l2lURjIXk0&hl=en&sa=X&ved=0ahUKEwjQ3__d_bLbAhXByVMKHf5XDps4ChDoAQhAMAU#v=onepage&q=Jesus%20the%20son%20of%20panther&f=false.
73. Ibid. Maltz, Steve. "Bad Names for Jesus."
    Also see:
    Contra Celsum by Origen, Henry Chadwick 1980, page 32.
    Patrick, John. "The Apology of Origen in Reply to Celsus," 2009, pages 22–24.

Student, Gill. "The Jesus Narrative In The Talmud," Accessed June 12, 2018, http://talmud.faithweb.com/articles/jesusnarr.html,.

74. Ibid. Maltz, Steve. "Bad Names for Jesus."
75. Dr. Sloyan, Gerard S. "Christian Persecution of Jews over the Centuries," U.S. Holocaust Memorial Museum, accessed April 22, 2018, https://www.ushmm.org/research/the-center-for-advanced-holocaust-studies/programs-ethics-religion-the-holocaust/articles-and-resources/christian-persecution-of-jews-over-the-centuries/christian-persecution-of-jews-over-the-centuries.
76. Rabbi Singer. "Outreach Judaism," (*About Rabbi Singer*), accessed May 2, 2018, https://outreachjudaism.org/about-us.
77. Dr. Adler, Rivkah Lambert. "Rabbi Kaduri 'Jesus as Messiah' Claim Proven as False," *Breaking Israel News*, 06-17-15, https://www.breakingisraelnews.com/43554/rabbi-kaduri-jesus-as-messiah-claim-discredited-as-false-jewish-world.
78. Ibid.
79. James D. Price Publications, "Personal History," accessed 8-26-18, http://www.jamesdprice.com/personalhistory.html.
80. Dr. Price, James. "The Names Yeshua and Yehoshua," Essene.com, accessed April 12, 2018, http://www.essene.com/Yeshua/yehoshua.htm.

81 Also see:

a.) O.T. 3442. "Yeshua," (NAS Exhaustive Concordance), Biblehub.com, http://biblehub.com/hebrew/3442.htm.

b.) "Yeshua, in turn, is a shortened form of the name Yehoshua ("Joshua" in English Bibles)." (*The Hebrew Meaning of Jesus*), Hebrew Streams, Accessed May 12, 2018, http://www.hebrew-streams.org/frontstuff/jesus-yeshua.html. *Yahshua*. "Etymology and Claimed Hebrew Origins," Accessed June 12, 2018, http://dictionnaire.sensagent.leparisien.fr/Yahshua/en-en/#cite_ref-0. See: Ilan, Tal. "Lexicon of Jewish Names in Late Antiquity Part I: Palestine 330 BCE–200 CE," (2002). (*Texte und Studien zum Antiken Judentum* 91). Tübingen, Germany: J.C.B. Mohr. p. 129. See also: Stern, David. *Jewish New Testament Commentary*. Clarksville, Maryland: Jewish New Testament Publications. (1992), pp. 4–5.

82. Dr. Adler, Rivkah Lambert. "Rabbi Kaduri 'Jesus as Messiah' Claim Proven as False."
83. Schneider, Aviel. "The Rabbi, the Note and the Messiah," Israel Today, Thursday, May 30, 2013, http://www.israeltoday.co.il/NewsItem/tabid/178/nid/23877/Default.aspx.
84. Yosef Mizrachi is a Sefardi Haredi rabbi and founder of DivineInformation.com, an Orthodox Judaism outreach organization, based in Monsey, New York. Mizrachi was born in 1968 in Israel. After his mandatory military service

in the Israel Defense Forces, he worked in finance in New York City. In 1994, Mizrachi began dedicating himself to Orthodox Judaism outreach, and in 1997, he left his professional career and began learning and teaching Torah at Yeshivat Ohr Yisrael in Monsey. See: "DivineInformation.com – Torah and Science – Rabbi's Bio," www.divineinformation.com. Accessed June 21, 2018.

85. YouTube Video, "Rabbi Yosef Mizrachi on Rabbi Yitzhak Kaduri Supposed Prophecy on Christian Messiah," Posted Nov. 18, 2014, accessed June 15, 2018, https://www.youtube.com/watch?v=0NkEqTkuoQQ.
86. Ibid.
87. I am not aware of any credible, documented source wherein Kaduri's webmaster or ministry organization flatly denies posting the note and the story that went with it. Of course, it would be impossible to deny that it was actually posted in the first place, since it was seen by the world and reported upon by Israeli media. The question is *who posted it*? Presumably, only the webmaster would have had access to the site. And if he didn't post it, why would the note and the story have remained on the site for nearly two months?
88. *Yeshua*. OT #3444. (See: Strong's Concordance, Brown-Driver-Briggs, NAS Exhaustive Concordance, Strong's Exhaustive Concordance), http://biblehub.com/hebrew/3444.htm.
89. Hebrew Streams, "The Hebrew Meaning of Jesus," Hebrew-Streams.com, accessed May 23, 2018, http://www.hebrew-streams.org/frontstuff/jesus-yeshua.html. Also see: *Yeshua*, Lexicon: Strong's H3444, https://www.blueletterbible.org/lang/lexicon/lexicon.cfm?t=kjv&strongs=h3444.
90. "'Jesus' is an Anglicized form of the Greek name *Yesous* found in the New Testament. *Yesous* represents the Hebrew Bible name Yeshua." See: "The Hebrew Meaning of Jesus," Hebrew-Streams.com, accessed May 23, 2018, http://www.hebrew-streams.org/frontstuff/jesus-yeshua.html.
91. What person who is familiar with the New Testament cannot here consider the passage from the gospel of John, wherein Jesus is talking with the woman at the well and called Himself the "living water"? More than likely, Jesus was directly identifying Himself with Isaiah 12:2–3.
92. Yasha. OT 3467. This is the verb form of *yeshua*. It, among other forms of translation depending upon the context, means "having yeshua, endowed with yeshua, be given yeshua, and brought yeshua." See: http://biblehub.com/hebrew/3467.htm.
93. Ibid. *Yasha*. OT 3467.
94. Bivin, David. "The Amidah Prayer," CBN, Accessed May 11, 2018, http://www1.cbn.com/biblestudy/the-amidah-prayer.
95. Kaduri apparently claimed to have had his vision of Messiah (the one that would eventually be revealed in the famous note) on Cheshvan 9, 5764 (November 4, 2003). This date was said to have been gleaned from Kaduri's

own website, then translated and archived on a website called "Nazarene Judaism: The Original Followers of Yeshua as Messiah." This information is in the section of the article labeled (My Notes), and is at paragraph 5. Trimm, James, Scott. "The Profound Revelation of Rabbi Kaduri." Nazarene Judaism, accessed April 22, 2018, http://nazarenejudaism.com/?page_id=513.

96. **Was Rabbi Kaduri "crazy," even in his last days?** Much documentation exists to prove that Kaduri was constantly praised for the sharpness of his mind and conduct right up to the last hours of his life. I have yet to find (and I've been researching this topic for years) any credibly documented evidence that Kaduri had "lost his mind" prior to his death and prior to the deciphering of his Messiah note. "Rabbi Yitzhak Kaduri was known for his photographic memory and his memorization of the Bible, the Talmud, Rashi and other Jewish writings. He knew Jewish sages and celebrities of the last century and rabbis who lived in the Holy Land and kept the faith alive before the State of Israel was born. Kaduri was not only highly esteemed because of his age of 108. He was charismatic and wise, and chief rabbis looked up to him as a Tsadik, a righteous man or saint. He would give advice and blessings to everyone who asked" (http://www.israeltoday.co.il/NewsItem/tabid/178/nid/23877/Default.aspx.)
97. "Jew of the Week: Rav Yitzhak Kaduri," *Jew of the Week: Highlighting Jewish Contributions to the World, With Interesting Links and Tidbits of Wisdom,* accessed April 7, 2018, https://www.jewoftheweek.net/tag/nachalat-yitzchak.
98. *WND*. "Messiah Mystery Follows Death of Mystical Rabbi," WND.com, 5-18-07, http://www.wnd.com/2007/05/41669/.
99. Schneider, Aviel. "The Rabbi, the Note and the Messiah," *Israel Today*, Thursday, May 30, 2013, http://www.israeltoday.co.il/NewsItem/tabid/178/nid/23877/Default.aspx.
100. Ibid.
101. Baruch, Gordon. "Kabbalist Urges Jews to Israel Ahead of Upcoming Disasters," Arutz Sheva, 09-2105, https://www.israelnationalnews.com/News/News.aspx/89850.
102 Schneider, Aviel. "The Rabbi, the Note and the Messiah."
103. Ibid.
104. Ibid.
105. Yad L'Achim (Israeli anti-missionary organization). Accessed April 27, 2018. http://yadlachim.org. At an article page titled: "Hundreds of Missionaries Participate in Massive Independence Day Campaign," are these words: "No fewer than 250 missionaries from Canada, the United States, Britain, South Korea and Russia have been circulating around Israel as part of a widespread campaign of the Christian cults... Our activists go to wherever

the missionaries operate, to warn passersby of the danger they pose." http://yadlachim.org/?CategoryID=192&ArticleID=1129.

106. Hamodia. "Harav David Kaduri, zt"l," *Hamodia: The Daily Newspaper of Torah Jewry*, 07-07-15, http://hamodia.com/2015/07/07/harav-david-kaduri-ztl.

107. The **Hasidic movement** is a faction among the Jewish Orthodox groups specifically devoted to both the revealed, outer aspect and hidden, inner aspect of the Torah. See https://www.jewishvirtuallibrary.org/hasidism. **The Chabad-Lubavitch movement** formed from the writings of Rabbi Shneur Zalman of Liadi. According to Zalman's followers, his writings contain the keys to Jewish mystical and spiritual awareness. Rabbi Menachem Mendel Schneerson was chosen as the seventh Lubavitcher Rebbe in 1950. Schneerson, known as the Rebbe, served as the heart and soul of Chabad for forty-four years, he was the spiritual leader, as well as, intellectual and organizational leader of the movement. See https://www.jewishvirtuallibrary.org/lubavitch-and-chabad.

108. 25 Questions and Answers about Kabbalah, "What does the word Kabbalah actually mean?" Accessed April 3, 2018, http://www.azamra.org/Kabbalah/FAQ/02.htm.

109. Jewfaq.org describes the Sephardic Jew as follows: "*Who are Sephardic Jews?* Sephardic Jews are the Jews of Spain, Portugal, North Africa and the Middle East and their descendants. The adjective 'Sephardic' and corresponding nouns Sephardi (singular) and Sephardim (plural) are derived from the Hebrew word 'Sepharad,' which refers to Spain. …Rabbi Kaduri was from Iraq—in the heart of the Middle East—making him a Sephardic Jew." "Ashkenazic and Sephardic Jews," (Judaism 101), Accessed April 23, 2018, http://www.jewfaq.org/ashkseph.htm.

110. "The Preparation of Paul." Ligonier Ministries, accessed April 12, 2018, https://www.ligonier.org/learn/devotionals/the-preparation-of-paul.

111. Acts 11:26, *Ellicott's Commentary for English Readers*, Biblehub.com, http://biblehub.com/commentaries/acts/11-26.htm.

112. Acts 11:26, *Expositor's Greek Testament*, Biblehub.com, http://biblehub.com/commentaries/acts/11-26.htm.

113. 1 Peter 4:16, *Vincent's New Testament Word Studies*, Biblehub.com, http://biblehub.com/commentaries/acts/11-26.htm.

114. 1 Peter 4:16, *Ellicott's Commentary for English Readers*, Biblehub.com, http://biblehub.com/commentaries/1_peter/4-16.htm.

115. 1 Peter 4:16, *Cambridge Bible for Schools and Colleges*, Biblehub.com, http://biblehub.com/commentaries/1_peter/4-16.htm.

116. Paul uses the word "mystery" more than a dozen times between Romans and 1 Timothy. He uses the terms "mysteries" and "kept hidden" twice each.

In each case, he uses the word in the context of "receiving truth that was previously hidden, through a mystical process of revelation." That is the very definition of the foundational understanding of the Hebrew word *kabbalah*.

117. 25 Questions and Answers about Kabbalah, "What does the word Kabbalah actually mean?" Accessed April 3, 2018, http://www.azamra.org/Kabbalah/FAQ/02.htm.
118. Dr. Edersheim was a Jewish convert to Christianity and a renowned biblical scholar. He was widely known for his book *The Life and Times of Jesus the Messiah* (1883). He authored at least a dozen scholarly works in his lifetime (some of them containing multiple volumes) that expounded upon Jewish life, customs, practices, and biblical understanding.
119. Edersheim, Alfred, *Brief Outline of Ancient Jewish Theological Literature: Sketches of Jewish Social Life*, Biblehub.com, accessed May 3, 2018, http://biblehub.com/library/edersheim/sketches_of_jewish_social_life/chapter_18_brief_outline_of.htm.
120. Miller, Elliot. "What Is Kabbalah?" *Christian Research Institute* (CRI), accessed April 30, 2018, http://www.equip.org/article/what-is-kabbalah.
121. Acts 19:12, *Expositor's Greek Testament*, Biblehub.org, http://biblehub.com/commentaries/acts/19-12.htm.
122. Acts 5:15, *Expositor's Greek Testament*, Biblehub.org, http://biblehub.com/commentaries/acts/5-15.htm.
123. Acts 5:15, *Robertson's Word Pictures (NT)*, Bibletools.org, https://www.bibletools.org/index.cfm/fuseaction/Bible.show/sVerseID/27075/eVerseID/27075/RTD/rwpnt/version/nasb.
124. Acts 5:15, *Barnes' Notes on the Bible*, Biblehub.org, http://biblehub.com/commentaries/acts/5-15.htm.
125. Matthew 9:21, *Pulpit Commentary*, Biblehub.com, http://biblehub.com/commentaries/matthew/9-21.htm.
126. Matthew 9:21, *Matthew Henry's Concise Commentary*, Biblehub.com, http://biblehub.com/commentaries/matthew/9-21.htm.
127. Matthew 9:21, *Ellicott's Commentary for English Readers*, Biblehub.com, http://biblehub.com/commentaries/matthew/9-21.htm.
128. Hila Ratzabi and MJL Admin. "What Is Gematria? Hebrew Numerology, and the Secrets of the Torah," *My Jewish Learning*, accessed March 29, 2018, https://www.myjewishlearning.com/article/gematria.
129. Revelation 13:17, *Cambridge Bible for Schools and Colleges*, Biblehub.com, http://biblehub.com/commentaries/revelation/13-17.htm.
130. Revelation 13:17, *Vincent's Word Studies in the New Testament*, Biblehub.com, http://biblehub.com/commentaries/revelation/13-17.htm.
131. Revelation 13:17, *Benson Commentary*, Biblehub.com, http://biblehub.com/commentaries/revelation/13-17.htm.

132. Edersheim, Alfred, "Brief Outline of Ancient Jewish Theological Literature: Sketches of Jewish Social Life," Biblehub.com, accessed May 3, 2018, http://biblehub.com/library/edersheim/sketches_of_jewish_social_life/chapter_18_brief_outline_of.htm.
133. Ibid.
134. Remember, as you examine this distinctly Jewish teaching, just as there are varying degrees of "denominations" among the Orthodox Jews, there are also varying beliefs among those sects regarding the Two Messiah teaching. Following are several sources for a further study of the Two Messiahs:
    - Jewish Roots, "Two Messiahs," accessed April 2, 2018, http://jewish-roots.net/library/messianic/two-messiahs-2.html.
    - Smith, Garrett. "The Returning King: The Two Messiahs in Zechariah," Jews for Jesus, 05-01-04, https://jewsforjesus.org/publications/issues/issues-v15-n05/the-returning-king-the-two-messiahs-in-zechariah.
    - Sper, David. "The Jewish Tradition of Two Messiahs," RBC Ministries: Discovery Series, accessed April 23, 2018, https://d3uet6ae1sqvww.cloudfront.net/pdf/discovery-series/the-jewish-tradition-of-two-messiahs.pdf.
    - FGBT. "Two Messiahs—I know Jesus but who is Messiah ben Joseph?" *Full Gospel Business Men's Training*, Accessed May 3, 2018, http://www.fgbt.org/Lessons/two-messiahs-i-know-jesus-but-who-is-messiah-ben-joseph.html.
135. Babylonian Talmud. Sukkah 52a; Psalm 21:4, v. 5 in the Hebrew Bible.
136. Berkowitz, Adam Eliyahu. "Was Arizona Pillar of Fire Connected to Passing of Righteous Rabbi?" *Breaking Israel News*, 07-17-18, https://www.breakingisraelnews.com/110994/biblical-pillars-smoke-fire-arizona.
137. "Because these two aspects of Messianic prophecy seem contradictory, many in the ancient Jewish community could not understand how such diverse prophetic sentiments could be fulfilled in a single individual. Due to this conundrum, ancient and modern Jews have posited the idea that two Messiahs (will come to Israel)." IPP Foundation Gold Ltd. "The Predicted Messiah—Jesus Christ The Messiah—Lamb Of God—Eternal Father—Prince Of Peace," 04-13-17, http://www.iprayprayer.com/predicted-messiah-jesus-christ-messiah-lamb-god-eternal-father-prince-peace.
138. Of the sixty-six books in the Bible, only three give rise to any real question concerning whether or not they were written through the hand of Jewish writers. They are as follows:
    1. **Job** (Old Testament) is about a non-Jew. He probably existed before the Jewish people were established through Abraham, but the book of Job itself was likely authored by a Jew and not written by Job.
    2. **Luke and Acts:** The two New Testament books that are often claimed

to have been written by a Gentile are Luke and Acts. Both books were written by Luke, the physician and historian. Some believe Luke may have been a Gentile convert to Judaism. However, Dr. Thomas S. McCall, who holds a ThM in Old Testament and a ThD in Semitic languages and Old Testament, makes a strong argument (biblical and historical) that Luke was in fact a Jew. If this is so, then there is a very high likelihood that every one of the biblical writers were thoroughly Jewish. Dr. McCall says in that article: "My conclusion is, then, that we must infer that Luke was a Jew. The idea that he was a Gentile appears to be based on nothing more than wishful thinking and tradition. The biblical evidence strongly supports the position that Luke was a Jew, and we should always believe the Scriptures over tradition, when there is a conflict between the two." For Dr. McCall's detailed treatise on the issue, see: https://www.levitt.com/essays/luke. For further confirmation of this treatise, see the following:

a.) http://www.learnthebible.org/luke-was-he-a-gentile.html.
b.) http://www.bpnews.net/18466/luke-was-jewish-speaker-tells-messianic-fellowship.
c.) https://israelstudycenter.com/luke-jewish-possibly-part-1.

139. Dr. Adeney, W. F. "The Second Advent, Biblehub.com, http://biblehub.com/sermons/auth/adeney/the_second_advent.htm.
140. "The Lubavitcher Rebbe, Rabbi Menachem Mendel Schneerson, of righteous memory (1902–1994), the seventh leader in the Chabad-Lubavitch dynasty, is considered to have been the most phenomenal Jewish personality of modern times. To hundreds of thousands of followers and millions of sympathizers and admirers around the world, he was—and still is, despite his passing—'the Rebbe,' undoubtedly, the one individual more than any other singularly responsible for stirring the conscience and spiritual awakening of world Jewry." Chabad Staff. "The Rebbe: A Brief Biography," *Chabad*, accessed May 3, 2018, https://www.chabad.org/therebbe/article_cdo/aid/244372/jewish/The-Rebbe-A-Brief-Biography.htm.
141. Yardley, Jim. "Messiah Fervor for Late Rabbi Divides Many Lubavitchers," *New York Times,* 06-29-98, https://www.nytimes.com/1998/06/29/nyregion/messiah-fervor-for-late-rabbi-divides-many-lubavitchers.html.
142. Grossman, Lawrence. "Was the Lubavitcher Rebbe Really the Messiah?" *Haaretz*, 12-01-10, https://www.haaretz.com/1.5084898.
143. Boster, Mark. "The Revered," *Los Angeles Times*, 2018, Accessed April 23, 2018, http://www.latimes.com/la-chabad2_hzfhnokf.jpg-photo.html.
144. Sharon, Jeremy. "Trump's Election Heralds Coming of Messiah' says Deri," *Jerusalem Post*, 10-10-16, https://www.jpost.com/Israel-News/Trumps-election-heralds-coming-of-Messiah-says-Deri-472282.

145. Berkowitz, Adam Eliyahu. "Trump Upset Victory Divinely Sent to Begin Messianic Process: Rabbis," *Breaking Israel News*, 11-09-16, https://www.breakingisraelnews.com/78288/trump-upset-victory-divinely-sent-begin-messianic-process-rabbis.
146. *Israel Today* Staff Report. "Top Israeli Rabbi Believes Trump Will Build Third Temple in Jerusalem," *Israel Today*, 03-29-18, http://www.israeltoday.co.il/NewsItem/tabid/178/nid/33685/Default.aspx.
147. Maza, Christina. "Will Trump Hasten the Arrival of the Messiah? Jews and Evangelicals Think so." *Newsweek*, 12-11-17, http://www.newsweek.com/jews-trump-persian-king-babylonian-exile-third-temple-judaism-744698.
148. Burston, Bradley, "Opinion: Trump's Jerusalem Syndrome: Whose End of Days Messiah Does He Think He Is?" *Haaretz*, 12-09-17, https://www.haaretz.com/israel-news/trump-s-jerusalem-syndrome-whose-end-of-days-messiah-does-he-think-he-is-1.5628063.
149. *News 24*. "The Turning of Ariel Sharon," 01-16-14, https://www.news24.com/MyNews24/The-Turning-of-Ariel-Sharon-20140116.
150. Schneider, Aviel. "The Rabbi, the Note and the Messiah," *Israel Today*, Thursday, May 30, 2013, http://www.israeltoday.co.il/NewsItem/tabid/178/nid/23877/Default.aspx.
151. Jeanviete. "Rabbi Kaduri Predictions about the Coming of the Messiah/Moshiach," Steemit.com, accessed April 4, 2018, https://steemit.com/judaism/@jeanviete/rabbi-kaduri-predictions-about-the-coming-of-the-messiah-moshiach.
152. Gordan, Baruch. "Leading Kabbalist Urges Jews to Israel - More Disasters Coming," Israel National News, Oct. 19,05, https://www.israelnationalnews.com/News/News.aspx/91417#.UYgOWqKsiSo.
153. Schneider, Aviel. "The Rabbi, the Note and the Messiah," *Israel Today*, Thursday, May 30, 2013, http://www.israeltoday.co.il/NewsItem/tabid/178/nid/23877/Default.aspx.
154. Gordon, Baruch. "Kabbalist Urges Jews to Israel Ahead of Upcoming Disasters,"*Arutz Sheva 7: Israel National News*, 09-21-05, https://www.israelnationalnews.com/News/News.aspx/89850.
155. Gordon, Baruch. "Leading Kabbalist Urges Jews to Israel—More Disasters Coming," *Israel National News*, 10-19-05, https://www.israelnationalnews.com/News/News.aspx/91417.
156. Ibid. Gordon, Baruch. "Leading Kabbalist Urges Jews to Israel—More Disasters Coming."
157. Rabbi Pinchas Winston (Pinchas Winston), Wikipedia, accessed May 11, 2018, https://en.wikipedia.org/wiki/Pinchas_Winston.
158. Dr. Adler, Rivkah Lambert. "Why Hasn't the Messiah Revealed Himself? End of Days Expert Weighs In," *Breaking News*

Israel, 06-20-16, https://www.breakingisraelnews.com/70138/end-days-expert-declares-final-redemption-door.

159. From the ABOUT AISH.com page: "Headquartered in Jerusalem near the Western Wall, Aish.com is a division of Aish HaTorah, an apolitical network of Jewish educational centers in 35 branches on five continents. This partnership enables Aish.com users to experience the richness of community at an Aish branch. The name Aish HaTorah literally means 'Fire of Torah.' As Elie Wiesel said: 'Aish HaTorah means to me the passion of teaching, the passion of learning. The study of Torah, the source of Jewish values, is the way to Jewish survival.' http://www.aish.com/about/About_Aishcom.html.
160. Rabbi Simmons, Shraga. "Why Jews Don't Believe in Jesus" (Waiting for the Messiah) Aish.com, May 6, 2004, http://www.aish.com/jw/s/48892792.html.
161. Trimm, James Scott. "The Profound Revelation of Rabbi Kaduri."
162. Jackson, Wayne, "Paul's Two-Year Roman Imprisonment," Accessed May 23, 2018, https://www.christiancourier.com/articles/144-pauls-two-year-roman-imprisonment.
163. I am in possession of an audio copy of a twenty-five-minute, nationally broadcast radio interview with Mr. Farber on 01-17-14. The quote represents the exact words of Mr. Farber, starting at the six-minute mark in the interview.
164. The 25 Greatest Radio Talk Show Hosts of All Time, Talkers Magazine Online. (Barry Farber) Accessed April 30, 2018, http://www.talkers.com/greatest/; also see http://www.talkers.com/greatest/9rfarber.htm.
165. I am in possession of an audio copy of that entire twenty-five-minute nationally broadcast radio interview with Mr. Farber on 01-17-14. The quote I have just related contains the exact words of Mr. Farber, starting at the six-minute mark in the interview, and then right after the commercial break following that mark.
166. Ginsburg, Mitch. "Israel's Indomitable Protector, Ariel Sharon Emblemized Military Audacity, Evolving Politics," *Times of Israel*, 01-11-14, https://www.timesofisrael.com/israels-indomitable-protector-ariel-sharon-emblemized-military-audacity-evolving-politics.
167. Avnery, Uri. "To Understand Ariel Sharon, Look to His Mother," *Times of Israel*, 03-26-16, https://www.haaretz.com/life/books/.premium-to-understand-ariel-sharon-study-his-mother-1.5422379.
168. Robert D. Mock MD. "Who Is Sephardic Orthodox Rebbe Yitzchak Kaduri," Biblesearchers.com, accessed May 12, 2018, http://www.biblesearchers.com/hebrews/jewish/messiah1.shtml.
169. Wagner, Matthew. "Kaduri," (Obituary), *The Jerusalem Post*, 01-25-06, https://www.jpost.com/Jewish-World/Jewish-News/Kaduri-obituary.

170. Michael Tzadok Elkohen, "Hilulah HaRav Kaduri 5771," An Aspiring Mekubal (blog), Accessed January 4, 2011, http://mekubal.wordpress.com/2011/01/04/hilulah-harav kaduri-5771/.
171. Jewish Virtual Library, "Kabbalah: The Ten Sefirot of the Kabbalah," Accessed May 11, 2018, http://www.jewishvirtuallibrary.org/the-ten-sefirot-of-the-kabbalah. The foundations of Kabbalah terminology are what is known as "the ten spheres." These are ten sources or "lights" through which God supposedly communicates with His world. The spheres also represent the ten different ways, or levels of understanding, in which God is said to reveal Himself.
172. Joffe, Lawrence, "Rabbi Yitzhak Kaduri," *Guardian*, 1-30-06, https://www.theguardian.com/news/2006/jan/31/guardianobituaries.israel.
173. The *Baal Teshuva* movement is a description of the return of secular Jews to religious Judaism. The term *baal teshuva* is from the Talmud, meaning "master of repentance." See Lisa Aiken, "The Baal Teshuva Survival Guide," Rossi Publications; First edition (February 1, 2009), p.1.
174. Yitzhak Kaduri (Final Days and Death), Wikipedia, Accessed 05-12-2018, https://en.wikipedia.org/wiki/Yitzhak_Kaduri#cite_note-2.
175. Chmaytelli, Heller, and Ferrell. "With Jews Largely Gone from Iraq, Memories Survive in Israel," Reuters, 05-02-18. https://ca.news.yahoo.com/jews-largely-gone-iraq-memories-survive-israel-190613942.html.
176. Rosenberg, David. "Living in Fear: Iraq's Last Jews," *Arutz Sheva 7*, 3-13-16, https://www.israelnationalnews.com/News/News.aspx/209316.
177. Farrell, Stephen. "With Jews Largely Gone from Iraq, Memories Survive in Israel," Reuters, May 2, 2018, https://ca.news.yahoo.com/jews-largely-gone-iraq-memories-survive-israel-190613942.html.
178. Zev Porat's family names are:
Father- Rabbi Shay Porat
Mother – Ruth Porat
Paternal Grandfather- Pinhas Porat
Maternal Grandfather – Zeev Goldman (member of the Knesset)
Paternal Great Grandfather - Rabbi Abraham Porat.
179. **The Sanhedrin and the Chief Rabbinate Council:** The term "Sanhedrin" is used by Zev in this context as being synonymous with the officially recognized ruling class of Orthodox rabbinic elite who were present and operating *by government edict* in Israel, since its rebirth in 1948. The current recognized Sanhedrin, often called the nascent Sanhedrin, was officially established in 2004 (http://www.thesanhedrin.org/en/index.php/Organization_of_the_Nascent_Sanhedrin).
During the period of the British Mandate of Palestine, British authorities, in 1921, instituted the Orthodox Rabbinate (also called the Chief Rabbinate

of Israel, or the Chief Rabbinate Council). The Chief Rabbinate of Israel is currently recognized *by law* as the supreme rabbinic and spiritual authority for Judaism in the State of Israel.

In 1947, David Ben-Gurion and the prevailing religious parties developed an official covenant, which included an understanding that matters of personal status in Israel would continue to be determined by the existing Chief Rabbinate of Israel. This arrangement has remained the existing state of affairs despite numerous changes of government since the beginning.

This body of Jewish religious authority consists of two Chief Rabbis: an Ashkenazi rabbi and a Sephardi rabbi. The Chief Rabbis are elected for ten-year terms and the two alternate in its presidency.

The Rabbinate has jurisdiction over a number of important aspects of Jewish life in Israel. Its jurisdiction includes personal status issues, such as Jewish marriages and divorce, as well as burials, conversion to Judaism and kosher laws, the immigration of Jews to Israel, supervision of Jewish holy sites, and working with various ritual baths (mikvaot) and yeshivas (rabbinic training schools). Most importantly, they oversee the powerful Rabbinical Courts in Israel.

The body does not have "constitutional authority" over the civil government and its affairs. However, those who live in Israel understand that they do indeed wield great influence and strong indirect political influence over many of Israel's most important leaders. It was from this group of supremely influential rabbis that the *current official Sanhedrin* body was formed. Thus, the Sanhedrin, in one form or another, has effectively been in place in Israel, by legal decree, since 1921, even though that body may not have always been called by the name Sanhedrin.

180. Messiah of Israel Ministries, Tel Aviv, Israel. https://www.messiahofisraelministries.org.

181. The "Kaduri Revival" is a term coined by Messianic Rabbi Zev Porat. He explains that Kaduri's Yeshua note has opened doors all over the world to lead Jews and Gentiles to *Yeshua Ha' Mashiach*. Zev is always quick to point out that, of course, true salvation comes only through the Holy Spirit of God. However, Zev says, "The Lord is using Rabbi Kaduri's handwritten revelation to unlock doors that otherwise would have been shut and sealed tightly. This revelation has opened those doors and sparked a true revival of opportunity for Jews to come to Yeshua for salvation."

182. Amazingly, Zev's family name, *Porat,* in the Hebrew language means "fruitful." Zev and his wife, Lian, have certainly proven to be globally fruitful in the Kingdom work since the day they both believed in Yeshua as Messiah. The divine connections that were set in motion from the beginning were now coming to that ordained "fruition." See "Porat," https://dbs.bh.org.il/familyname/porat.

183. Yad L'Achim (Israeli anti-missionary organization). Accessed April 27, 2018. http://yadlachim.org. On an article page titled: "Hundreds of Missionaries Participate in Massive Independence Day Campaign," are found these words: "No fewer than 250 missionaries from Canada, the United States, Britain, South Korea and Russia have been circulating around Israel as part of a widespread campaign of the Christian cults.... Our activists go to wherever the missionaries operate, to warn passersby of the danger they pose" (http://yadlachim.org/?CategoryID=192&ArticleID=1129).
184. *The Jerusalem Post*, founded in 1932 by Gershon Agron, is the leading Israeli English newspaper. https://www.jpost.com/LandedPages/AboutUs.aspx.
185. Zieve, Tamara. "Will Israel Ever Accept Messianic Jews?" *The Jerusalem Post*, Dec. 16, 2017, https://www.jpost.com/Israel-News/Diaspora-Affairs-Will-Israel-ever-accept-Messianic-Jews-518129.
186. "Antinomianism, (Greek anti, 'against'; nomos, 'law'), doctrine according to which Christians are freed by grace from the necessity of obeying the Mosaic Law. The antinomians rejected the very notion of obedience as legalistic; to them the good life flowed from the inner working of the Holy Spirit. In this circumstance they appealed not only to Martin Luther but also to Paul and Augustine." See: *Encyclopaedia Britannica*. "Antinomianism," accessed April 22, 2018, https://www.britannica.com/topic/antinomianism.
187. Trimm, James Scott. "The Profound Revelation of Rabbi Kaduri," Nazarene Judaism, accessed 02-22-18, http://nazarenejudaism.com/?page_id=513.
188. Aliya: "A modern Hebrew word which means—**the immigration of Jews to Israel**." See *Merriam-Webster Dictionary*, "Aliya," https://www.merriam-webster.com/dictionary/aliyah.
189. Zieve, Tamara. "Will Israel Ever Accept Messianic Jews?"
190. Ibid.
191. Rabinowitz, Aaron. "Messianic Jews Cannot Be Married as Jews in Israel, Rabbinical Court Rules," *Haaretz*, 8-31-17, https://www.haaretz.com/israel-news/.premium-rabbinical-court-messianic-jews-cannot-be-married-as-jews-in-israel-1.5447252.
192. Ibid.
193. Bar, Eitan. "If Jesus Is the Messiah, How Come No Rabbis Believe in Him?" One For Israel, accessed May 8, 2018, https://www.oneforisrael.org/bible-based-teaching-from-israel/if-jesus-is-the-messiah-how-come-no-rabbi-believes-in-him.
194. Ibid.
195. Messianic Good News, "Rabbis Who Believed in Jesus the Messiah," Accessed May 4, 2018, http://www.messianicgoodnews.org/rabbis-who-believed. Israel in Prophecy, "A Brief List of the Most Famous Messianic Jews," Accessed May 8, 2018, http://www.israelinprophecy.org/ENGLISH/

live_site/brief_list-most_famous_messianic_jews.html. An updated PDF list as of 2008: http://www.israelinprophecy.org/ENGLISH/live_site/in_depth/bibliographies/mfmj023_010808.pdf. Also, see this page at the same site: http://www.messianicgoodnews.org/jewish-converts.

196. Again, to revisit the origin of this term, the "Kaduri Revival" was a moniker initially used by Messianic Rabbi Zev Porat in his own video and website reporting of the Kaduri note phenomenon. Eventually, he and this author began using the term in national and international interviews. Zev Porat has been very careful to explain that the revival attached to this story is from the Lord Himself. Kaduri's revelation is merely being used as an important vehicle to foster a global revival.

197. Kotel: "A remnant of the retaining wall that underlay the second Temple in Jerusalem. The Western Wall is now a site of pilgrimage, lamentation, and prayer by Jews. Also called Wailing Wall." See https://www.thefreedictionary.com/The+Kotel.

198. Video testimonials and published reports of many of Rabbi Porat's witnessing encounters using the Kaduri note may be viewed on his website and in numerous other places on the Internet. Messianic Rabbi Zev Porat's website is found at http://www.messiahofisraelministries.org. From there you may contact Rabbi Porat directly and view the numerous articles, videos, written reports, and testimonials that are referenced in this book.

199. Hickory Hammock Baptist Church: http://www.hickoryhammockbaptist.org.

200. Kogan, Shmuel. "Why Are Ten Men Needed for a Minyan?," Chabad.org, accessed July 12, 2018, https://www.chabad.org/library/article_cdo/aid/543104/jewish/Why-Are-Ten-Men-Needed-for-a-Minyan.htm.

201. Jewish Voice, "Forbidden Chapter in the Tanakh," (Isaiah 53), 6-2-16, https://www.jewishvoice.org/read/blog/forbidden-chapter-of-the-tanakh.

202. The Cardo of Jerusalem begins at the Damascus Gate in the north and crosses the city southwards until the area of the Zion Gate. A *cardo* was the Latin name given to a north-south street in Ancient Roman cities.

203. "The [Cardo] menorah which stands today in Jerusalem's old city Jewish Quarter, overlooking the Temple Mount, is the work of the Temple Institute. It was created exclusively to be used in the new Holy Temple." See http://www.templeinstitute.org/history-holy-temple-menorah-1.htm. The Temple Institute's ultimate goal is to see Israel rebuild the Holy Temple on Mount Moriah in Jerusalem, in accord with the biblical commandments. See https://www.templeinstitute.org/.

204. Zev Porat has left the city unnamed for the purposes of this book. The official identification of this particular locale could prove to be dangerous, even life-threatening, to the people in the story who are still living in Israel.

205. Isaiah 40:22. "Parallel Translations," Biblehub.com, http://biblehub.com/isaiah/40-22.htm. Examples of other scholarly translations of Isaiah 40:22 from the Hebrew word *chugh*:
Douay-Rheims Bible
It is he that sitteth upon **the globe of the earth**, and the inhabitants thereof are as locusts: he that stretcheth out the heavens as nothing, and spreadeth them out as a tent to dwell in.
New American Standard 1977
It is He who sits above **the vault of the earth**, And its inhabitants are like grasshoppers, Who stretches out the heavens like a curtain And spreads them out like a tent to dwell in.
New English Translation Bible (NET)
He is the one who sits on **the earth's horizon**; its inhabitants are like grasshoppers before him. He is the one who stretches out the sky like a thin curtain, and spreads it out like a pitched tent.
Contemporary English Version
God is the one who **rules the whole earth**, and we that live here are merely insects. He spread out the heavens like a curtain or an open tent.
Examples of commentary attestations of Isaiah 40:22, and its various forms of translation concerning the Hebrew word *chugh*:
Barnes' Notes on the Bible
The circle of the earth—Or rather, "above" (al) the circle of the earth. The word rendered "circle" (*chûg*) denotes "**a circle, sphere, or arch**"; and is applied to the arch or vault of the heavens, in Proverbs 8:27; Job 22:14.
Jamieson-Fausset-Brown Bible Commentary
Circle—applicable to **the globular form of the earth**, above which, and the vault of sky around it.
Gill's Exposition of the Entire Bible
It is he that sitteth upon the circle of the earth… **Or, "the globe"** of it.
See Isaiah 40:22, "Commentaries," Biblehub.com, http://biblehub.com/commentaries/isaiah/40-22.htm.

206. *Gill's Exposition of the entire Bible* (Proverbs 8:27 where the same word is used)
Made the earth with the sea **globular**, which make one terraqueous **globe**: or "made a circle" (p); all around it, called the circle of the earth, on which he sits, Isaiah 40:22; this compass may design the vast expanse or firmament of heaven, which is stretched and drawn around the terraqueous **globe** as a canopy or curtain. See Proverbs 8:27, "Commentaries," Biblehub.com, http://biblehub.com/proverbs/8-27.htm.
The imam's real name is not used here in order to preserve his personal safety.

207. These accounts and statistics can be found documented all over the Internet and on radio programs and television shows, as well as various video channels on the Net. Following is a list of a few of those reports and videos to get your research started:
   - Janelle P., "Muslims Turn to Christ in Unprecedented Numbers," Open Doors USA, 6-28-17, https://www.opendoorsusa.org/christian-persecution/stories/muslims-turn-to-christ-in-unprecedented-numbers-pt-1.
   - CBN. "Visions of Jesus Stir Muslim Hearts," Accessed May 12, 2018, http://www1.cbn.com/onlinediscipleship/visions-of-jesus-stir-muslim-hearts.
   - Muslims in Media Statistics. "Al-Jazeerah: 6 Million Muslims Convert to Christianity in Africa Alone Each Year," 12-14-12, accessed April 12, 2018, https://muslimstatistics.wordpress.com/2012/12/14/al-jazeerah-6-million-muslims-convert-to-christianity-in-africa-each-year.
   - YouTube video testimony. "This Jewish Professor Saw Jesus in a Vision," One for Israel Ministry, https://www.youtube.com/watch?v=eu4BaZyweuE.
   - Gardner, Charles. "Passover Miracle. Orthodox Jew Dreams of Jesus," *Israel Today*, 04-02-18, http://www.israeltoday.co.il/NewsItem/tabid/178/nid/33713/Default.aspx.
   - Jones, Emily, "'Jesus is My Messiah': Jewish Woman Comes Face to Face with an Angel, Gives Life to Christ," *CBN News*, 12-21-17, http://www1.cbn.com/cbnnews/cwn/2017/december/jesus-in-my-messiah-jewish-woman-comes-face-to-face-with-an-angel-gives-life-to-christ.

208. CBN. "Visions of Jesus Stir Muslim Hearts," Accessed May 12, 2018, http://www1.cbn.com/onlinediscipleship/visions-of-jesus-stir-muslim-hearts.
209. Dr. Strauss, Lehman. "Bible Prophecy (A Principle of Prophetic Interpretation; Isaiah's Prophecies; Micah's Prophecies)," Bible.org, accessed November 4, 2017, https://bible.org/article/bible-prophecy. Author's note: A compound prophecy, or a compound reference, is one that either contains several layers of meaning and context, or one that begins as a reference to one thing, or person, but then shifts to a symbolic reference to something or someone else. See examples of this well-known biblical phenomenon in the above-listed reference material by Dr. Strauss.
210. Isaiah 49, *Expositor's Bible Commentary*, Biblehub.com, http://biblehub.com/commentaries/expositors/isaiah/49.htm.
211. Isaiah 49:11, *MacLaren's Exposition of the Scriptures*, Biblehub.com, http://biblehub.com/commentaries/maclaren/isaiah/49.htm.

212. Isaiah 49:12, *Keil and Delitzsch Biblical Commentary on the Old Testament*, Biblehub.com, http://biblehub.com/commentaries/isaiah/49-12.htm.
213. Isaiah 49:22, *Pulpit Commentary*, Biblehub.com, http://biblehub.com/commentaries/pulpit/isaiah/49.htm.
214. Isaiah 49:22, *Jamieson-Fausset-Brown Bible Commentary*, Biblehub.com, http://biblehub.com/commentaries/isaiah/49-22.htm.
215. Isaiah 49:22, *Matthew Henry's Concise Commentary*, Biblehub.com, http://biblehub.com/commentaries/isaiah/49-22.htm.
216. Isaiah 49:22, *Ellicott's Commentary for English Readers*, Biblehub.com, http://biblehub.com/commentaries/isaiah/49-22.htm.
217. The Word China in Hebrew, "China," Accessed May 23, 2018, http://www.hebrewpod101.com/blog/2011/09/30/hebrew-word-of-the-day-china/.
218. *International Standard Bible Encyclopedia* Online, s.v. "Sinim, Land of," accessed May 9, 2018, http://www.internationalstandardbible.com/S/sinim-land-of.html.
219. Isaiah 49:12, *Ellicott's Commentary for English Readers*, Biblehub.com, http://biblehub.com/commentaries/isaiah/49-11.htm.
220. Isaiah 49:12, *Jamieson-Fausset-Brown Bible Commentary*, Biblehub.com, http://biblehub.com/commentaries/isaiah/49-11.htm.
221. Isaiah 49:12, *Pulpit Commentary*, Biblehub.com, http://biblehub.com/commentaries/isaiah/49-11.htm.
222. Isaiah 49:12, *Barnes' Notes on the Bible*, Biblehub.com, http://biblehub.com/commentaries/isaiah/49-11.htm.
223. O.T. 5515. Sinim. *Strong's Exhaustive Concordance*, Biblehub.com, http://biblehub.com/hebrew/5515.htm.
224. O.T. 5515. Sinim. "Brown-Driver-Briggs," Biblehub.com, http://biblehub.com/hebrew/5515.htm.
225. Rahn, Wesley. "In Xi We Trust—Is China Cracking Down on Christianity?" Deutsche Welle, 01-19-18, https://www.dw.com/en/in-xi-we-trust-is-china-cracking-down-on-christianity/a-42224752. "The Jindengtai ('Golden Lampstand') mega-church, which reportedly had a congregation of 50,000 people, was one of many so-called 'underground churches' in China that religious activists say are being targeted by China's Communist government. These independent congregations are not registered with the government, which all religious organizations in China are legally required to do."
226. Eleanor Albert, "Christianity in China," Council on Foreign Relations, May 7, 2015, http://www.cfr.org/china/christianity-china/p36503.
227. From: "History of the Jews in China," https://en.wikipedia.org/wiki/History_of_the_Jews_in_China. Though a small minority, Chinese Jews have had an open presence in the country since the arrival of the first Jewish immigrants during the seventh or eighth century CE. Relatively

isolated communities of Jews developed through the Tang and Song Dynasties (seventh to twelfth centuries CE) all the way through the Qing Dynasty (nineteenth century), most notably the Kaifeng Jews (the term "Chinese Jews" is often used in a restricted sense in order to refer to these communities).

228. Isaiah 49:12, *Whedon's Commentary on the Bible*, StudyLight.org, https://www.studylight.org/commentaries/whe/isaiah-49.html.
229. Isaiah 49:12, *Barnes' Notes on the Bible,* Biblehub.com, http://biblehub.com/commentaries/isaiah/49-12.htm.
230. Isaiah 49:12, *Keil and Delitzsch Biblical Commentary on the Old Testament*, Biblehub.com, http://biblehub.com/commentaries/isaiah/49-12.htm.
231. Isaiah 49:12, *Barnes' Notes on the Bible*, Biblehub.com, http://biblehub.com/commentaries/isaiah/49-12.htm.
232. Isaiah 49:12, *Matthew Poole's Commentary*, Biblehub.com, http://biblehub.com/commentaries/isaiah/49-12.htm.
233. Isaiah 49:12, *Gill's Exposition of the Whole Bible*, Biblehub.com, http://biblehub.com/commentaries/isaiah/49-12.htm.
234. Fox News. China Ramps Up Persecution of Christians and Other Religious Groups, Report Finds," 02-28-17, http://www.foxnews.com/world/2017/02/28/china-ramps-up-persecution-christians-and-other-religious-groups-report-finds.html.
235. Dr. Michael Brown, "Does the Bible Really Say That Things Will Only Get Worse?" *Charisma News*, July 15, 2013, http://www.charismanews.com/opinion/in-the-lineof-fire/40236-does-the-bible-really-say-that-things-will-only-get-worse.
236. Rabbi Singer, Tovia. "Who Is God's Suffering Servant? The Rabbinic Interpretation of Isaiah 53," *Outreach Judaism*, accessed June 12, 2018, https://outreachjudaism.org/gods-suffering-servant-isaiah-53.
237. Rabbi Frydland, Rachmiel. "Why I Believe That Yeshua (Jesus) Is the Jewish Messiah," Association of Messianic Congregations, accessed May 23, 2018, http://www.messianicassociation.org/bio-frydland.htm.
238. Rabbi Frydland, Rachmiel. "The Rabbis' Dilemma: A Look at Isaiah 53," Jews for Jesus, accessed June 12, 2018, https://jewsforjesus.org/publications/issues/issues-v02-n05/the-rabbis-dilemma-a-look-at-isaiah-53/.
239. Bar, Eitan. "Isaiah 53—The Forbidden Chapter," *One For Israel*, Accessed June 11, 2018, https://www.oneforisrael.org/bible-based-teaching-from-israel/inescapable-truth-isaiah-53.
240. The *Haftarat* is a series of selections from the Books of the Prophets of the Old Testament. They are read publicly in synagogue as part of Jewish religious practice.

241. Ungurean, Geri. "Isaiah 53 is the 'Forbidden' Chapter in the Tanakh," January 1, 2018, https://grandmageri422.me/2018/01/01/isaiah-53-is-the-forbidden-chapter-in-the-tanakh.
242. Rabbi Frydland, Rachmiel. "The Rabbis' Dilemma: A Look at Isaiah 53," Jews For Jesus, Accessed June 11, 2018, https://jewsforjesus.org/publications/issues/issues-v02-n05/the-rabbis-dilemma-a-look-at-isaiah-53.
243. Isaiah 53:1–12. From the *English Translation of The Holy Scriptures, Revised in Accordance with Jewish Tradition and Modern Biblical Scholarship*, by Alexander Harkavy, published by the Hebrew Publishing Company, New York, 1916.
244. Rabbi Sacks, Jonathan. "Congregational Leader," Hope in Messiah, Accessed June 11, 2018, http://www.hopeinmessiah.org/staff.
245. Rabbi Sacks, Jonathan. "What Rabbis Have Said about Isaiah 53," *Hope In Messiah*, 08-21-15, http://www.hopeinmessiah.org/what-rabbis-have-said-about-isaiah-53.
246. Ibid Rabbi Sacks draws heavily upon the work titled, *The Fifty-Third Chapter of Isaiah According to the Jewish Interpreters*, (translations by S. R. Driver and A. D. Neubauer), KTAV Publishing House, New York, 1969.
247. Heart of G-d Ministries. "Sharing the Gospel with Israelis," *The Yeshua Project*, Accessed June 2, 2018, https://heartofg-d.org/yeshua-project.
248. The Yeshua Project (The Forbidden Chapter in the Hebrew Bible—Isaiah 53), accessed June 2, 2018, https://www.youtube.com/watch?v=cGz9BVJ_k6s.
249. Ibid. These words are found in the "Description" section immediately under the video at the current URL of https://www.youtube.com/watch?time_continue=1&v=cGz9BVJ_k6s.
250. YouTube Video. "Jewish Man Turns to Jesus and Explains Why in a Way You Never Heard Before!" Accessed June 12, 2018, *John Matthews* Channel, posted 6-2-15, https://www.youtube.com/watch?v=-tKbO_Yxolc. Mottel Baleston is the director of the Messengers of the New Covenant of New Jersey, an organization first established in 1940 to communicate the good news of the arrival of Messiah Yeshua. Mottel was born in a Jewish home in Brooklyn, New York City, and attended both Jewish and public schools there. All four of his grandparents were born into Jewish homes in Europe. Mottel came to faith in Messiah as a result of a search for spiritual truth. After a careful reading of the Messianic prophecies of the Jewish Bible, it was evident to him that only Jesus has fulfilled these.
251. See Messengers of the New Covenant, Biography of Mottel Baleston, Director, http://www.messiahnj.org/director.htm.
    In the United States, this act would be an illegal one. Nothing can be placed in a US mailbox without proper postage attached. In Israel, however, this

is not an illegal act and Messiah of Israel Ministries distributes much of its material in this manner.

252. Messiah of Israel Ministries can be contacted at www.messiahofisraelministries.com.
253. Yad L'Achim Staff. "The Missionary Campaign of Distributing Hundreds of Thousands of Disks Continues; Yad L'Achim Responds in Preemptive War," Accessed July 12, 2018, http://www.yadleachim.co.il/?CategoryID=363&ArticleID=1762. Note: This site is published in Hebrew only. However, some Internet browsers allow for translation of the site's content into English. The quoted portion of that article is from the English translation option. Also, a video presentation of the CD distribution and Yad L'Achim's response to it can be seen, with Zev Porat reporting, at the following YouTube link: "BREAKING! The Rabbi Who Found Messiah Continues to Explode in Israel Messianic Rabbi Zev Porat," https://www.youtube.com/watch?v=njCiODDjWhs&t=10s.
254. See biblical passages (among others): Ezekiel 37–39; Hosea 3:4–5; Ezekiel 20:34; Isaiah 11:11–12; Jeremiah 32:44; Isaiah 66:8; Isaiah 43:5–6, 21; Zephaniah 3:8–10; Isaiah 26:6; Deuteronomy 30:1–9). Also see: Shuva Global. "Return to the Promised Land: 70 Biblical Reasons to Stand with and Support Israel," Accessed June 23, 2018, http://www.shuvaglobal.com/media/israel-70-biblical-reasons.
255. Peters, Ralph. "Turkey and Erdogan: Here Comes the (Real) Caliphate," Fox News, 07-21-16, http://www.foxnews.com/opinion/2016/07/21/turkey-and-erdogan-here-comes-real-caliphate.html.
256. Genetics Home Reference. "What Are Genome Editing and CRISPR-Cas9?" Accessed July 12, 2018, https://ghr.nlm.nih.gov/primer/genomicresearch/genomeediting.
257. I examine in detail all these prophetic signs and more in my book titled, *When the Lion Roars: Understanding the Implications of Ancient Prophecies for Our Time*, WND Books, 2016.
258. "The Bible code, also known as the Torah code, is a purported set of secret messages encoded within the Hebrew text of the Torah. This hidden code has been described as a method by which specific letters from the text can be selected to reveal an otherwise obscured message. Although Bible codes have been postulated and studied for centuries, the subject has been popularized in modern times by Michael Drosnin's book *The Bible Code* and the movie *The Omega Code*," https://en.wikipedia.org/wiki/Bible_code. Also see: Doron Witztum; Eliyahu Rips; Yoav Rosenberg (1994). "Equidistant Letter Sequences in the Book of Genesis," *Statistical Science*, 9 (3): 429–38.
259. CJCUC. "Orthodox Rabbinic Statement on Christianity," December 3, 2015, http://cjcuc.org/2015/12/03/orthodox-rabbinic-statement-on-christianity.

260. See Mishneh Torah, Laws of Kings 11:4 (uncensored edition); Kuzari, section 4:22. (This was referenced in the CJCUC article.).
261. Ibid. CJCUC. "Orthodox Rabbinic Statement on Christianity."
262. Ibid.
263. By Editorials. "Ariel Sharon, Lion of Israel," *New York Daily News*, January 14, 2018, http://www.nydailynews.com/opinion/ariel-sharon-lion-israel-article-1.1576467.
264. *Sunday Times*. "Ariel Sharon: The 'Lion of God' departs," January 5 2014, https://www.thetimes.co.uk/article/ariel-sharon-the-lion-of-god-departs-bgg8llk72sf.
265. *Newsroom*. "The Lion of Israel—Ariel Sharon," 01-21-14, https://thejewishnews.com/2014/01/21/the-lion-of-israel-ariel-sharon/.
266. Lazaroff, Tovah. "Sharon, The Life of a Lion," *Jerusalem Post*, 01-12-14, https://www.jpost.com/Opinion/Op-Ed-Contributors/Sharon-The-life-of-a-lion-337867.
267. Leve, Ariel Sharon. "My Name Is Ariel Sharon," *Guardian*, 04-13-2003, https://www.theguardian.com/theguardian/2003/apr/14/features11.g2.
268. Sagiv, Assaf. "The Left Is Waiting for a Messiah," *Haaretz*, 04-16-17, https://www.haaretz.com/opinion/.premium-the-left-is-waiting-for-a-messiah-1.5461429.
269. Weizman, Eyal. "The Architecture of Ariel Sharon," *Aljazeera*, 01-11-14, https://www.aljazeera.com/indepth/opinion/2014/01/architecture-ariel-sharon-20141111417103088 55.html.
270. Gordon, Baruch. "Kabbalist Urges Jews to Israel Ahead of Upcoming Disasters," *Arutz Sheva* 7, 09-21-05, https://www.israelnationalnews.com/News/News.aspx/89850.
271. As an example of this idea, see: "The Third Temple—Physical or Spiritual?" https://www.thepathoftruth.com/teachings/third-temple-physical-spiritual.htm.
272. For a thorough study of every OT and NT Scripture that could be interpreted to be about a Third Temple in Jerusalem in the last days, see: Gallups, Carl. For PNN. "A New Temple Has to Be Rebuilt for Jesus to Return?" PNN News and Ministry Network, 09-08-16, http://ppsimmons.blogspot.com/2016/09/a-new-temple-has-to-be-rebuilt-for.html.
273. Littman, Shany. "Following the Dream of a Third Temple in Jerusalem," *Haaretz*, 10-04-12, https://www.haaretz.com/chasing-the-dream-of-a-third-temple-1.5176045.
274. Berkowitz, Adam Eliyahu. "Government Announces 'Majority of Jews in Israel' Sanhedrin Responds 'Time for Jubilee,'" *Breaking Israel News*, 07-08-18, https://www.breakingisraelnews.com/110564/messianic-tipping-point-majority-jews-israel.
275. Ibid.
276. Littman, Shany. "Following the Dream of a Third Temple in Jerusalem."

277. Ibid.
278. Berkowitz, Adam Eliyahu. "Sanhedrin Calls on Arabs to Take Their Role in Third Temple as Prophesized by Isaiah," *Breaking News Israel*, 3-19-18, https://www.breakingisraelnews.com/104480/sanhedrin-calls-on-arabs-to-take-their-role-in-third-temple-as-prophesized-by-isaiah.
279. Gordon, Baruch. "Kabbalist Urges Jews to Israel Ahead of Upcoming Disasters," *Arutz Sheva* 7, 09-21-05, https://www.israelnationalnews.com/News/News.aspx/89850.
280. Berkowitz, Adam Eliyahu. "Sanhedrin Calls on Arabs to Take Their Role in Third Temple as Prophesized by Isaiah," *Breaking News Israel*, 3-19-18, https://www.breakingisraelnews.com/104480/sanhedrin-calls-on-arabs-to-take-their-role-in-third-temple-as-prophesized-by-isaiah.
281. Berkowitz, Adam Eliyahu. "Sanhedrin Calls on Arabs to Take Their Role in Third Temple as Prophesized by Isaiah," *Breaking Israel News*, March 19, 2018, https://www.breakingisraelnews.com/104480/sanhedrin-calls-on-arabs-to-take-their-role-in-third-temple-as-prophesized-by-isaiah.
282. Staff, "Top Israeli Rabbi Believes Trump Will Build Third Temple in Jerusalem," *Israel Today*, 03-29-18, http://www.israeltoday.co.il/NewsItem/tabid/178/nid/33685/Default.aspx.
283. Sommer, Allison Kaplan. "Christians and Jews Now Compare Trump to Persian King Cyrus—Will He Build the Third Temple?" *Haaretz*, 12-16-17, https://www.haaretz.com/israel-news/trump-s-compared-to-persian-king-cyrus-will-he-build-the-third-temple-1.5628538.
284. Maza, Cristina. "Will Trump Hasten the Arrival of the Messiah? Jews and Evangelicals Think So," *Newsweek*, 12-11-17, http://www.newsweek.com/jews-trump-persian-king-babylonian-exile-third-temple-judaism-744698.
285. The Persian Empire's King Cyrus issued what is often called the Edict of Restoration. The edict, described in the Bible as made by Cyrus the Great, left a lasting legacy on the Jewish religion, where, because of his policies in Babylonia, he is referred to by the Jewish Bible as "messiah" (lit., "His anointed one," Isaiah 45:1). The edict ordered the refurbishing of the destroyed Jerusalem and the rebuilding of the Temple that had previously been destroyed by the Babylonians. See: Jona Lendering (2012). "Messiah—Roots of the Concept: From Josiah to Cyrus," livius.org. Retrieved January 26, 2012, through Wikipedia article: "Cyrus the Great." https://en.wikipedia.org/wiki/Cyrus_the_Great.
286. Berkowitz, Adam Eliyahu. "Global Support for Third Temple Coin," *Breaking Israel News*, 03-05-18, https://www.breakingisraelnews.com/103700/global-support-third-temple-coin.
287. Ibid. Berkowitz, Adam Eliyahu. "Global Support for Third Temple Coin."
288. Hamikdash.org, "The Temple Coin," Accessed June 24, 2018, http://en.hamikdash.org.il/about/we-need-your-support/the-temple-coin.

289. Holloway, Henry. "'Messiah has been born' rabbi claims saviour is already here…and end times are imminent. A rabbi claims the Messiah has been born this weekend. The world is now entering the final stages of the end times," *Star*, July 22, 2018, https://www.dailystar.co.uk/news/weird-news/718138/messiah-jewish-israel-end-times-born-jerusalem-temple-rabbi-chaim-kanievsky-arrival.
290. YouTube video of Netanyahu's live Embassy dedication speech. "The Temple in Jerusalem Will Be Rebuilt!" Randy Vild, 5-14-18, https://www.youtube.com/watch?v=xJiBu79Bids.
291. Blau, Uri. "Netanyahu Allies Donated to Groups Pushing for Third Temple," *Haaretz*, 12-09-15, https://www.haaretz.com/netanyahu-allies-donated-to-groups-pushing-for-third-temple-1.5434678.
292. Ibid
293. Ibid.
294. Silow-Carroll, Andrew. "Who Is King Cyrus, and Why Did Netanyahu Compare Him to Trump?" *Times of Israel*, 03-08-18, https://www.timesofisrael.com/who-is-king-cyrus-and-why-is-netanyahu-comparing-him-to-trump.
295. *Newsmax*. "Israel Declares Itself 'Jewish State,' Jerusalem as Eternal Capital," 07-19-18, https://www.newsmax.com/newsfront/israel-netanyahu-nation-jerusalem/2018/07/19/id/872553.
296. Ibid.
297. Dan Cohen and David Sheen. "'When I have the opportunity to do it, I will': Likud Lawmaker Vows to Demolish Al-Aqsa Mosque," *Mondoweiss*, 02-29-16, http://mondoweiss.net/2016/02/when-i-have-the-opportunity-to-do-it-i-will-likud-lawmaker-vows-to-demolish-al-aqsa-mosque.
298. The four quoted rabbinic statements were taken from a *Breaking Israel News* article. See: Berkowitz, Adam Eliyahu. "An End-of-Days Guide to the Embassy Move," *Breaking Israel News*, May 14, 2018, https://www.breakingisraelnews.com/107721/an-end-of-days-guide-to-the-embassy-move.
299. Editor, Yeni Safak. "What If a Muslim Army Was Established against Israel?" Yeni Safak, 12-12-17, https://www.yenisafak.com/en/world/what-if-a-muslim-army-was-established-against-israel-2890448.
300. *Yeni Şafak* ("New Dawn") is a conservative Turkish daily newspaper. The newspaper is known for its hardline support of President Recep Tayyip Erdoğan and the AK Parti and has a very close relationship with the Turkish government. See: "Yeni Safak," https://en.wikipedia.org/wiki/Yeni_%C5%9Eafak; Usluata, Ayseli; Rosenbaum, John (2005). *Shaping the Future of Communication Research in Europe*. İstanbul: Yeditepe University Pub. p. 140; Tziarras, Zenonas (April 2015). "State-Media Relations in Turkey: Daily Sabah and Yeni Şafak as a Tactical Arm of the AKP's Foreign Policy." *Asian Politics & Policy*. 7 (2): 323–327.

301. Editor, Yeni Safak. "What If a Muslim Army Was Established against Israel?"
302. Al Jazeera Media Network is a major global news organization with eighty bureaus around the world. Al Jazeera Media Network is owned by the government of Qatar. According to the *Atlantic* magazine, Al Jazeera presents a far more moderate, Westernized face than Islamic jihadism or rigid Sunni Orthodoxy, and though the network has been criticized as "an 'Islamist' stalking horse," it actually features "very little specifically religious content in its broadcasts." See: Bakshian, Aram, Jr., "The Unlikely Rise of Al Jazeera," https://www.theatlantic.com/international/archive/2012/01/the-unlikely-rise-of-al-jazeera/251112/.
303. *Al Jazeera*, "Erdogan Calls on Muslim Countries to Unite and Confront Israel," May 18, 2018, https://www.aljazeera.com/news/2018/05/erdogan-calls-muslim-countries-unite-confront-israel-180518185258629.html.
304. *FrontPage Magazine* is a project of the David Horowitz Freedom Center. The "About Us" page says: "The David Horowitz Freedom Center combats the efforts of the radical left and its Islamist allies to destroy American values and disarm this country as it attempts to defend itself in a time of terror.... FrontPage Magazine, the Center's online journal of news and political commentary, has 1.5 million visitors and over 870,000 unique visitors a month (65 million hits) and is linked to over 2000 other websites." See https://www.frontpagemag.com/about.
305. Puder, Joseph. "The Threat of Erdogan: And What the U.S. Must Do about It," *FrontPage Magazine*, May 29, 2018, https://www.frontpagemag.com/fpm/270269/threat-erdogan-joseph-puder.
306. Voorwinde, Stephen. "Hebrews' Use of the Old Testament," Accessed June 30, 2018, http://www.rtc.edu.au/RTC/media/Documents/Vox%20articles/Hebrews-Use-of-the-Old-Testament-SV-73-2008.pdf?ext=.pdf. Also see: "Old Testament Direct Quotations from the Book of Hebrews," PDF download, accessed June 30, 2018, ww.sbsinternational.org/resource-material/hebrews/?wpdmdl=1075&ind=2.
307. Rudd, Steve. "A List of Old Testament Quotes in the New Testament: Books Quoted by Jesus and other New Testament Writers," Accessed June 12, 2018, http://www.bible.ca/b-canon-old-testament-quoted-by-jesus-and-apostles.htm.
308. Wagner, Matthew. "Judaism: The Magic of the Late Rabbi Yitzhak Kaduri," *Jerusalem Post*, 02-02-06, https://www.jpost.com/Features/Judaism-The-magic-of-the-late-Rabbi-Yitzhak-Kaduri.
309. The Hebrew word rendered "anointed" in most English translations of this verse is actually O.T. #4899: *Mashiach,* from where we get our word "Messiah."
310. Tetragrammaton. A Greek word, neuter of *tetragrammatos*, meaning "having four letters." See also: *Agape Bible Study*, "The Many Names of God,"

Accessed 07-12-18, http://www.agapebiblestudy.com/documents/The%20Many%20Names%20of%20God.htm.

311. Ibid.
312. Judaism 101, "The Name of G-d," (Pronouncing the Name of God), Accessed July 27, 2018, http://www.jewfaq.org/name.htm. Also see: Jewish Virtual Library. "Jewish Concepts: The Name of God," Accessed July 27, 2-18, https://www.jewishvirtuallibrary.org/the-name-of-god.
313. Keyser, John D. "The True Pronunciation of the Sacred Name," Accessed August 12, 2018, http://www.hope-of-israel.org/tetragram.html.
314. "Tetragrammaton," *New International Dictionary of New Testament Theology* (1984, Volume 2, page 512).
315. "Tetragrammaton in the New Testament," *Anchor Bible Dictionary*, Volume 6, Edited by David Noel Freedman, Anchor Bible: New York. 1992.
316. Gallups, Carl. "Hebrew Alphabet/Pictograms Chart," Carlgallups.com, accessed July 12, 2018, http://www.carlgallups.com/hebrewpictograms.gif.
317. See my two previous books, *Gods and Thrones* and *Gods of Ground Zero* for a deeply thorough examination of the word *elohim* and its use throughout the Scriptures, both in the Old and New Testaments.
318. Gallups, Carl. *Gods of Ground Zero*, (chapter 36, "I Will Put My Name There"), Defender Publishing, August 24, 2018, p. 228.
319. *Mezuzah:* A decorative case containing a tiny scroll upon which the first two sections of the Shema (Deuteronomy 6) are handwritten. That section begins with the declaration "Hear O Israel, the Lord is our God, the Lord is One." This passage also contains God's instruction to affix the *mezuzah*: "You shall write them on the doorposts of your house and on your gates." The *mezuzah* is meant to signify that the name of the LORD is upon the home, the business, and the people within.
320. Gallups, Carl. *Gods of Ground Zero: The Truth of Eden's Iniquity, Why It Still Matters, and the Mystery Surrounding What's Coming Next.* (Defender Publishing. August 2018).
321. Weber, Jeremy, "'Worst Year Yet': The Top 50 Countries Where It's Hardest to Be a Christian," *Christianity Today*, 01-11-17, https://www.christianitytoday.com/news/2017/january/top-50-countries-christian-persecution-world-watch-list.html.
322. Ibid.
323. Gallups, Carl, *Gods of Ground Zero*.
324. Philip was a Jewish follower of Jesus who bore a Greek name. He is not to be confused with the original disciple named Philip. We first meet this particular Philip in the book of Acts (6:5) as one of "seven deacons." Those first deacons were chosen to calm the murmurings of the Hellenists against the Hebrews. Philip appears several times in the book of Acts (Acts 6, 8, 21).